A-LEVEL
AND AS-LEVEL

GOVERNMENT AND POLITICS

George Tyrrell

Longman
London and New York

LONGMAN A-LEVEL AND AS-LEVEL REVISE GUIDES

Series editors:
Geoff Black and Stuart Wall

Titles available:
Accounting
Art and Design
Biology*
Business Studies
Chemistry*
Computer Science
Economics*
English
French
Geography*
German
Government and Politics
Law
Mathematics*
Modern History
Physics*
Psychology
Sociology*

*New editions

Addison Wesley Longman Ltd.
Edinburgh Gate, Harlow,
Essex CM20 2JE, England
and Associated Companies throughout the world.

First Published 1996

ISBN 0582 28702-2

British Library Cataloguing in Publication Data
A catalogue record for this title is available from the British Library

Set in 10/12 pt Century Old Style by 8QQ

Produced by Longman Singapore Publishers Pte
Printed in Singapore

CONTENTS

	Editors' Preface	iv
	Acknowledgements	iv
1	The syllabuses and examinations	1
2	Political culture	6
3	The constitution	21
4	The Prime Minister	35
5	The Cabinet	49
6	Parliament	64
7	The civil service	83
8	Political parties	99
9	Pressure groups	115
10	Public opinion and elections	129
11	Voting behaviour	144
12	Local government	158
13	The European Union	173
	Review Sheets	183
	Index	207

EDITORS' PREFACE

Longman A-level Revise Guides, written by experienced examiners and teachers, aim to give you the best possible foundation in your course. Each book in the series encourages thorough study and a full understanding of the concepts involved, and is designed as a subject companion and study aid to be used throughout the course.

Many candidates at A-level fail to achieve the grades which their ability deserves, owing to such problems as the lack of a structured revision strategy or unsound examination techniques. This series aims to remedy such deficiencies by encouraging a realistic and disciplined approach in preparing for and taking examinations.

The largely self-contained nature of the chapters gives the book a flexibility which you can use to your advantage. After starting with the background to the A-level and AS-level courses and details of the syllabus coverage, you can read all the other chapters selectively, in any order appropriate to the stage you have reached in your course.

Geoff Black and Stuart Wall

ACKNOWLEDGEMENTS

I am indebted to the following examination boards for permission to reproduce questions which have appeared in their examination papers.
   The Associated Examination Board
   Northern Examinations and Assessment Board
   Oxford and Cambridge Examinations Council (responsible for examinations
      previously conducted by OCSEB, UCLES and UODLE)
   University of London Examinations and Assessment Council
The examination boards are not responsible for the suggested answers to the questions. Full responsibility for these is accepted by the author.

We are also grateful to the following for permission to reproduce copyright material: Crown copyright is reproduced with the permission of the controller of HMSO for the map of England in Figure 12.2, and with the permission of the Welsh office for the map of Wales in Figure 12.2.

Many thanks to Geoff Black for compiling the index and to Stuart Wall for helpful encouragement at the initial stage of the project.

NAMES AND ADDRESSES OF THE EXAM BOARDS

Associated Examination Board (AEB)
Stag Hill House
Guildford
Surrey GU2 5XJ
(01483) 506506

Northern Examinations and Assessment Board (NEAB)
Devas Street
Manchester M15 6EX
(0161) 9531180

University of Cambridge Local Examinations Syndicate
(covers OCSEB, UCLES and UODLE)
Ewert House
Summertown
Oxford OX2 7BZ
(01865) 54291

University of London Examinations and Assessment Council (ULEAC)
Stewart House
32 Russell Square
London WC1B 5DN
(0171) 3314000

To my wife Margaret and sons Edward and Kenneth
for their patience during the writing of this book.

THE SYLLABUSES AND EXAMINATIONS

STUDYING POLITICS

USING THIS BOOK

TOPICS AND SYLLABUSES

ASSESSMENT

REVISION AND EXAMINATION

GETTING STARTED

WHY THIS BOOK HAS BEEN WRITTEN

This book has been written as a revision aid for students taking A-level and AS-level examinations in British Government and Politics and as an up-to-date supplement to any text books used throughout a course. One problem with studying Politics at Advanced Level needs to be dealt with at the outset. The Labour Prime Minister Harold Wilson is credited with the saying 'A week is a long time in politics', meaning that you cannot predict future political events and that everything can and usually does happen quickly in politics.

Information gained in this subject will therefore quickly date – more so than in Sociology or History for example. The obvious way round this problem is to keep abreast of political events as and when they occur. You could through your teacher or lecturer, be reviewing political controversies on a regular basis, or if you are working on your own (as a distance learning correspondence student, for example) you can perform this function yourself. This does not mean that the basic arguments in British Politics continually change – there is a body of academic knowledge built up in Political Science as in all other social sciences that needs to be acquired and there is no simple short cut to the hard work of studying to gain this knowledge.

ESSENTIAL PRINCIPLES

Besides using this book and your mainstream course text books I hope you will read a newspaper on a regular basis – it can but does not have to be a heavyweight broadsheet, there are plenty of adequate popular tabloids that give sufficient political information. Cut out and keep any particular articles that you think add to your knowledge and file them for later use. Television (news, current affairs and discussion programmes) is now well established as a major source of information for Politics students and little needs to be said about content or bias in presentation. Most students are aware that newspapers are more partisan in their reporting of politics than television which is subject to greater controls over objectivity.

One way of keeping your study of politics 'alive' is to hear guest speakers and study specialist journals which are referred to in this book. The examiner's report on the 1994 Oxford A-level Politics commented on the wide range of material now available to students in the following way:

> The advantage that today's Politics students enjoy over both their predecessors and their peers *in other disciplines* [my emphasis] is a consequence of the availability of up-to-date material in journals, and has been commented on before. In addition, the activities of the Politics Association, in venues around the country, make it possible for students to attend lectures by experts who address a whole range of syllabus themes.

POLITICS AND HISTORY

I am often asked by students about the historical content of modern politics as they are worried that their lack of specialised knowledge of this subject will penalise them in the examination. I always reply that most of the current examination boards do not expect a detailed academic knowledge of the interpretation of modern British history but obviously politics cannot be studied in a vacuum. British politics is rich in history – it informs our understanding of the institutions in the State and you will be expected to have some appreciation of post 1945 events. Here it is instructive to quote from the NEAB (Northern Examinations and Assessment Board) British Government and Politics (Advanced) Syllabus for 1996:

> The Common Core concentrates on contemporary British government and politics. Historical perspectives should be developed only to the extent that they are necessary to the understanding of the existing system. Of necessity, therefore, the historical span will differ from topic to topic.

Noting the above, some topics like Voting Behaviour will contain very little history; others like Parliament or Culture will examine historical inputs, but only as they contribute to understanding concepts such as **Butskellism**, which describes the consensus prevailing between the Conservative and Labour Parties in the 1960s.

APPROACHES TO THE STUDY OF POLITICS

As the sources of information open to today's students of Politics are greater than at any previous time, they are expected to be able to produce answers of a higher quality. One way to do this is to attempt to see politics in the round – to take each topic and see how it fits into the greater order of things. This will aid your organisational and analytical skills which are now tested in the examination. There are three broad approaches to the study of British Government and Politics that you will encounter in your A-level work:

1 **The institutional** Here the focus is on the institutions of the state including Parliament, the constitution and administration.

2 **Policy cycle** The main attention here is on policy making and the processes that accompany it. The executive including the Prime Minister and Cabinet and other policy influencers are examined.

3 **Socio-political** The socio-political approach is concerned with the sociological

content of politics and focuses on the aspects of class, power and structures in British government that inform the wider perspective.

USING THIS BOOK

Each chapter in this book has been written to provide a succinct and up-to-date coverage of one of the major topics contained in the Common Core of the A-level Government and Politics syllabuses of the major examining boards – AEB, NEAB, OXFORD, OXFORD and CAMBRIDGE and ULEAC (LONDON). The first half of the chapter identifies the current academic debate in the topic, then breaks this down using theoretical and empirical studies so it can be easily assimilated. Diagrams are used where relevant as a descriptive aid to learning which are taken from my course of lectures to first and second year A-level students. Academic sources have been extensively identified throughout these chapters as well as in the textual references to each section. Time permitting, these could be used as guides to reading and as background for further study.

The second half of each chapter is dedicated to assessment of the material in the form of actual examination questions. Each question is provided with an outline answer, a student's answer and a tutor's answer. Student essays are given as guidance with helpful examiner's comments and a suggested A-level grade to demonstrate the level of work falling into the approximate mark bands. Examiner essays are not meant to be taken as model answers but are given as samples as to what can be written. All were written without the aid of notes roughly in the 45 minutes allowed in the examination. Look at them critically, try to improve them and test your analytical powers. Remember there is no right or wrong answer in politics. What examiners are looking for in A-level Politics answers are quality of thought, a good range of knowledge, and demonstration of understanding and evaluative skills – in other words, the ability to advance good arguments on paper.

Finally, do try to work through the set of review sheets for each chapter, found at the end of the book. These are based on key areas in the chapter and should act as aids to learning. Although we do not advocate learning by rote, you still have to strengthen your powers of recall to be able to use them eventually under examination conditions. There are numerous books written on study skills – all refer to the ability to increase memory powers. Practising recall is one way of doing this.

TOPICS AND SYLLABUSES

All the topics in this book are covered by the following examination boards:

Chapters and topics	Examination boards				
	AEB	NEAB	ULEAC	Oxford	Oxford and Cambridge
2 Political culture	✓	✓	✓	✓	✓
3 Constitution	✓	✓	✓	✓	✓
4 Prime Minister	✓	✓	✓	✓	✓
5 Cabinet	✓	✓	✓	✓	✓
6 Parliament	✓	✓	✓	✓	✓
7 Civil service	✓	✓	✓	✓	✓
8 Political parties	✓	✓	✓	✓	✓
9 Pressure groups	✓	✓	✓	✓	✓
10 Public opinion/elections	✓	✓	✓	✓	✓
11 Voting behaviour	✓	✓	✓	✓	✓
12 Local government	✓	✓	✓	✓	✓
13 Europe	✓	✓	✓	✓	✓

Table 1.1 Topics and examination boards

Most of these topics are embedded in the new syllabuses of the examining boards either in a Common Core or Paper One format.

SYLLABUSES

With the exception of the Oxford Board, all the syllabuses below allocate 50 per cent of marks to the compulsory or Common Core Paper One (on British Politics). Oxford allocates 40 per cent. The breakdown of Paper One of the main boards is as follows:

AEB	1	Representation
	2	Decision Making
NEAB	1	Context of Politics in Britain
	2	Representation and Participation in Theory and Practice
	3	The Machinery of Government
ULEAC	1	Political Institutions and Concepts
OXFORD	1	British Political Culture
	2	The Constitutional/Legal Framework
	3	Participation and Representation
	4	The Institutions of Government
OXFORD AND CAMBRIDGE	1	Modern British Politics

ASSESSMENT

You will take two examination papers of three hours each (one British Politics plus one option paper) unless you choose to offer a personal study which will reduce your second paper. Most papers still contain essay questions plus a combination of short answer and data/stimulus response questions. Short answer questions (ULEAC) are designed to test factual knowledge together with the ability to analyse and differentiate between ideas and concepts. Data response questions (NEAB) test understanding and interpretation of data based on selected passages or simple statistics. Questions are usually stepped. Those with the lowest mark (4) can be answered from the text. Those with the middle range mark (7) demand a textual response supported with understanding acquired in your studies. Those with the highest mark (14) test analytical skills and demand a more complex response. Finally stimulus response questions (AEB) demand the combination of all three skills found in data response as the student is expected to display the three levels of understanding, description, explanation and analysis.

KNOWLEDGE AND ABILITIES TESTED

All the A-level Government and Politics syllabuses are approved by SCAA (Schools Examinations and Assessments Authority) and variously test skills, knowledge and understanding. More emphasis is now placed on understanding and skills than on knowledge – it is no longer possible (if it ever was) to score high marks in a Politics A-level paper by simply presenting facts. The NEAB syllabus for 1996 weights ability tested in the examination as follows:

- Knowledge – 30 per cent
- Understanding – 20 per cent
- Application – 20 per cent
- Evaluation and synthesis – 30 per cent

Breaking this down further, the AEB Summer 1995 Chief Examiner's Report on Government and Politics gives allocations for each question marked out of 40 as follows:

1	Knowledge	10	(Objective 1)
2	Behaviour	10	(Objective 2)
3	Analysis	10	(Objective 3)
4	Synthesis	10	(Objective 4)

With **Objective 1** examiners look for a knowledge of the facts. For **Objective 2** they require an understanding of how conflicts are resolved. For **Objective 3** students must display evidence of ability to unpick and identify the components of a proposition bringing them together in a refocused way that answers the question. Finally, **Objective 4** tests synthesis, relevance, structure/organisation and reasoned conclusion. The point is made that examiners now like to see outlines of conclusions at the beginning of the answer as an aid to the development of that answer.

REVISION AND EXAMINATION

REVISION

Keep your revision **active and organised**. You will be given plenty of advice by your teachers or tutors. If you are working alone, consult one of the many books written on this subject from your local library.

Revising for an examination is like preparing for a race – you must gradually build up your stamina, skills and speed for the day when all will be brought into action. Treat it like a long campaign – always think of your studies over a nine month period and plan accordingly, for the second half of the academic year will involve you in taking the examination.

Try to **get organised** at the outset in your studies using file cards or other ways of keeping your notes in order – this will help in revision. If you have been studying effectively throughout the year, you will be surprised at the amount of material you have retained. A revision period should enable you to bring your material to the forefront of your mind. Practise answering examination questions at home within the time limits and gradually improve on your performance each time. **Use your memory and recall powers** to good effect – practise strengthening them whenever you can. Do this orally or in writing. Take a topic – say voting behaviour – and attempt to reproduce all the associated themes, ideas and writers on this subject on one side of A4 paper. Do this for all the topics in this book and rework and reread your file notes, lecture notes and relevant sections in books and articles.

THE EXAMINATION

Apart from the obvious advice like arriving on time, a few simple guidelines can be offered here:

1 **Make sure you know** the time available to answer the paper and allocate it to questions accordingly.
2 **Read the paper carefully** and select only those questions you plan to answer. Avoid panicking at this stage.
3 **Carefully plan each answer** on the examination answer sheet at the head of each question on your paper. Leave the answer plan for the examiner to see and give credit for if necessary.
4 **Time each answer carefully** – do not write longer than the allocated time on one answer. If you squander time on one answer the others will suffer.
5 **Remember the skills** examiners are looking for – essays must be analytical and well answered.
6 **If you make a mistake**, cross it through neatly and carry on, or select a new question if time.
7 **At the end of the examination** – if you have spaced your answers carefully you should have a little time left to read through what you have written and make any last minute corrections. That is why you should leave plenty of space between each answer and always start a new question on a fresh page of the answer book.

POLITICAL CULTURE

THE IDEA OF POLITICAL CULTURE

CONTINUITY IN THE STATE

SOCIAL COHESIONS

POLITICAL CONSENSUS

PROCEDURAL CONSENSUS

THE UNCERTAIN FUTURE

GETTING STARTED

This is one of the most confusing areas of the syllabus for students of British Government. Largely because descriptions and understandings of political culture must rely on concepts borrowed from history, sociology and the social sciences generally, it is difficult to reach precision on what in effect is a study of attitudes, values and acceptances of a whole political system. A study of political culture contributes to our understanding of the finer points of political toleration, obedience and survival of parliamentary government. It can also help our appreciation of how the modern state has accommodated to new social divisions or cleavages in the British public.

The following are the main themes of questions on political culture:

■ Discussions of public support for the political system and the extent to which this has changed.

■ Examination of the nature and context of British political culture in so far as these can be identified.

■ Comparisons of political dissent against political consensus.

■ An appreciation of political toleration and its implications for the British state.

ESSENTIAL PRINCIPLES

THE IDEA OF POLITICAL CULTURE

66 Definitions 99

THE SOCIAL WORLD

Sociologically the idea of a culture relates to descriptions of the norms and values that regulate the conduct of people's lives. These are transmitted from one generation to the next largely by the primary agencies of socialisation – families – and the secondary agencies of schools, institutions and the political system. Borrowing from the **Functional School** in sociology (*Emile Durkheim, Talcott Parsons*) a culture is therefore essential for the maintenance and survival of a social system – it serves to integrate members of society.

THE POLITICAL WORLD

66 Substance and procedure 99

A political culture describes the **values, beliefs, attitudes and emotions** that people display towards their political system. According to *Moran (1994)*, it covers the political culture of a community focusing on both procedural aspects of how we are governed and the substantive questions of what the government should do. People will therefore adopt attitudes to the political system which are dependent very much on upbringing and political socialisation, occupation and other sectoral cleavages like consumption which cut across social class divisions. For example, attitudes to the monarchy in Britain may be changing but they are still generally supportive of the institution despite criticisms over lifestyles and royal marriages in the mid nineties.

Attitudes to the conduct of politics through parliamentary channels as opposed to violence are still prevalent. Generally speaking the British people believe in parliamentary as opposed to anti-parliamentary politics (street demonstrations, direct action protests and extremist or terrorist violence) and this belief has become a **cultural norm**. Although British political culture has never been totally quiet (*Pimlott 1989*), there is widespread support for the institutions of the state and for the idea that elections and the ballot box rather than the bomb and the bullet are the accepted way of transmitting opinions to the politicians. Cultural studies of British politics have attempted to explain British conformity and acquiescence to the status quo using the concept of a civil culture.

CULTURAL STUDIES

66 Civic culture 99

Pioneering work on British political culture was carried out as early as 1963 by the Americans *G Almond and S Verba* using a functionalist perspective. Puzzled as to why British participatory democracy exhibited considerable degrees of subservience to established authority in comparison with other European democracies, they introduced the idea of a civility model. British political culture was neither completely parochial, subject or participant, all of which exhibit variations of involvement or subjection by people to ruling elites. British political culture had a **mix of participant and subject characteristics**. There was a degree of participation through elections transmitting authority to ruling elites, but it was not particularly active. Parochialism was very evident also in the deferential trust placed in the political elite – they were free to govern in the interests of the people provided public opinion was accommodated.

ATTITUDINAL ISSUES

Almond and Verba's descriptions of political culture rested heavily on the ideas of a placid deferential populace subservient to those in authority (probably truer for the working classes who did not form part of the administrative or professional elites necessary for the maintenance of the social system) and in this sense they were repeating the findings of the nineteenth-century writer *Walter Bagehot*. In his classic work on the English constitution first published in 1867, *Bagehot* drew attention to the deferential attitudes of the British people manifested in respect for law and order and

❝ Deferential attitudes ❞

reverence for the monarchy. Pointing to a dichotomy between the form and function of the constitution, *Bagehot* made it clear that the general populace were ignorant of the political power aspects surrounding the dignified monarchy. The Prime Minister and Cabinet held real or efficient political power, but the monarch received the deferential respect of the people who were unaware of this situation. These developments contributed to the long period of quite peaceful politics which the British state had experienced and partially explained why the working class (the masses) accepted political institutions dominated by an aristocratic elite.

During the 1960s there was a tendency for functionalist writers to approach British political culture from this deferential perspective, the only substantive evidence of political attitude towards the state. Studies of voting behaviour had shown how deferential to the Conservative Party certain sections of the working class were (*Parkin 1967, Butler and Stokes 1969*).

MARXISTS

Marxist writers unhappy at this explanation of working class servility began to develop counter theories of **hegemony** to explain continued passive working class adherence to the political and capitalist economic system. Developing the ideas of the Italian writer *Antonio Gramsci, Miliband (1972)* showed how the ruling class dominated the value system of the working class by control of the ideological institutions – the media, education and political parties in the state. Such a view presupposes the working class suffer from a false consciousness in the sense that they cannot see that the political institutions and ideas in the state (which they absorb) are the product of a dominant class ideology.

Modern sociologists working in this field have refined these ideas to take account of more sophisticated explanations of working class cultural attitudes. According to *Marshall (1988)* working class people's attitudes can fall into either **instrumentalism** (acceptance that capitalism works in their interests) or **ambivalence** (neither fully committed to capitalism nor wholeheartedly opposed to it). If either of these positions is accurate, working class attitudes to a dominant ruling class cultural model are no longer capable of simplistic interpretations (see Figure 2.1).

❝ Values ❞

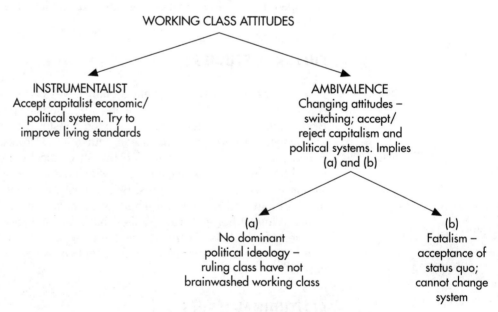

Fig. 2.1 Working class cultural attitudes to the state and economic system

CONTINUITY IN THE STATE

The British have a long historical continuity for their political state. Although there was a civil war in the seventeenth century this was not the revolutionary break with the past experienced later in some countries. Parliamentary government was restored after Cromwell together with a redefined monarchy ruling through representatives of the people. By the nineteenth century Britain was moving towards representative and popular government as we know it. Political power was flowing towards a newly enfranchised working class and their representatives. The twentieth century saw the completion of the franchise and the establishment of total representative government. Other developments as a result of the growth of the political party system meant the virtual dominance of the House of Commons by an executive assuming power through a Prime Ministerial governmental system backed by a Cabinet operating on collegiate or monocratic power guidelines. According to *Madgwick (1994)*, there was a circular development to British political history which passed through the following stages:

1 **Supreme monarch** – dominant executive to seventeenth century
2 **Dual power** – monarch and Parliament sharing power (eighteenth century)
3 **Dominant Parliament** – eighteenth to nineteenth century
4 **Dual power** – Parliamentary executive managing House of Commons
5 **Supreme executive** – dominant executive (Prime Minister and Cabinet) based on Parliament

The past therefore presses heavily on the present practice of British politics and its stability may explain conservative attachment to the institutions of the state. (*Madgwick 1994*). The past cannot be changed but successive British governments have substantive choice of policies within this operational framework.

SOCIAL COHESIONS

CULTURAL DIVERSITY

Britain has become descriptively a culturally homogeneous society – the majority of the population have an English, Welsh or Scots ethnic background; the minority are descended from immigrants who entered the country at various times. In the nineteenth and early twentieth centuries the British host population absorbed immigrants from Ireland and Europe and from the 1950s from the Commonwealth, the West Indies and the Indian sub-continent. Britain has been painfully transformed into a multi-cultural society with both Labour and Conservative governments eventually forced to restrict immigration (in the hope that this would improve race relations) and pass race relations laws.

The majority of immigrants from the New Commonwealth have settled in areas of high population concentration, for example in London and the cities of the North and Midlands where they have been made welcome by other immigrants. There are a number of cultural perspectives applicable to an understanding of immigrant-host relations.

1 **Assimilation** Assimilationists tend to the view that ethnic communities should adapt to the British way of life. They argue that the problems faced by immigrants are cultural rather than racist and they can be overcome by conformity to the institutions of the host country (*Patterson 1965*).
2 **Ethnic pluralism** This view points to the wide variety of cultural groups in Britain. There is already a multi-cultural society in existence and it is easy to over simplify by focusing on a single ethnic culture (*Gilroy 1987*). Pluralists tend to see the relationship between host majority and ethnic minority as one of coexistence rather than dominance by English cultural values.
3 **Class culture** Marxists tend to regard ethnic culture as less important than class culture for purposes of analysis. They believe the focus should be on dominant and subordinate class positions rather than minority – majority cultures. From this perspective migrant labourers constitute a fraction of the working class and share all the disadvantages of this group (*Westergaard and Resler 1976*).

ETHNICITY AND THE VOTE

It is often claimed that ethnic minority voters are preponderantly Labour largely because that party has a softer image on race relations and immigration issues generally. The three Race Relations Acts were all passed under Labour governments (*Denver 1989*). Apart from ethnicity other factors put forward as explanations of the ethnic vote include class and political geography. If the majority of immigrants fall into a working class category then the same influences pressing on the host working class will operate. The difficulty with this simplistic view is that there is little evidence to support the notion of either a united ethnic or working class. The evidence for geographical concentrations of black Labour votes is stronger. As immigrants have tended to concentrate in areas of Britain where ethnic communities are preponderant, so this has increased the tie between the Labour Party and this category of voter.

CELTIC NATIONALISM

" Parts of Britain "

The cultural cohesion of Britain is further affected by celtic nationalism. Of the four constituent parts of what *Rose* (*1971*) calls a multi-national state – comprising England, Scotland, Wales and Northern Ireland – all groups except the English have some self government aspiration. The Scottish National Party is now in favour of a completely independent Scotland, whilst the Welsh National Party concentrates on keeping the Welsh language and culture alive. In Northern Ireland, despite (or because of) the 1994 cease-fire and 1995 ongoing peace talks and the resumption of the bombing campaign in 1996, Irish nationalists and Sinn Fein are intent on securing an all Ireland government whilst Ulster Unionists seek to maintain their identity within the United Kingdom. The implications of this aspect are that growing minorities in these former separate nations feel alienated from the governing British party at Westminster (in the 1995 local elections the Conservatives failed to gain control of a single authority in Scotland) and are prepared to support parties which advocate some form of self governing arrangement with the centre.

CLASS AND SECTORAL DIVISIONS

The social fabric of Britain still exhibits class and sectoral divisions although there is a remarkable degree of self control among the different groups. Some writers claim that the passivity of the British in the face of what is an unequal society economically rests on the acceptance of the status quo. Working class attitudes have come to terms with the capitalist economic system, partly through rising living standards and cultural change. The **embourgeoisement debate** may have been discredited in the sense that possession of a higher living standard did not change the Labour-voting working class into Conservative (*Goldthorpe, Lockwood, Bechofer and Platt 1969*) but it was the first to pick up the growing scepticism or development of instrumental polit-

" Skilled working class "

ical attitudes. Margaret Thatcher successfully attracted the skilled working class vote (the C2s) in the three Conservative election victories of 1979, 1983 and 1987, largely because of policy voting for issues which offered greater shares of wealth to that section (*Crewe 1992*). Popular capitalist measures of sales of council houses, privatisation of public utilities and lower taxation attracted large sections of the working class vote. However, by the 1992 general election the effects of these advantages were wearing thin with the result that the Labour Party regained the majority share of its traditional C2 vote for the first time in twelve years, even though it lost the election again.

As **class and party dealignment** theories have been developed to show post war electoral volatility breaking monolithic Labour and Conservative support, so new explanations tend to focus on other cleavages in the populace. Class categories are no longer permanent. *Crewe* (*1985*) first distinguished between the more affluent new working class, who were predominantly owner occupiers and working in private industry, and the poorer northern traditional old working class, who were living in council houses and were still reliant on trade unions and the Labour Party. Changes in middle class culture have opened new divisions between traditional and new professions and salariat and service classes so increasing contradictory class locations in these groups. This again makes pronouncements about political behaviour difficult (*Wright 1976*).

The class structure of Britain is more fluid than at any time since 1945 due in large measure to changes in industrial and employment patterns, educational opportunities and increased social mobility. Vertical consumption patterns divide and cut horizontal class categories on the basis of those who are self-reliant and those who need the State – those with wealth and those without (*Dunleavy 1979*). One consequence of this is that although talk of a classless society is premature, class is having less of an impact on British politics and culture generally.

POLITICAL CONSENSUS

Political consensus or agreement contradicts the idea that politics and political activity exist because of disagreements, that politics is the settlement of disputes. Clearly if politics ended, political society as we know it would cease. Yet party politicians make rhetorical public statements whilst privately agreeing on many policy issues (*Kavanagh 1992*). Analysis of consensus demands that we separate the substantive from the procedural, since consensus about ends (policy) is clearly different from consensus over means (procedure). Some critics claim that substantive or policy con sensus disappeared under the governments of Margaret Thatcher only to return in a different form with John Major. But discussion of consensus also involves an examination of the part played by the opposition reacting to government policies.

POLICY CONSENSUS

❝ Post war consensus ❞

The classic period of substantive or policy consensus occurred after 1945 – the post war consensus – when there was broad agreement and no great ideological difference between the Conservative and Labour parties in certain areas. According to *Seldon (1994)* there were six features of continuity or overlap between Conservative and Labour policies where divisions between the two parties were insignificant:

1   Commitment to full employment.

2   Acceptance of a mixed economy of state and private enterprise.

3   Support for the welfare state idea of providing state security in health and welfare for the majority.

4   Close relationships maintained with trade unions as representatives of organised labour.

5   Promotion of policies designed to reduce inequality in society through progressive taxation.

6   Bilateral approach between Conservative and Labour Parties towards foreign and defence policies.

It is not difficult to find the origins of the post war consensus for they lay in the general desire of politicians of all parties to improve the lot of the people of Britain immediately preceding and after the Second World War. Plans were laid for improvements to the welfare benefits system (**the Beveridge Report 1942**) which were acceptable to both sides together with positive steps to increase government intervention in regulation of the economy to ensure a better match between supply and demand. The moderate Conservative *Harold Macmillan* had argued as early as the 1930s for a better 'middle way' solution to the problem of mass unemployment and the party under *Winston Churchill* (Prime Minister 1940–45 and 1951–55) came to accept **Keynesian** monetary policy (after the economist *John Maynard Keynes*) which appeared to find the solution to managing inflation with full employment.

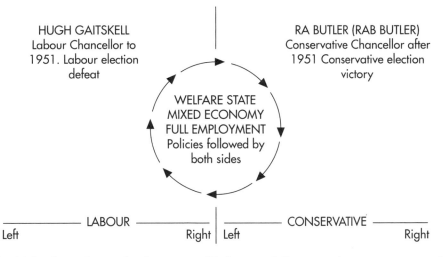

Fig. 2.2 Consensus 1951–55. Moderate Conservative economic and monetary policy (Butskellism)

The fairly short alternation in power of Labour and Conservative governments during the 1950s and the fact that the Conservative Party were returned to office in 1951 with a small majority contributed to feelings of policy consensus in the electorate with the result that governments did not depart too far from the centre ground. This was particularly evident in the field of economic and monetary policy where **Butskellite** policies of the moderate Conservative Chancellor, *R A Butler*, bore a striking resemblance to those of his predecessor in post, the moderate Labour Chancellor, *Hugh Gaitskell* (see Figure 2.2).

CHANGING CONSENSUS

It is difficult to be precise over the date when the post war consensus or consensual policies between the two major parties began to diverge. Certainly government and opposition throughout the 1960s and 1970s were not widely different in their support for the status quo and consensus policies – Harold Macmillan, Alec Douglas Home, Harold Wilson, Edward Heath and finally James Callaghan all in their own ways followed middle ground substantive ideas. Despite party rhetoric (mainly for the benefit of party activists) Conservative and Labour governments to 1979 presided over or reached what came to be called the **high point of consensus** (*Holmes and Horsewood 1988*). From that point on consensus would become a term of abuse as the new radical Margaret Thatcher sought to lead the Conservative Party into a new direction.

MARGARET THATCHER AND CONSENSUS POLITICS

Consensus politics broke down under the Conservative governments from 1979 for a number of reasons – some practical, some ideological. Economically the policies of Keynesian money management were discredited as economic growth slowed and unemployment throughout the eighties rose. *Margaret Thatcher* turned to the economic philosophies of the 'New Right' to overcome the fiscal crises of the state whereby state incomes do not keep up with state expenditure. The removal of the commitment to full employment allowed tighter control over the money supply as advocated by the monetarist philosophies of *Milton Friedman.* In return this meant that state spending could be targeted on welfare benefits whilst maintaining a reduced form of welfare state system. In many policy areas, for example housing, privatisation, local government, education and the civil service, the intention was to drive down public expenditure by the introduction of market forces principles in line with new Conservative thinking on the advantages of free enterprise as opposed to state involvement. In this Margaret Thatcher was successful – British political culture was radically altered along with the cosy world of consensus politics.

❝ **New Right ideas** ❞

As the political divide began to open again there were those who felt the Conservative Party was pushing its radicalism to unpopular extremes. Yet the party was successful in three consecutive general elections under its radical leader. Paradoxically it was fear of losing a fourth general election that prompted the party to remove Margaret Thatcher and replace her by the more consensual John Major in 1990.

CONSENSUS POLITICS IN THE NINETIES

Margaret Thatcher succeeded in one of her stated aims in changing the course of socialism for she compelled the Labour Party to move closer ideologically to the centre ground after a radical shake-up of policy first under Neil Kinnock (to 1992), then John Smith (to 1994) and finally Tony Blair (from 1994). In abandoning the more extremist socialist policies under Tony Blair, then accepting many of the policy changes of Margaret Thatcher and John Major, the Labour Party moved back to the right of the political spectrum raising the probability of an end to **adversary politics** as the two major parties became locked in popularity contests for votes at general elections.

Although John Major has continued with the broad drift of Thatcherite policies since 1990, he has been anxious to stamp his own personality on the party, particularly since he was elected in his own right in the 1992 general election. Many former Conservative policies have continued, such as those concerned with management of the economy, whilst there have been initiatives in making state services more responsive to the public – the Citizens' Charter of 1991 could be seen in this light.

ELECTORAL PROBLEMS OF CONSENSUS

66 Centre ground 99

A major difficulty for John Major as the next election approaches will be reasserting his party's identity in the face of a new Labour Party also crowding into the centre ground where the median voters are found. As Labour is now a respectful party of government, not protest, it will endeavour to show how it will run the state better than the existing Conservatives since most elections are lost on a government's record rather than opposition appeal. Throughout 1995 and 1996 the Conservatives were anxious to establish **clear blue water** between themselves, the Labour Party and the Liberal Democrats. If there is a new consensus between John Major and Tony Blair, both parties will be fighting on the same territory unless they return to their activist wings as is the usual practice during general election contests, reasserting again their different philosophies (see Figure 2.3).

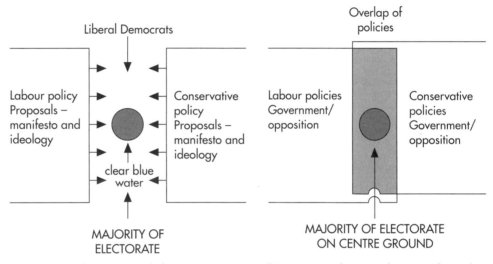

Fig. 2.3 a) and b) Consensus during general elections and consensus during Parliaments (the reality)

a) Consensus during general elections

b) Consensus during Parliaments (the reality)

In practical terms, therefore, the political parties cannot afford to alienate the electorate by appearing too extreme, yet they have to distance themselves from each other for identification reasons. General election campaigns are often fought using rhetorical statements giving an impression of intense cultural, ideological and class division in the conduct of British politics. The reality in administration and parliamentary politics may be further from this appearance, however, as even the radical Margaret Thatcher had less of an impact on the culture than is popularly supposed (*Vincent 1987*).

PROCEDURAL CONSENSUS

Procedural consensus implies that there is agreement about the means of conducting political debate even if there are substantive disputes over the content of political ideologies. There is still widespread acceptance of parliamentary channels or the law in settlement of grievances by the majority. A minority might be prepared to use violence against the state to achieve the replacement of laws they perceive as illegitimate as a last resort. This has occurred on relatively few occasions – discounting events in Northern Ireland – and includes opposition to industrial relations legislation and the Miners Strike in 1984, inner city riots in the early eighties and nineties and demonstrations against the Community Charge or Poll Tax 1988–1990.

66 Violence and state 99

Although criminal acts are clearly different to civil disobedience by virtue of motive – the one selfish, the other moral – demonstrations and anti-political activity are close to the dividing line between lawful and unlawful activity (*Heywood 1994*). Occasional outbreaks of violence also lead to claims of ungovernability, breakdown in law and order or support for the government. Marxist writers regard this as evidence of a **legitimation crisis** in the capitalist state – as people lose faith in the ability of government to reconcile conflicting demands so the state loses its legitimacy to govern. There is a corresponding lack of motivation to participate in the democratic processes with the result that citizens turn to other forms of political activity (*Habermas 1976*).

Without accepting this pessimistic view of the state, there is clearly some evidence that people came to expect too much of governments after 1945. The so-called revolution of rising expectations for a continual improvement in living standards, which could not be delivered by governments despite increased spending on the welfare state and the use of Keynesian economic management, affected public confidence in politicians' ability to govern. The rejection of consensus politics by Margaret Thatcher after 1979 was in part a reaction to what had been perceived as an over-generous state, and a realisation that people could no longer look to government for solutions.

CONSTITUTIONAL DISPUTES

Politically, procedural consensus breaks down over debates on the fairness of the electoral system. Although there is still all-party support for the idea that major constitutional change (altering the electoral system for example) requires the support of all the parties, there is a growing realisation that nothing will change until after the next general election. The Liberal Democrats wish to move to a more equitable proportional system of election, the Labour Party are equivocal and the Conservatives reject outright any ideas of changing the status quo. Until this question is solved there will be a sizeable proportion of the electorate (17.8 per cent of the total electorate supported the Liberal Democratic Party in the 1992 general election) who feel alienated from the democratic process. From the Liberal Democratic viewpoint, there is no justice in the existing British system of counting the vote and a proportional system will bring a fairer distribution of parliamentary seats.

66 Liberal Democratic support 99

The question of the continuation of the constitutional arrangements for Wales and Scotland was settled in the devolution debates and referendums of the late seventies, but again there is measurable electoral support for separate Welsh and Scottish Parliaments. The whole question of the British unitary constitution arrangement is bound up with the future direction of Northern Ireland, the British government's reaction to the original IRA cease-fire from 1994 to 1996 and the restoration of democratic government to the province of Ulster. If the Northern Irish people are again given their own parliament (the Protestant dominated Stormont Parliament lasted from 1921 to 1972) there will be demands from Welsh and Scottish Nationalists to be treated in the same way.

MODERATE GOVERNMENT

British governments usually command a majority in Parliament with the result that they can claim legitimate power or authority to rule. Although this legitimacy gives them authority over a vast governmental machine, they still depend on cooperation (consent willingly given) and acceptance from the electorate to achieve their programme. Little is to be gained in a democratic state from **coercion** and outright control over the people who have ultimate sovereignty to remove their rulers through parliamentary elections. Clearly there will be disputes in any political system and democratic governments usually display **toleration** towards the expression of minority opinion. Clearly, if such opinion coalesces into anti-democratic movements that threaten the survival or security of the state, then the government will use coercion and security forces to remove that threat.

66 State power 99

The case of Northern Ireland is illustrative. Here, on a simplistic level, the IRA and its nationalist allies sought to achieve by violence what they failed to achieve through democratic argument and persuasion. Since republicans could not convince the Unionist majority to support unification with all Ireland (Catholics were in a difficult Protestant tyranny of the majority statehood situation) they turned to anti-state revolutionary or war tactics as a last resort. In using the armed forces to defeat or neutralise republicanism, the British government had to avoid over-reacting to the IRA threat by the massive use of fire power. As a result, British troops were never allowed by the politicians to mount a full scale war against nationalist and republican forces (the use of battle tanks was either considered unnecessary against a guerilla enemy or considered provocative, for example) with the result that the army fought an anti-insurgency campaign from 1969 to 1994 – the date of the original IRA cease-fire. As long as the IRA felt it had more to gain politically by continued armed resistance to the British government, it kept fighting. The signing of the Downing Street Declaration in December 1993 and the original cease-fire were recognition that the nationalists at last had a realistic opportunity to advance their aims through democratic methods. The resumption of the bombing capaign in 1996 demonstrated IRA impatience with the progress of the peace initiative and was used as a bargaining device to bring pressure on the British government.

THE UNCERTAIN FUTURE

It is difficult to generalise about British political culture. Commentators saw the fifties as a time of restraint with quiet political activity and remarked on the acquiescent attitudes of the people towards their rulers (*Beer 1965*). The high point for the post war consensus came during the sixties and seventies paradoxically during a period of pessimism when the survival of British parliamentary democracy was being questioned. The eighties marked a retreat from consensus to conviction politics under the radical government of Margaret Thatcher with a noticeable change in public attitudes to the state. Some detected a move away from political movements, the so called 'end of ideology' debate; others detected a 'post material' outlook manifested in concerns for the environment and new social movements (*Inglehart 1977*).

❝ New attitudes ❞

The nineties have witnessed consolidations in the cultural make-up of the United Kingdom and changed attitudes to the institutions of the state, for example the monarchy and electoral system have lost the element of certainty they once had. As a Conservative government continues into its seventeenth consecutive year in 1996, there are those who begin to doubt that the present two party system is functioning as it should. This may have a connection to the increasing apathy and uncertainty felt by many opposed to the present party system that excludes one major and one significant minor party from power.

EXAMINATION QUESTIONS

1 'The British political system no longer enjoys the high degree of public support it once did.' Discuss. *(25)*

(NEAB)

2 (a) Why is the British system of government described as parliamentary?

(b) Distinguish between extra-parliamentary and anti-parliamentary actions.

(20)

(ULEAC)

3 'Dissension and division rather than consensus and homogeneity are now the key features of British political culture.' Discuss. *(25)*

(NEAB)

ANSWERS TO EXAMINATION QUESTIONS

OUTLINE ANSWER TO QUESTION 2

a) This question demands a knowledge of the theoretical position of parliamentary government. An answer could discuss the idea of sovereignty of the people giving way to parliamentary sovereignty. It is important to show an understanding of the theory of the representative and the relationships to constituents prevailing in an indirect democracy.

b) Discuss the importance of extra-parliamentary activity as an adjunct to the legislature. This includes pressure groups and other organisations representing interests in the state usually working through democratic channels which may include protests. Anti-parliamentary actions may be political as opposed to criminal but they focus on public opinion as leverage over politicians. Some anti-parliamentary activity involves violence as a tool against government and is clearly anti-democratic. Other anti-parliamentary action (e.g. street demonstrations) is designed to draw political attention to a pressing issue demanding resolution.

TUTOR'S ANSWER TO QUESTION 1

Democratic politics in the true sense of having an enfranchised and educated electorate is relatively new in the life of the British state. All women did not achieve the vote until 1928 and compulsory secondary education was not introduced much before 1900. Attachment to British parliamentary democracy by the mass of the people is therefore surprising considering the short time in which Parliament has been democratised. The degree of public support for a democratic political system is manifested in a number of ways or passes through a number of tests. There must be political parties, pressure groups and a free mass media to transmit public opinion from the electorate to the rulers. The machinery of government must include arrangements for free elections and other tests of public opinion to ensure the periodic replacement of one party by another, and the people must feel political activity is worthwhile. In terms of alternatives, the British state is democratic for opposition parties can challenge the government and if elected by consent can respond to new popular demands.

In any political system there will be a relationship between the minority – usually the government – and the majority – usually the electorate. Attitudes of the electorate towards a government will be conditioned by a number of factors and will vary according to political situations. In one sense the electorate are not monolithic – there are divisions of class, culture, section and interest. Talk of electoral apathy or satisfaction with government and the political system must therefore be used with care. The relationship between the governing minority and electoral majority may be harmonious or one of conflict. Fortunately the British have evolved a system of representative democracy which does not demand active participation of the majority in the political activity of the country. It is too easy to read into this the idea of a subservient populace acquiescing in all the decisions of the government contributing to the long period of stability and respect for the British political system (*G. Almond and S. Verba*). Studies of political consensus have passed through a post war period when the main political parties agreed on welfare state policies to a high point in the seventies when strains first appeared in the arrangement. Margaret Thatcher from 1979 was the first post war Prime Minister to set her government's direction against the continuation of consensus for ideological reasons and this would have far reaching consequences.

A major difficulty with the conviction politics style of Margaret Thatcher in terms of political attachment to a democratic government was the emphasis on sectional as opposed to majoritarian policies. Despite winning three consecutive general elections (1979, 1983 and 1987) the Conservative government was elected on a minority of the popular vote (less than 50 per cent), as all governments of whatever political persuasion have been since 1945. It could be argued, therefore, that to proceed with a radical programme of reform to the institutions and culture of the state (the introduction of market forces philosophy, privatisation, changes to the welfare state benefit and tax system and departure from the policies of full employment) was an exercise in minority government power at the expense of majority interests. Yet many of the measures were popular, for example the sale of council houses and the privatisation programme which spread the level of wealth downwards to the working class. On the other hand, unpopular policies like the introduction of the community charge or poll tax created great resentment and protest and the poll tax had to be withdrawn – after damaging both the political culture, the Conservative Party and Margaret Thatcher herself. It was claimed that the poll tax destroyed the tradition of regular and obedient payment of local taxes which had long been a feature of local government and replaced it by a surly, rebellious and resentful populace.

The period of Conservative government under Margaret Thatcher 1979–90 placed serious stresses on the body politic and political culture. Although many gained from the prosperity engendered during those years, the losers in the state were the disadvantaged, the unemployed and those opposed to Thatcherism. For example, the urban unrests culminating in inner city riots in the early eighties had as their cause unemployment, deprivation and racial disadvantage (*Benyon 1986*). These and other actions increased feelings of public apathy to the political system felt by a large number of the electorate.

At the level of local government, growing Conservative centralisation and reduction of local power antagonised those councils under Labour control. These oppositional councils developed a variety of urban socialist techniques whereby they could maintain spending on the disadvantaged in their areas in the face of central restrictions on finance. Changes to the system of local government finance (capping, standard spending assessment, abolition of the rates) and finally the abolition of the Greater London Council and metropolitan councils in 1986 further reduced the areas of resistance to the policies of Margaret Thatcher.

The arrival of John Major as Conservative Prime Minister in 1990 ushered in a new period of consensual politics with a more compliant style of governing. Although he continued with many of the reforms of his predecessor in the political system, he was quick to replace the community charge with the more acceptable council tax. This one act restored the faith of many local Conservatives disillusioned with the departure from traditional Tory one-nation values.

Public support for the political system has always suffered from those opposed to the existing constitutional arrangement of unitary government and the electoral system. Welsh and Scottish Nationalist feeling was tested in two referendums in 1979 which resulted in the rejection of plans for separate assemblies in those countries. Despite this, as *Mitchell* (*1994*) notes, the majority of people living in Scotland did not vote for the four successive Conservative governments in power since 1979. Welsh Nationalism has never been such a force in that country but nevertheless a considerable number of Welsh voters are Labour supporters and that party has been out of power for seventeen years. Whether this means a majority of Welsh and Scottish people have been effectively disenfranchised under the Conservative governments of Margaret Thatcher and John Major is debatable. The British system of parliamentary representation has never placed doctrinal and ideological support behind the idea that the member of Parliament is delegated to the legislature to represent a particular interest or section. Under the Burkian view, MPs represent all their constituents whether they supported them or not.

The arguments over representation are more serious for those in Northern Ireland where Catholics and nationalists have suffered political discrimination in the past. The IRA campaign of violence contributed to the general feelings of ungovernability and apathy from a sizeable minority in that part of Ireland which had repercussions for the rest of Britain. The attempts to settle this conflict are continuing and the original IRA cease-fire of 1994 reduced tension in the province to the benefit of all citizens of both Protestant and Catholic persuasion.

Finally, there is some evidence that public apathy and disillusionment with government owed something to misplaced unrealistic economic expectations that governments from the 1960s would continue to bring prosperity – the Harold Macmillan 'never had it so good' arguments. Because of the economic difficulties and recessions of the seventies and eighties, there is now less public reliance on a continual revolution of rising expectations. If this idea is coupled with the general decline in the belief in political ideology – the end of ideology thesis – Margaret Thatcher's emphasis on self reliance and less state involvement in people's lives may have been more in keeping with modern attitudes to the state. People now expect less from government but conversely are not as strongly committed to either major political party. That does not imply that democracy is in danger – only that attitudes are changing.

STUDENT'S ANSWER TO QUESTION 3 WITH EXAMINER'S COMMENTS

> Britain has had a relatively stable political culture throughout her history with change coming about more by evolution compared to America or Russia's revolutionary background. To say, however, that Britain has an entirely peaceful past would be untrue; the Glorious Revolution of 1688 is testimony to this.
>
> Part of the reason for such continuity may be the degree of political consensus that has been present in the country over the years and also the social and cultural cohesion of Britain has added to her stability. There has

66 Good historical beginning 99

been a string of quite moderate governments too, recently, who have never really strayed too far from a liberal compromise of public ideals and opinions. This is another considerable factor adding to Britain's reputation of being a homogenised political culture.

In 1959-60 two American political scientists Almond and Verba, when studying political culture, put Britain forward as an excellent example of a balanced political society. They characterised the culture as having respect from its citizens who were confident in what their political system did for them and believed themselves able to effectively take part in it as and when they felt the need. There was a healthy mix of active participant citizens and passive deferential subjects. This attitude of deference provides a useful and important factor which could be related to peaceful change in Britain.

However, many have argued that things have changed considerably since Almond and Verba's work. The eighties brought about a new abrasive and rebellious youth culture, liberalisation of sexual behaviour, some street riots and phenomena such as football hooliganism. An altogether more conflictive culture was becoming apparent. Britain's characteristic cohesion, a lot of which was based on tradition, was breaking up.

The idea of political consensus can be seen as going through highs and lows but generally neither party has done anything too out of step with public values. There was a high degree of consensus in the fifties where after the setting up of the welfare state by the Labour government, the Conservatives accepted much of Labour's work. There also emerged the term 'Butskellism' which referred to the high amount of agreement on economic policy between the Conservative and Labour Chancellors, R A Butler and Hugh Gaitskell. This consensus broke down somewhat in the eighties with the radical Mrs Thatcher taking office and taking measures to privatise 10 per cent of the economy in her eleven years in power.

It seems now, though, that the two main parties are moving back towards the centre of the political spectrum with the election of a very moderate Labour leader Tony Blair and the pragmatic John Major holding much in common. There are writers who argue that the idea of a political consensus is largely a myth. Ben Pimlott is one such writer, who sees the voters 'sandbagged in two great trenches battling it out with the Liberals floundering in no-man's land'. Lowe makes an interesting and very relevant distinction on the issue of defining consensus. He asks whether what is meant is what each party has done in the past or what each say they intend to do, whilst in opposition. If we take the first definition then a consensus could arguably be said to exist.

Public opinion on politics has also seemingly changed. There seems to be no more of the deference which was apparently measured by Almond and Verba but a sort of indifference and cynicism has replaced it. The pomp of Parliament and the dated pseudo-mysticism of the monarchy have disillusioned the electorate on what politics is actually about. Numerous scandals involving politicians and respected members of the public and royalty have led to a decline in confidence in authority figures by most

❝ Could be more clearly expressed ❞

66 Innaccurate reference 99

people, so whilst the legitimacy of politicians and people in power positions does not go unquestioned, there does seem to remain a society clearly based around order with no revolutionary action arising from a degree of public discontent. There are those who are not overcome with apathy on matters where abuses of power have been seen to happen. A contemporary example would be the coalition against the new Criminal Justice Act which violates around eight of the sub-sections in the EU documentation for the protection of civil liberties and human rights. Indeed the British populace has not always been entirely subservient; in 1649 Charles I was beheaded for breaching his contract with his people. Similarly it would be naive to say conflict is an inherent part of most developed trading and capitalist societies. Employers and employees contrive to demonstrate their opposite interests even today. The most recently publicised example would be the Railtrack signal workers' dispute, with the workers wanting better pay and conditions and the executives wanting to maximise profits.

There is, I would argue, a degree of dissension and division in politics today with groups like the British National Party aggravating demonstrations from various anti-Nazi groups and an increased campaigning effort on behalf of the left wing Socialist Workers Party on issues such as the signal workers dispute, VAT on fuel and the privatisation of the Post Office (or at least its proposal). The main parties, those who have a reasonable chance of gaining power, however, remain in agreement on many things while fundamental ideological differences still divide the two and the participating active citizen and deferential subject which Almond and Verba talked of have now been replaced by the indifferent apathetic cynical voter.

66 A very competent essay even if a little confused in parts. There is little reference to Celtic Nationalism or the ethnic make up of the United Kingdom but you have included numerous points. Certainly worthy of a high C or low B grade. 99

REFERENCES IN THE TEXT

Almond, G and S Verba 1963 *The civic culture, political attitudes and democracy in five nations*, Princeton University Press

Beer, S 1965 *Modern British Politics*, London: Faber

Benyon J 1986 Turmoil in the cities, *Social Studies Review*. January

Butler, D and D Stokes 1969 *Political change in Britain*, London: Macmillan

Crewe, I 1985 Can Labour rise again?, *Social Studies Review* **1**

Crewe, I 1992 Why did Labour lose (yet again)?, *Politics Review* **2** September

Denver, D 1989 *Elections and voting behaviour in Britain*, Hemel Hempstead: Philip Allan

Dunleavy, P 1979 The urban basis of political alignment, *British Journal of Political Science* **9**

Gilroy, P 1987 *There ain't no Black in the Union Jack*, London: Hutchinson

Goldthorpe, J H, D Lockwood, F Bechofer and J Platt 1969 *The affluent worker in the class structure*, Cambridge University Press

Habermas, J 1976 *Legitimation crisis*, London: Heinemann

Heywood, A 1994 *Political ideas and concepts*, London: Macmillan

Holmes, M and N Horsewood 1988 The consensus debate, *Contemporary Record* Summer

Inglehart, R 1977 *The silent revolution*, Princeton University Press

Kavanagh, D 1992 *British politics: continuities and change*, Oxford: Oxford University Press

Madgwick, P 1994 *A new introduction to British politics*, Cheltenham: Stanley Thornes (Publishers)

Marshall, G 1988 Some remarks on the study of working class consciousness. In D Rose (ed.) *Social Stratification and Economic Change*, London: Hutchinson

Miliband, R 1972 *The state in capitalist society*, London: Weidenfeld and Nicholson

Mitchell, J 1994 Devolution. In W Wale (ed.) *Developments in politics* **5** Ormskirk: Causeway Press

Moran, M 1994 Political culture and political participation. In B Jones et al. *Politics UK*, 2nd edn. Hemel Hempstead: Harvester Wheatsheaf

Parkin, F 1967 Working class Conservatives, *British Journal of Sociology*

Patterson, S 1965 *Dark strangers*, Harmondsworth: Penguin

Pimlott, B 1989 Is the postwar consensus a myth? *Contemporary Record* Summer

Rose, R 1971 *Governing without consensus: an Irish perspective*, London: Faber

Seldon, A 1994 The rise and fall (and rise again?) of the post war consensus. In B Jones et al. *Politics UK*, 2nd edn. Hemel Hempstead: Harvester Wheatsheaf

Vincent, J 1987 Mrs Thatcher's place in history, *Contemporary Record* Autumn

Westergaard, J and H Resler 1976 *Class in a capitalist society*, Harmondsworth: Penguin

Wright, E O 1976 Class boundaries in advanced capitalist societies, *New Left Review* **98**

CHAPTER 3

THE CONSTITUTION

DESCRIBING THE CONSTITUTION

CENTRAL FEATURES

PROBLEMS IN THE CONSTITUTION

CONSTITUTIONAL REFORM

GETTING STARTED

The British constitution has many admirers; as an ancient institution it is one of the oldest in continuous existence. It has changed by adaptation to political circumstances (not by revolution) so has remained uncodified or consolidated in a single format. But for a variety of reasons there is now less satisfaction with the **traditional evolutionary route** to constitutional change. It is now more difficult to accommodate current political forms within old structures; the **new** wine in old bottles argument is less acceptable. There is greater pressure for structural change to the constitution itself than at any time in its long history.

Questions on this subject centre around the following themes:

- The impact of the European Union on the constitution.
- Arguments for and against a written constitution.
- Whether Britain should introduce a Bill of Rights.
- Different party political views on the constitution.

Useful definitions

- **Constitution** – an arrangement within a political state regulating the allocation of power – between the government and the governed.
- **Executive** – the branch of government dealing with policy making and its implementation. In Britain the Prime Minister and Cabinet fall within this description.
- **Legislature** – the parliamentary branch of government where laws are made – the House of Commons and House of Lords.
- **Judiciary** – the system of courts and judges who operate the administration of the law.

ESSENTIAL PRINCIPLES

DESCRIBING THE CONSTITUTION

❝ Political reality ❞

CONFUSION IN DESCRIPTIONS

There is no one single document that encompasses all descriptions of the British constitution. This may have led to confusion in the past as to what the constitution really was, but if it is remembered that no constitution can completely describe all political arrangements within a modern state, then the lack of a written document is not a handicap.

A constitution describes the relationships prevailing between the government and the governed within certain parameters, laws, customs and precedents (*Hood Phillips 1978*). It also regulates behaviour between the various branches of government: executive, legislative and judicial. The British constitution is generally regarded as **prescriptive** or informal because of the lack of a single written document to describe or formalise this arrangement. According to *Norton (1988)* it is this lack of abstract principles found in **descriptive** constitutions which has allowed the British constitution to work so effectively in the past.

STRUCTURES

Structurally the modern British constitution can be described as a constitutional monarchy governed by ministers in the name of the Queen (see Figure 3.1). The executive includes these ministers and the Prime Minister who are responsible for policy formulation and implementation. The legislature involves Parliament where the laws are passed. The judiciary through judges and the courts operates the laws. Finally, the European Union makes legislation which is binding on the whole system.

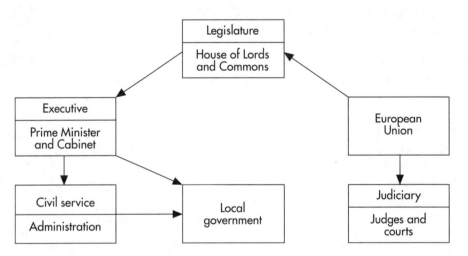

Fig. 3.1 The structure of the British constitution

THE SEPARATION OF POWERS

The three branches of government – the executive, legislature and judiciary – are kept separate according to the principle of the separation of powers. The eighteenth-century political theorist Baron Montesquieu first observed that a **concentration of power** in a political system could best be avoided by separating government branches. This structure was adopted in the American constitution (1787), but has evolved differently in Britain. In the British constitution the principle is accepted in that the judicial branch is formally separated from the executive and legislature and functions without political interference. But for procedural reasons the personnel in the branches are not separated so there is an overlapping of power. The executive (Prime Minister and Cabinet Ministers) are drawn from and responsible to the legislature (the House of Commons and House of Lords). This has two implications:

❝ Executive–legislative overlap ❞

■ There is a lack of formal check and balance over the powers of the executive.

■ The powers of the executive have grown at the expense of the legislature.

Both these features weaken the separated powers argument and lead to a concentration of authority in the hands of the executive. Early criticism of this overlapping power was made by the jurist *Lord Hewart* in his 'new despotism' arguments in 1929. This found an echo in *Lord Hailsham's* 'elective dictatorship' arguments of 1976.

WRITTEN OR UNWRITTEN

❝ Uncertainty ❞

Constitutions are often classified according to whether they are formally written down in a descriptive document or informally organised in a prescriptive arrangement. The fact that the British constitution is unwritten is no disadvantage in deciphering the political arrangement. It does not, as some claim, lead to uncertainty or a political vacuum because ideas and values are not clearly characterised (*Peele 1993*). The drawbacks of not having a written constitution in Britain have been overstated for no document can entirely encompass the political practices of a nation. The political reality is closer to the constitutional arrangements for both written and unwritten constitutions according to *Finer* (*1979*).

FLEXIBLE OR INFLEXIBLE

❝ Legal basis ❞

A similar simplistic comparison between constitutions is often applied to the mechanism for change and amendment. The British constitution is flexible in the sense that no special majorities or arrangements are needed to effect it. The **normal legislative** process of passing Acts through Parliament is sufficient to change the constitution and this can be done quickly, as in the case of the annual passage of the Prevention of Terrorism Act which has a bearing on a person's individual rights and freedoms. It can be argued that since the British constitution has a legal basis – various Acts of Parliament, for example Act of Union 1707, Parliament Acts 1911, 1949, have a bearing on the political system – careful thought would be given to any changes in the law which had a constitutional significance. This in turn introduces a degree of **inflexibility**, for governments would not repeal or change the above-mentioned Acts without all party **consultation**.

The comparisons with the inflexible American constitution are not productive either. Although special majorities are needed from the constituent States in the United States Congress to change the constitution, the inflexibility of this arrangement is balanced by the activity of the US Supreme Court. The Court has acted as a separate legislative branch on occasions, adding a degree of flexibility to the written document.

EVOLUTIONARY NATURE

❝ History ❞

The British constitution has evolved over the centuries **successfully adapting** to changed political circumstances. This partly explains the lack of a written document (*Kavanagh 1992*). Feudal monarchy surrendered power to lesser barons (the effects of Magna Carta 1215). Parliament experimented with a republic after the overthrow of the monarchy in the seventeenth century. The Revolution Settlement of 1688 reformulated the rights of monarchy against Parliament. The nineteenth century introduced the beginning of democracy with a series of Reform Acts, each one increasing the size of the electorate. The early part of this century saw the completion of the constitution – votes were extended to women and the competing Conservatives and Liberals were joined by a Labour Party representing working class interests.

THEORETICAL CONSTRUCTS

The evolutionary nature of the British constitution can be tracked through theoretical descriptions which are grounded in history. There are three theoretical constructs that can be examined:

1 **A balanced constitution** The idea of a balanced constitution **emerged** in the seventeenth century and was classically described by Sir William Blackstone at that time. The Revolution Settlement of 1688 placed restrictions over royal power

– now the King had to **accept** the authority of Parliament. The system was described as balanced because the powers of the monarch were **checked or balanced** by Parliament. Each House of Parliament (Lords and Commons) could **check the other** and the King's ministers were also restrained by the legislature.

2 **A liberal constitution** Using an historical framework, *Birch* (*1964*) described the nineteenth-century 'liberal' constitution as parliamentary. The middle classes were anxious to establish the supremacy or sovereignty of Parliament over the executive, and for a brief period (1830–40, the so-called **Golden Age**) this came into existence. Descriptions of the 'liberal' constitution tended to overlook the monarchy in their focus on Parliament. Writing in 1867, *Walter Bagehot* allocated a dignified constitutional role to the monarch, leaving Parliament as the efficient part – an accurate description of the situation prevailing at that time.

3 **A Liberal Democratic constitution** Descriptions of the current Liberal Democratic constitution include the influence of a mass electorate working through political parties choosing representatives for Parliament. We can detect two positions in this approach:

- **The Whitehall view** *Birch* (*1964*) produced a model of the constitution that focused on executive and administrative power. Parliament was now playing a subordinate role to the executive which decided on and implemented policy through the civil service. Parliamentary supremacy in this view has largely given way to executive dominance and control of both the House of Commons and House of Lords.

- **An empirical view** Some modern descriptions of the constitution go beyond the political institutions to include extra-parliamentary opinion formers. In an empirical view of the constitution, *Foreman* (*1985*) includes the media, industrial interests and pressure groups. Such a view is similar to the corporate model of the constitution popularised by the Labour governments during the seventies. These views may be descriptions of a pluralist political system rather than solely of a constitution.

CENTRAL FEATURES

SOURCES OF THE CONSTITUTION

Since the British constitution is unwritten and uncodified, there is no one single source where it can be found. This is not particularly advantageous or disadvantageous. Part of the constitution will have a legal basis; part will lie in the political arrangements of the state. The main sources are:

- Acts of Parliament;
- common law;
- conventions;
- European law;
- constitutional writings.

Acts of Parliament

Acts of Parliament as statute law constitute the most important source of the British constitution. They illustrate two important features:

1 Legislation gives a legal basis or footing to the constitution. Where so much is based on unwritten principles this is important.

2 They demonstrate the principle of parliamentary sovereignty.

Parliament is the supreme law making body and can produce new laws and change existing ones as it pleases. The following important Acts of Parliament all have a bearing on the constitution:

66 Acts with political bearing 99

- The Parliament Acts 1911 and 1949 regulate the relationship between the House of Lords and House of Commons.

- The Representation of the People Acts 1949 and 1969 regulate elections.

- The European Communities Act 1972 regulates relationships between the UK Parliament and the European Union.

There are many examples of legislation having a political bearing and thus a constitutional significance. The important point is that all are capable of ordinary reversal (repeal) by the orthodox legislative process. Compared to a written constitution, this procedure has the greater flexibility.

Common law

Common law has a number of ingredients. Rules made by judges form a customary basis on which many court decisions are made. Since parliamentary statutes need judicial interpretation in the courts, the case law which is built up over the years forms an important backdrop to the constitution.

The rules surrounding the monarchy also fall within the common law. Much of the royal prerogative power is protected by the courts on these grounds and can rarely be challenged. The residual powers of the monarch are now operated solely by ministers of the crown either directly (the prerogative of mercy, the granting of honours, the selection of the Cabinet) or indirectly by Prime Ministerial advice to the monarch (the decision when to dissolve Parliament, the content of the Queen's Speech opening a new session of Parliament).

Conventions

Conventions of the constitution are rules or understandings generally observed by politicians, but not enforceable at law (see Figure 3.2). They add substance to the constitution by providing a framework against which politics can operate – 'the flesh on the bones of the constitution'. They are followed because it is expedient to do so; there would be political difficulties for a government if they were ignored or breached. The 1911 Parliament Act stipulates that general elections must be held every five years, but conventionally the selection of the date is left to the Prime Minister. Clearly this convention cannot be breached because it is sanctioned by an Act of Parliament.

Area of politics affected	Conventional behaviour	Why followed
MONARCH	The monarch keeps out of political controversy. Always acts on advice from Prime Minister/ministers	To protect impartiality of constitutional monarchy
PRIME MINISTER	Since 1900 the Prime Minister has come from the House of Commons	Recognition of primacy of House of Commons as electorally accountable to the people

Fig. 3.2 Examples of conventions of the constitution

This situation demonstrates the loss of flexibility if conventions are given the force of law. Sometimes this is necessary, as in the case of the Ministers of the Crown Act 1937 which statutorily recognised the leader of the opposition by the payment of a special salary. Prior to 1937 the opposition leader was only conventionally recognised. Conventions underpin the working of government; collective responsibility allows the Cabinet to operate with a degree of secrecy and accountability. They add flexibility to the constitution because they are easily discarded if no longer of use. By adjusting to the current political climate, they move the constitution forward.

European law

Since Britain joined the European Community in 1973 (now the European Union or EU) European law has been a source of the constitution because of its impact on Parliament and English law. European law and some EU rules take precedence over British law and are applied without further parliamentary debate. This in turn has consequences for parliamentary sovereignty – the UK Parliament has lost some of its **exclusivity in law making** power over UK citizens. But a future government could always take Britain out of the EU by renouncing the Treaty of Rome. Such a step is

66 Maastricht Treaty 99

now unlikely to happen, especially as the movement towards greater unity is quickening. The passing of the Maastricht Treaty and the Single European Act of 1986 together with the demands for European Monetary Union by the end of the decade are further areas where the British government's sovereignty is being reduced (*Nugent 1991*).

Constitutional writings

Constitutional writings are an important source of the constitution because they give guidance to politicians in the grey area where conventional practice operates. Much of the procedure surrounding the working of Parliament is unwritten in the sense of being contained in Acts. **Authoritative books** like *Erskine May's Parliamentary Practice* (*1844*) therefore become important in any confusion over **interpretation** of the rights and privileges of Parliament. A similar status has been conferred on the constitutional writer *A V Dicey* whose *Study of the Law of the Constitution* was first published in 1885. Dicey is now regarded as an authority on the rule of law – an important constitutional principle that we will examine later (see p. 27).

CENTRAL CONSTITUTIONAL PRINCIPLES

Since there is no written British constitution, there will always be a dichotomy (division) between the **form** (description) and **function** (practice) of the constitution. This is particularly obvious in the operation of the three main characteristics or principles of the constitution: parliamentary sovereignty, the rule of law and the unitary state.

Parliamentary Sovereignty

The legal supremacy of Parliament is the central characteristic of the constitution. In principle this translates into the following aspects:

- There are no limits to the authority of the Queen in Parliament expressed through an Act of Parliament.
- One Parliament cannot bind another since all legislation is repealable by Parliament.
- Parliament can extend its life as it did during the 1914–18 and 1939–45 wars.
- Judges apply the law but do not determine the constitutionality of statute law.

The political reality of parliamentary sovereignty qualifies many of the above features. Parliamentary sovereignty itself is now taken to mean electoral sovereignty expressed through a Parliament of representatives indirectly responsible to the people. Since Parliament must submit itself for periodic re-election by the people, the doctrine of a mandate acts as a real restraint on the government.

It has been argued that the use of **referendums** has undermined parliamentary sovereignty because they by-pass Parliament. The 1975 referendum on European Community membership actually passed the decision whether to accept renegotiated terms back to the electorate from a divided Cabinet. The referendum offered Prime Minister James Callaghan a lifeline from which to escape internal Labour Party feuding on this issue.

From another perspective, although referendums are foreign to the constitution, where used they reinforce parliamentary sovereignty as there are no clear rules governing their use. All require parliamentary approval and must be included in statutes, as with any other law. The failed Welsh and Scottish referendums on devolution (1 March 1979) were both included in separate Acts – the 1978 Wales Act and 1978 Scotland Act. Both were passed subject to confirmation in positive referendum results. The loss of these referendums (Parliament amended the two bills against the Labour government's original intentions by insisting that the Acts would not be effective without at least 40 per cent of those entitled to vote, together with a simple majority of the actual vote, agreeing to the measures) actually damaged the Labour government and contributed to its defeat in the Commons vote of confidence of March 1979.

66 Scotland and Wales Acts 99

The British government is **obligated to other states** by two main treaties: the North Atlantic Treaty and the Treaty of Rome, which was incorporated into British law by the provisions of the European Communities Act 1972. Both of these commitments can be viewed over the long term and in this sense breach the sovereignty principle by **committing future Parliaments** to a course of action decided by their predecessors. Although Parliament retains the ultimate right to withdraw from the Rome Treaty and the EU (and this would have occurred if the 1975 referendum on continuing membership of the EC had been lost) it is at the present time not conceivable that a government will renege on these obligations. British parliamentary sovereignty is therefore affected but not destroyed by continuing membership of the EU.

British subordination to the laws of the European Union is demonstrated by the **1991 Factortame case** (see p. 177). By signing the 1986 Single European Act the British government committed itself to a European fisheries policy which could not be affected adversely by British fishing law. The European Court of Justice ruled in this case that the UK courts had the power to suspend Acts of Parliament that appeared to be in breach of European law. Sections of the British Merchant Fishing Act of 1988 were therefore held inoperative (*Peele 1993*).

    66 EU fisheries policy 99

Rule of Law

The rule of law was classically seen by *A V Dicey* as a second central feature of the constitution alongside parliamentary sovereignty. Described as equality before the law, procedural fairness and supremacy of the law in the courts, the rule of law has ensured that political life is governed by legal principles.

Although governments observe these principles and are not above the law themselves, the expansion of administrative and executive power has produced cases of conflict between the courts and the executive. In the **Pergau Dam Affair** of 1994 the Foreign Secretary, Douglas Hurd, was found to have broken the law in agreeing to a deal that linked part of an overseas budget to **arms** sales to Malaysia. This case and others demonstrate that the principle of **judicial review** ensures that the executive keeps within the law applied by an independent judiciary.

Individual equality before the law is partially qualified by the cost of access; legal aid is available to those on low incomes but the cost of litigation can act as a deterrent. Individual rights are guaranteed by ordinary legal processes rather than any special constitutional Bill of Rights. Changes in the law have impacted in this area, for example the Criminal Justice Act of 1994 took away a person's right to silence in criminal trials.

    66 Criminal Justice Act 99

Challenges to the rule of law have been made by those who have refused to accept the law as impartial or just. Violence was used in protests against the Conservative government policy of reducing the coal industry during the eighties. The anti-poll tax movement of the early nineties refused to acknowledge the legality of the community charge as a replacement for council rates. And the republican and nationalist forces in Northern Ireland never accepted the authority of the British government over Ulster.

Unitary state

Centralisation is a key feature of British government with political power concentrated in the hands of the majority party at Westminster. Constitutionally this arrangement is supported by a unitary system of government. Although the United Kingdom comprises the three ancient kingdoms of England, Scotland and Wales together with the province of Northern Ireland, political power resides with England. Each constituent country has a different history and has retained a degree of local government vastly different to the powers enjoyed by the separate states in the truly federal United States of America.

    66 US federal system 99

Scotland has its own legal and educational system by virtue of its peaceful accession into the Union in 1707. Wales received different treatment from the English as a result of conquest and was brought into the Union in 1542. Northern Ireland was originally part of Ireland and joined the Union as a separate entity in 1921 with the partition of that country. From 1921 to 1972 Northern Ireland had its own form of self government with a separate Parliament at Belfast (the Stormont). The breakdown in the province's political institutions in 1972 caused the British government to impose direct rule with the closure of the Northern Irish Parliament.

Devolution

Devolution of power to Wales and Scotland has never been far from the political agenda in the United Kingdom. Described as the transference of political power away from Westminster to geographically elected bodies (*Bogdanor 1979*), devolution as an issue in United Kingdom politics first surfaced in the modern period in the 1970s.

Two features brought devolution to the forefront:

- Growing electoral support for the Scottish National Party in the general election of 1974.
- A Labour government with a precarious majority.

We have already seen how the weak government of James Callaghan legislated to set up structures for devolved assemblies in both Wales and Scotland dependent on referendum results in 1979 (see p. 26). Although the separate Wales and Scotland Acts (1978) were not introduced, the whole issue of power for the regions refused to disappear. Over the next decade support for Nationalism in both Scotland and Wales fluctuated; as the governing party, the Conservatives were opposed to any form of devolution. Conservative support in Scotland declined to a low point by the 1987 general election and recovered slightly by 1992. Support for Scottish Nationalism has increased as Conservative hold over the country has declined. This has led some commentators to claim that the Conservatives are an English party who fail to understand the demands of the Scottish people, even though they have governed the country since 1979 (*Mitchell 1994*).

66 Conservatives as English party 99

The **debate surrounding devolutionary proposals** is well documented (*Norton 1994*). Granting powers to separate Scottish and Welsh assemblies might have increased pressures for new constitutional arrangements for regional assemblies for other parts of England. In 1995 the Labour Party appeared to reverse its intention to establish regional governments as subnational tiers between Westminster and local councils in the face of public and political opposition.

Devolution of legislative power to Scotland and Wales would have been **unique** in the sense that Britain has no experience of **subordinate legislative assemblies** within a unitary state. Such an arrangement could produce legislative difficulties in settling disputes between the Westminster Parliament and its subordinates and even lead to the eventual break up of the United Kingdom. The least administrative difficulties could be caused by a more complex and expensive governmental structure with Scottish and Welsh assemblies becoming a problematic third tier of government above the existing counties and districts.

66 Scottish Constitutional Convention 99

The arguments for devolution are now embraced by a Scottish Constitutional Convention comprising the Labour Party, the Liberal Democrats and other groups seeking to bring about change. Paradoxically, the Scottish National Party has now turned away from devolution and is demanding independence for Scotland. Constitutionally the Conservative Party has always stood for the Union and sees devolution proposals as an unnecessary and undesirable expense.

PROBLEMS IN THE CONSTITUTION

The British constitution is never static – by its evolutionary nature it has accommodated to a variety of pressures which have had implications for the internal working of the state. The following developments have all had an impact on the distribution of power within the constitution, since they change the balance between the government and the governed:

- **Membership of the European Union** has added an additional tier of legislative authority above the United Kingdom Parliament. Parliamentary sovereignty has been affected as the laws and directives of the EU must be given effect.
- **A growing trend towards centralisation** of power into the hands of the executive. This has had consequences for traditional Cabinet government and policy making with the increasing tendency for decisions to be taken by a Prime Minister working in smaller Cabinet committees or advisory groups.
- **Executive dominance of the legislature** by a party guaranteed a working majority through an electoral system that favours larger parties. The Houses of Parliament (Commons and Lords), despite procedural and organisational changes in the select committee system, are not effective checks over what *Lord Hailsham (1976)* called 'elective dictatorship'.
- **The balance of power** in relationships between the centre and subnational government has shifted in favour of the executive. Local government powers and

democracy (localism) have to some extent been replaced by a growing centralism as reforming Conservative governments have sought to control the costs and function of localities.

■ **An expansion in the 'patronage state'**, of Non-Governmental Organisations (QUANGOS) exercising devolved executive administration powers. These various bodies (trusts, boards, regulatory and advisory councils and other agencies) are not elected and are theoretically accountable to the executive (government) which appointed them.

■ **Relationships between government and citizens** have changed as the state has further clarified civil liberties by amending the laws on criminal justice and official secrets.

APPROACHING REFORM

Although the British constitution has successfully adapted to problems faced by it, there have always been demands to introduce a new structure along the lines of a written or **codified format**, on the grounds that this would be preferable to the existing arrangement. Demands for a new constitutional arrangement became very evident in the decade 1970–80. Both Labour and Conservative governments began to tackle problems of administrative structural reforms and this lead inevitably to the constitution itself. Questions were raised about the nation's capacity to absorb the pressures of industrial society; resist demands for devolution; face problems of inflation/stagflation; deal with governmental overload and manage the impression of general ungovernability.

66 **Problems of government** 99

The long period of **Conservative rule** from 1979 excluding the Labour and Liberal Democratic Parties also gave the impression of a breakdown in the two party system, and highlighted defects in the electoral system. The Liberal Party (later the Liberal Democrats) felt more confident about arguments over electoral and constitutional reforms as their popularity increased during the eighties.

POLITICAL ATTITUDES

The political parties' position on constitutional reform reflected their ideological attitudes to the state. *Norton (1994)* in a seminal work on the constitution identified seven theoretical approaches to reform: **High Tory, Socialist, Marxist, Group, New Right, Liberal and Traditional**. Of these approaches the more important, Liberal and Traditionalist, have had greater impact on political debate in the nineties. The Liberals advocate a written constitution guaranteeing individual rights, proportional representation, a revised House of Lords and revitalised House of Commons. The Traditionalists recognise that the state must adapt if it is to survive. They tend to focus on the importance of reformed parliamentary institutions as a check against excessive executive powers. The most active pressure group in this area is **Charter 88** and their reform proposals have some party support (mainly Labour and Liberal Democratic) even if they are unlikely to be enacted. Charter 88 has twelve main proposals for constitutional reform centred around two goals: (a) a democratic written constitution and (b) a culture of citizenship which would empower citizens to take a greater part in the running of their country (see Figure 3.3). These radical ideas go

1 A Bill of Rights
2 Freedom of information
3 Accountable government
4 A fair voting system
5 A reformed House of Commons
6 A democratic House of Lords
7 Judicial reform
8 Redress for state abuses
9 Independence for local government
10 Parliaments for Scotland and Wales
11 Devolution of power
12 A written constitution

Fig. 3.3 Charter 88 proposals for a new British constitution

66 Great Reform
Programme 99

beyond any Traditionalist position but do find an echo in the Liberal view of a reformed constitution. In 1995 Charter 88 launched a Citizens' Enquiry into British Democracy campaign, arguing for a Great Reform Programme which would seek to implement constitutional changes within the lifetime of a single Parliament.

CONSTITUTIONAL REFORM

The arguments for and against a reformed constitution are long and complex; apart from theoretical positions, there is the practicality of introducing a totally new system of government. In a refined analysis, *Norton* (*1988*) makes the point that it may not be possible to introduce a new constitution because the mechanism for enactment does not exist. Even if all-party talks could produce a consensus over the form a new constitution should take, Parliament does not have the legitimacy to overturn the existing arguments.

66 Judges and
representation 99

Placing those technical arguments aside, it is doubtful if a new written constitution would be an improvement on the old. If the constitution were written, it would be entrenched or protected against change by a political party without the support of the mass electorate. In such a situation, unelected (some claim unrepresentative) judges would become the guardians of the constitution as in the American system of government. Although the system works well in the United States (mainly because of its federal structure) it does not follow it would function effectively in Britain with unelected judges.

Supporters of a written constitution often focus on the need to protect the rights of citizens with greater certainty than at present under the existing arrangements. The production of a Bill of Rights could initiate the process towards a written constitution, for such an enactment would give constitutional safeguards to British citizens. However, the problems of entrenchment (to protect the bill from political interference) again embrace judicial power operating in a constitutional court, which would need to check executive rights. In September 1995 the Conservative government's reaction to criticism from the European Court of Justice over British SAS killing IRA suspects in Gibraltar does not lead to confidence in this idea.

EXAMINATION QUESTIONS

1 'The case for a written constitution has become unanswerable.' Do you agree?

(25)

(UODLE)

2 'Membership of the European Community seriously threatens the British constitution.' Discuss. *(25)*

(NEAB)

3 Discuss the problems involved in drawing up a written constitution for Britain.

(100)

(ULEAC)

ANSWERS TO EXAMINATION QUESTIONS

OUTLINE ANSWER TO QUESTION 3

This essay expects the student to be familiar with the arguments surrounding the technical difficulty of Britain adopting a written constitution. Reference needs to be made to *Phillip Norton's* points about the problems of enactment and parliamentary sovereignty. The following points could be used in an answer:

1 Briefly say why you think Britain should have a written constitution – greater certainty in the law, protection of civil rights, checks and balances against an overpowerful executive.

2 Examine how this could be done. Start with a written Bill of Rights.

3 Look at the technical, legal and political problems.

   (a) Technical   How would Parliament enact a constitution that would take away parliamentary sovereignty? (*Phillip Norton's* points)

   (b) Legal   How could an unelected judiciary become guardians of the constitution?

   (c) Political   What would be the political implications to successive governments restricted or bound by a written document?

4 Make some evaluation of the above points and conclude with a definite argument.

TUTOR'S ANSWER TO QUESTION 2

Membership of the European Community (European Union) has had a marked impact on the British constitution and the practice of politics in the United Kingdom. As the British constitution is mainly prescriptive or informal without a single written or codified document, the act of joining a community with a descriptive constitution was bound to have repercussions over the political institutions and practices of Britain. Procedural changes in domestic laws have been imposed on the British bringing them into closer harmonisation with Europe. The constitutional implications arising from this have highlighted divisions within the major political parties and affected the working of the party system, the executive and Parliament.

The initial act of joining the European Community allied the British state to a written constitution through the Treaty of Rome for the first time in its long history. The British Parliament gave effect to the provisions of the Rome Treaty by passing the 1972 European Communities Act; this had two initial effects on the constitution, one parliamentary, the other legal.

Parliamentary sovereignty was affected by the need to apply legislation on its citizens originating from a separate sovereign Parliament (the European Parliament). There was no historical precedence for this dilution of legislative power of the British legislature. The House of Commons and House of Lords have now surrendered their claims to be the sole source of legislation for the British people. New interpretations of parliamentary sovereignty (and electoral sovereignty) were now needed to embrace this reality. Legislation from the European Parliament in effect breaches the principle that no Parliament can bind its successor. Clearly future governments will be bound by legislation from this source.

The effects on the British legal system of membership of the European Union have added a new dimension to statute law. Now the judiciary must apply European statutes and provisions that affect the United Kingdom directly, through the courts. British freedom of action under the law has therefore been curtailed. Legally, British citizens are now subject to European Community regulations that are binding and enforced through the courts with appeal to the European Court. In cases of conflict between British domestic law and European Treaty provision, European regulations prevail. Subordination to the laws of the European Union has thus added a new dimension to the rule of law principle. Now traditional judicial review of executive action that is regarded as '*ultra vires*' (beyond the powers given in statutes) also includes the European Court and judges taking decisions that affect the British executive. This has been demonstrated in a number of cases including the 1991 Factortame case, where sections of the British Merchant Fishing Act of 1988 were held in breach of European Community policies of free trade by the European Court.

Membership of the European Community was encouraged by successive British governments (although the Conservative Party was initially more enthusiastic) because of the benefits which flow from greater cooperation between the European member states. The initial 1972 European Communities Act has been supplemented by the signing of the Maastricht Treaty 1991 and the Single European Act of 1986, both of which have drawn Britain closer to the ideals of a United Europe. Although Britain achieved the principle of subsidiarity at Maastricht, she still gave up an element of national sovereignty under the Rome Treaty. By being a member of the EU,

Britain voluntarily restricted the action of future governments which in itself placed limits over parliamentary sovereignty. Eventually sovereignty over the British currency will be transferred to Europe by 1999 as an example of continuing development of the EU.

Although Britain has surrendered elements of national sovereignty to the European Union, it has the ultimate sanction of withdrawal from the Rome Treaty. The 1975 Referendum on the European Community gave the British people a choice on continuing membership. Formal safeguards include consultation over future changes in the structures of the EU. Margaret Thatcher was able to reduce Britain's contribution to the EU budget in 1979. Important new policy made in Brussels must have the consent of a British minister who is answerable to the government and Parliament. John Major and Douglas Hurd changed the wording in the Maastricht Treaty from a Federal Europe to one of a closer union, to satisfy both the Euro-enthusiast and Euro-sceptic wings of the Conservative Party rather than Parliament itself. As a last safeguard, the British Parliament has the ability to discuss draft regulations and express opinions through the House of Commons Select Committee on European Legislation.

There is little doubt that Britain's membership of the European Union has affected the constitution, but whether this threatens the political system is a matter for debate. *Lord Denning's* comment that British sovereignty was affected by European law which restricted the autonomy of the legal system was accurate. But by redefining the traditional concept of parliamentary sovereignty to embrace EU law, the constitution is altered rather than damaged. Adaptability has always been a feature of the constitution and membership of the EU can be seen against a background of adjustment to political reality.

STUDENT'S ANSWER TO QUESTION 1 WITH EXAMINER'S COMMENTS

66 Good critical start 99

Britain's current constitution is uncodified – the framework for our government is dispersed over many areas and working out what constitutes strictly constitutional behaviour is more often than not a matter for lawyers and/or judges only. This predicament has been coming under attack for some time now, it is feared that governments are able to manipulate the law to their own advantage and in doing this that British democracy is increasingly becoming nothing but a façade to keep the public settled.

So if the British constitution does not exist in one tangible written document where does it manifest itself? It has four main sources: firstly, the statute law. These are Acts of Parliament which define the structures and powers of government and the relationship between the government and the citizen. Secondly there is common law, which can effectively be broken down into three parts: rules of custom, which are so well established they are enforced by the courts; the royal prerogative, i.e. powers traditionally vested in the Crown which have not been displaced by statute law; and judicial interpretation. The third source of the constitution is conventions, which are not enforced by any authorities. They are essentially the oil in the machinery of the constitution. The final constitutional determinants are works of authority which comprise books which provide guidance and interpretation on uncertain aspects of the constitution. These works have persuasive authority only. Examples of authors include the nineteenth-century writer A V Dicey.

So it is evident that acts of constitutional significance are not drawn together in any one authoritative document. But it still comprises a number of constitutional essentials. What are these? Firstly, there is the doctrine of parliamentary sovereignty, which is taken as the corner-stone of the British constitution. Acts of Parliament cannot be set aside by the courts. Another constitutional prerequisite is the 'rule of law' which refers to certain procedural and substantive rights, for example an accused person's right to silence which comes from the democratic tradition that the prosecution should prove the case that it brings. Thirdly, a unitary state is a constitutional essential. This means that power rests in the central authority of the state, with no regional or local author-ities commanding any autonomous power other than that granted by the central authority. Lastly, parliamentary government is favoured. Over time this country has built up a political culture comprising a strong executive among other things. It has, however, always been bound by and been accountable to the political community which is that community represented by Parliament.

66 Accurate 99

Until recently the constitution of Britain was seen to be one of the country's political triumphs. The position changed in the sixties and seventies. Britain experienced economic, political and social problems which the existing system of government seemed increasingly unable to deal with. Calls began to be heard not just for tinkering with the existing structures of government but for wholesale reform, including a new and written constitution.

Some pioneers of this argument included *Lord Scarman* in 1974 who advocated a 'constitutional settlement', includ-ing a Bill of Rights and a supreme court to protect the constitution. In 1976 *Lord Hailsham* claimed that the existing constitution was 'wearing out'. His solution was 'nothing less than a written constitution … which limits the powers of Parliament and provides a means for enforc-ing these limitations, either legal or political.'

66 Need to develop this 99

Perhaps the most consistent support for radical consti-tutional change has come from the Liberal Party, who have been pressing for a new British constitution comprising a federal system of government and a Bill of Rights.

The principal argument for change derives from the per-ception that power in Britain has become too centralised. The old checks and balances identified by *Dicey* have been eroded, leaving the executive pre-eminent in the political system and able to get enacted, as Acts of Parliament, whatever measures it wants.

Thus two essential provisions of the current constitu-tion – the rule of law and parliamentary government – are being eroded through the power that now accrues to govern-ment by virtue of the principal provision of the constitution – the doctrine of parliamentary sovereignty.

There are two further arguments for change, however. One is that the doctrine of parliamentary sovereignty itself is being eroded by the increasing number of international obligations the government has become involved in, most notably and most recently the membership of the European Community. Here, not only is Britain a member in perpetu-ity but community law takes precedence over domestic law.

The other argument concerns the unitary state. There is growing pressure for elected assemblies in Scotland and Wales (as well as in English regions) with legislative and some executive powers. Such a form of autonomy would by definition bring to an end the unitary state and the

66 Give more detail 99

relationship between the national and regional governments would need to be delimited in a definitive constitutional document and the courts would then probably be expected to adjudicate in the event of any dispute.

The Conservatives see this as unnecessary and merely an expensive extra layer of bureaucracy. The other major parties, however, are both committed to some form of devolution, seeing one assembly in London as overloaded and too centralist.

A written constitution, then, is seen as necessary by its advocates to limit government and protect the rights of citizens and it is seen as inevitable given Britain's international obligations and pressure for radical constitutional change such as a federal system of government.

66 A very clear answer that gets to the point of the question. The essay could be improved by reference to more recent arguments, for example those of Charter 88. Indicative of a good C grade A level. 99

REFERENCES IN THE TEXT

Birch, A H 1964 *Representative and responsible government*, London: Allen & Unwin

Bogdanor, V 1979 *Devolution*, Oxford University Press

Finer, S E 1979 *Five constitutions*, Harmondsworth: Penguin

Foreman, F N 1985 *Mastering British politics*, London: Macmillan

Hailsham, Lord 1976 Elective dictatorship, the 1976 Dimbleby Lecture reprinted in *The Listener* 21 October

Hood Phillips, O 1978 *Constitutional and administrative law*, London: Sweet and Maxwell

Kavanagh, D 1992 *British politics: continuities and change*, Oxford University Press

Mitchell, J 1994 Devolution. In W Wales (ed.) *Developments in politics* **5**, Ormskirk: Causeway Press

Norton, P 1988 Should Britain have a written constitution? *Talking Politics* **1** Autumn

Norton, P 1994 The constitution in question, *Politics Review* **3** April

Nugent, N 1991 *The government and politics of the European Community*, London: Macmillan

Peele, G 1993 The Constitution. In P Dunleavy, A Gamble, I Holliday and G Peele (eds) *Developments in British politics* **4**, London: Macmillan

THE PRIME MINISTER

EXPLAINING PRIME MINISTERIAL POWER

MANAGING THE CORE EXECUTIVE

THE PRIME MINISTER'S ENVIRONMENT

FIELDS OF AUTHORITY

GETTING STARTED

Studies of the power, authority and role of Prime Ministers have become more sophisticated over the years. Early or **traditional** theories were mainly descriptive in their analysis (the Prime Ministerial versus Cabinet government debate). **Recent** theories focus on wider parameters – style, personality, environments and competing centres of power – and the student should be aware of these (core executive theories). Questions on the Prime Minister are often related to the Cabinet since as a chief executive the Prime Minister cannot really be divorced from it.

The main themes of questions set in this area are:

- Different theoretical explanations of Prime Ministerial power.
- Examination of the relationship between a Prime Minister and other members of the Cabinet.
- The central importance of the Prime Minister in the machinery of government.

Useful definitions

- **Chief executive** – description of the Prime Minister as the head of government used in a non-evaluative way, not implying dominance or weakness.
- **Core executive** – refers to the grouping of institutions that are central to policy making: Prime Minister, ministers, Cabinet, Cabinet committees, policy advisers and civil servants.
- **Machinery of government** – refers to the structures of government that make possible the art of public administration, for example, the Cabinet and its committees, the civil service or bureaucracy, the system of local government and the agencies or quangos responsible for implementing aspects of central policy.

ESSENTIAL PRINCIPLES

Prime Ministers today are vastly more powerful than their predecessors ever were. Government has expanded its activities over people's lives and this increasing centralisation of power has continued throughout the Conservative administrations of the eighties and nineties.

THE PRIME MINISTERIAL GOVERNMENT DEBATE

66 Traditional theories of
Prime Ministerial power 99

The focus here is on how the powers of Prime Ministers are used at the expense of the other branches of government – most noticeably the Cabinet and the House of Commons (see Figure 4.1).

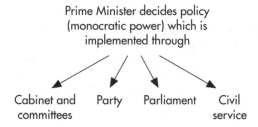

Fig. 4.1 The Prime Ministerial
government view

The principle arguments in this theory are:

1   A **dominant** or **monocratic** style of premiership prevents the development of traditional **collegiate** or **group** policy deliberation within the Cabinet.
2   Public policy decisions are now taken by the Prime Minister in **bilateral meetings** of small groups of advisers, ministers or officials before full Cabinet deliberations.

Secondary themes are:

1   Successive Prime Ministers have expanded their powers over the core executive to the limits of what is constitutionally possible.
2   The patronage system of rewards, honours and appointments in the gift of Prime Ministers has been personalised to the extent of devaluing or politicising its impartial nature.

The starting point for this debate was *Crossman (1963, 1977)*. His observation that Britain was moving towards a Presidential system of government was based on Cabinet experience in Harold Wilson's Labour government. Paraphrasing *Walter Bagehot's* analysis of English politics of 1874, Crossman relegated the Cabinet to the **dignified** or ceremonial side of the constitution alongside the monarch on the grounds that the Prime Minister had usurped the **efficient** role. The reasons given for this development were:

■   Weakening of the independence of MPs who were now more reliant on their parties for their careers.
■   Domination of the House of Commons by the executive which in effect meant the Prime Minister.
■   Improvements in Cabinet support staff around the Prime Minister which increased the Prime Minister's powers of control over the executive.
■   Creation of a unified civil service responsible to an official directly under the Prime Minister's authority made it easier for the Prime Minister to control the bureaucracy.

66 The ideas of Crossman,
Mackintosh and Benn 99

Mackintosh (1962) advanced similar ideas of a Presidential style of Prime Ministership replacing traditional Cabinet government. The growth of the powers of Prime Ministers over the machinery of government made it impossible to remove or challenge them outside a general election.

In his *Case For a Constitutional Premiership, Benn (1980)* appeared to support the Prime Ministerial view by claiming that the powers of Prime Ministers were now so great that they affected the rights of the electorate, undermined the role of Parliament and usurped some of the functions of the Cabinet. His solution was to remove the electoral advantage conferred on Prime Ministers of calling general elections by the devise of fixed term Parliaments.

Margaret Thatcher and Prime Ministerial government

66 **Applications to government** 99

Margaret Thatcher's premiership (1979–90) is cited as evidence that the Prime Ministerial government thesis was an accurate description of the relationships prevailing between a Prime Minister and a Cabinet. She made less use of full Cabinet meetings for policy making and gave the impression of governing through bilateral meetings of committees and ad hoc groups (*Hennessy 1986*). This inevitably reduced the role of the Cabinet to a committee with peripheral policy making power. Matters came before Cabinet for final sanction not full and frank discussion in the traditional sense. It is worth noting, however, that previous Prime Ministers had on occasion taken policy decisions in small groups of ministers (Inner Cabinets) before Margaret Thatcher. Her novelty lay in developing a style of leadership (discussed later in this chapter, p. 41) that took to the limits what a Prime Minister could do without the Cabinet (*Madgwick 1994*). This was itself a contributory factor in the Cabinet rebellion that removed her from office in 1990.

Evaluation of the Prime Ministerial debate

66 **Comparison of US President and Prime Minister** 99

Crossman, *Mackintosh* and *Benn* drew parallels between the British Prime Minister and the American President in order to demonstrate the dangers of the **over centralisation** of powers around a chief executive. Although these comparisons are historically useful in charting the gradual expansion of the office of Prime Minister, they must be used with care. Constitutionally a British Prime Minister's powers are limited by a different set of legislative arrangements to an American President's. Prime Ministers are members of the House of Commons and must operate successfully there. They are not elected in their own right but as a Member of Parliament. American Presidents face a more rigid separated power system of executive and Congress. They are elected directly – not as a result of party – and depend on strength of personality and a complex system of relationships for survival.

Other weaknesses in this perspective are:

1 A tendency to ignore the constraining influences pressing on a Prime Minister within the executive, Parliament and party.

2 Less attention is given to the mix of personality and style of governing of various Prime Ministers.

THE CABINET GOVERNMENT VIEW

Margaret Thatcher's removal as Prime Minister in 1990 reinforced the premise that in British politics it is difficult to govern without the support of the Cabinet. The traditional Cabinet government view of Prime Ministerial power was of a chief executive governing through a collegiate of ministers who were consulted and involved in policy making at the highest level.

The principle arguments of this theory are :

1 It is virtually impossible for a Prime Minister as one person to dominate a Cabinet of twenty other ministers.

2 Policy decisions can go to small bilateral groups of ministers including the Prime Minister but final authority remains with the full Cabinet.

Fig. 4.2 The Cabinet government view

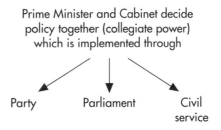

Prime Minister and Cabinet decide policy together (collegiate power) which is implemented through

Party   Parliament   Civil service

Secondary themes are :

1 Prime Ministerial patronage power over ministerial appointments is checked by the practicality of having a balanced Cabinet representative of the party spectrum.

2 The power to dissolve Parliament for a general election confers little political advantage on a Prime Minister.

66 Checks and balances on Prime Minister 99

Claiming that the restraints operating on a Prime Minister's power were as significant as the strengths (*Jones 1980, 1990* and *King 1985*), makes a convincing case against Prime Ministerial government; it is impossible for a Prime Minister to govern without the support of the Cabinet, the party, public opinion and Parliament. There are many examples: Clement Attlee's Labour Cabinet committee decision to develop the British nuclear force in 1945 was typical of defence and security matters being decided before full Cabinets. Harold Macmillan's removal of a third of his Conservative Cabinet in July 1962 lost him popularity from which he never recovered. In the eighties Margaret Thatcher was persuaded to accept the Rhodesian/Zimbabwe settlement and the necessity to enter the European Exchange Rate Mechanism against her will (*Thatcher 1993*). John Major faced difficulties in divided Cabinets over a European referendum, the privatisation of the Post Office, VAT on fuel and the Maastricht Treaty.

66 Applications to government 99

John Major and the restoration of Cabinet government

John Major's appointment as Prime Minister in 1990 signalled a return to traditional Cabinet government making Margaret Thatcher's period of office seem like an aberration. For a variety of reasons, including smaller Commons majorities, different personality, consensus approach to running the government, he appeared a less dominant **Cabinet chairman** to Margaret Thatcher's **chief executive**. He restored Cabinet discussion to its central place in policy making and endeavoured to hold together a balanced Cabinet of left, centre and right deeply divided over Europe. From 1992 to 1995 he attempted to assert his hold over the Cabinet, party and Parliament and passed through a series of crises each deeper than the other: withdrawal from the Exchange Rate Mechanism in 1992; vote of confidence over the ratification of the Maastricht Treaty in 1993; expulsion of the Euro-rebels from the party in 1994 and the Conservative leadership election of 1995. Margaret Thatcher's Premiership was characterised by certainty and conviction, John Major's by comparison was continually dogged by fears for his own survival (*Young 1994*).

The Conservative leadership election of June/July 1995

Mounting criticism of his premiership caused John Major to call a Conservative leadership election in the summer of 1995, the first contest since he replaced Margaret Thatcher in 1990. Calling for a vote of confidence, the main objective of the election was to attempt to **restore his authority** over the party and forestall a later challenge to his leadership which could have removed him from office. By calling the election early John Major successfully outflanked his critics on the left and right of the party. It was expected that a '**stalking horse**' candidate would stand against him in the first round. The former Chancellor Norman Lamont's name was suggested, but in the event the Welsh Secretary, John Redwood, broke ranks from the Cabinet and challenged for the leadership. The other '**heavyweights**' in the Cabinet, notably Michael Heseltine and Michael Portillo, refused to enter the contest and publicly supported John Major.

The long term factors leading to this situation were:

66 Criticisms of John Major 99

1 Failure to heal the rifts over Europe in his party and Cabinet.

2 Disastrous local election results in Scotland (1994) and in England and Wales (1995).

3 Slump in Conservative popularity – 39 to 40 points behind Labour in the opinion polls by June 1995.

4 Fear of electoral defeat in the general election of 1996 or 1997.

The short term factors were:

1 Media destabilisation of John Major by his opponents throughout June.

2 Lady Thatcher's criticisms of his administration in the promotion of the second volume of her autobiography.

3 Criticisms the Prime Minister received in a meeting with the Euro-sceptic **Fresh Start** group of MPs.

4 Media speculation over his leadership that was continually raised during his visit to the Canadian G7 Economic Summit in June.

In the first ballot (4 July 1995) John Major gained a convincing 2:1 win over John Redwood. Of the 329 Conservative MPs eligible to vote, 218 voted for the Prime Minister, 89 for John Redwood, with eight abstentions, twelve spoiled ballot papers and two non-voters. This victory for John Major succeeded in the short term in re-establishing his authority over the separate factions within the Conservative Party, but more importantly it removed the threat of further leadership challenges before the next general election. In this sense it strengthened John Major's premiership and enabled him to carry out the most sweeping Cabinet reshuffle of his years in office.

Evaluation of the Cabinet government view

The survival of John Major in the Conservative leadership election contest paradoxically strengthens the traditional Cabinet government viewpoint. For although John Major was confirmed as Prime Minister and his authority re-established over the Cabinet and Party, circumstances kept him in power. Cabinet opponents from the left of centre (Michael Heseltine) and right (Michael Portillo) refused for their separate reasons to challenge John Major at this time. Indeed it rather looked as if John Major was able to **broker** a deal before the contest with Michael Heseltine by promising him the post of Deputy Prime Minister in return for his support.

❝❝ How John Major survived ❞❞
As with Margaret Thatcher's removal in 1990, the events of the summer of 1995 demonstrate the importance of Cabinet support for any Prime Minister. The value of the Cabinet government view is that it demonstrates how the survival of a Prime Minister is inextricably bound up with relationships to the Cabinet. There seems little point in attempting to analyse the Prime Minister's position away from this construct.

CORE EXECUTIVE THEORIES

❝❝ The Prime Minister as chief executive ❞❞
Current theories of Prime Ministerial power are complex and all-embracing. They focus on the relationships surrounding the Prime Minister as a chief executive and recognise that the **power of other elites** and the **fragmentation of policy making** between them affect the Prime Minister's authority within the core executive.

As a **chief executive** the Prime Minister presides over and manages a core executive of institutions, networks and practices which include the Cabinet and its committees, ministerial groups, meetings and negotiations (*Dunleavy and Rhodes 1990*) In this role the Prime Minister's formal powers cover the armed services (Commander in Chief), the legislature (policy leader and head of the largest single party in both Houses of Parliament), the administration (head of the civil service as First Lord of the Treasury) and foreign affairs (chief spokesperson for the nation).

There are two basic core executive views:

1 **The segmented decision making model**

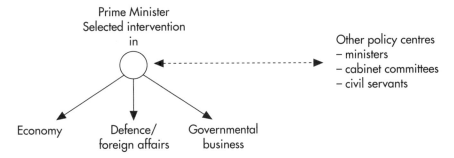

Fig. 4.3 The segmented decision making model

This view claims that power is now so fragmented in the British core executive that the Prime Minister only selectively intervenes in major policy areas, for example the economy, foreign affairs, state security/defence and governmental business (*Rose 1984, Dunleavy and Husbands 1985*). This narrow Prime Ministerial focus leaves other policy centres with ministers, Cabinet committees and civil servants.

2   **The bureaucratic coordination model**

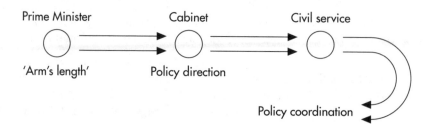

Fig. 4.4 The bureaucratic
coordination model

According to this view the civil service has an independent power in policy making forcing the core executive of Prime Minister and Cabinet into the background (*Heclo and Wildavsky 1981*). Policy making diffuses through a vast bureaucratic elite who have a vested interest in encouraging a Presidential arm's length style of leadership. This inevitably reduces the role of the Prime Minister to one of **tie-breaking** or **power-broking** interdepartmental and Cabinet disputes.

Evaluation of core executive theories

❝ **'Who governs' debate** ❞

Both theories are administrative in the sense of focusing on policy networks of ministers and officials around the Prime Minister and elitist in trying to show how there exist within the core executive competing elites and centres of power. In each position we can detect precedents in the arguments about the location of power in the core executive and the 'who governs' debate in the civil service. Although **conspiratorial** in nature, for example in the claim that no core executive can adequately control the modern state, core executive theories have moved forward the debates on Prime Ministerial power and authority.

**MANAGING THE
CORE EXECUTIVE**

❝ **Roles of the Prime
Minister** ❞

In managing the core executive a Prime Minister will be preoccupied with:

■ Deciding and implementing public policy at the highest level, primarily the aims and objectives of the political party (**policy initiation**).

■ Governing the country at the head of an administration, mainly through the Cabinet and civil service (**policy implementation**).

At any time performance in these roles will depend on a mix of factors: personality, style of leadership, environment and party political considerations. How they come together will affect the judgement made of a Prime Minister's handling of the **government machine**.

STYLES AND PERSONALITIES

Kavanagh (1991) identifies two styles of Prime Minister: **Mobilisers** and **Reconcilers**. Mobilisers are impatient for change, keen to press on with ideas and motivate others. Reconcilers try to maintain the consensus and cohesion of the Cabinet and will compromise if necessary to reach this position.

Norton (1988) uses a fourfold categorisation of the personalities of Prime Ministers: **Innovators, Reformers, Egoists** or **Balancers** (see Figure 4.5).

INNOVATORS Set the agenda; expect to lead others	REFORMERS Seek to implement the party programme
EGOISTS Enjoy the power of premiership for own sake	BALANCERS Seek a compromise or middle ground between functions

Fig. 4.5 Prime Ministerial
personalities (based on *Norton*
(1988))

Margaret Thatcher showed the traits of belonging to the Innovator category whilst John Major was clearly a Balancer. His apparent indecision and perceived weaknesses in governing were partially explained by his inability to control all the factions in the

Conservative Party. After his successful re-election as party leader in July 1995 he had more success in presenting a stronger public image.

Evaluation of Kavanagh and Norton

There are obvious similarities between the style and personality categories of *Kavanagh* and *Norton* (Mobilisers and Innovators, and Reconcilers and Balancers). Although Margaret Thatcher appeared to adopt a Mobiliser style of leadership – she had larger parliamentary majorities than John Major giving her more authority over the party (*Thatcher 1993*) – there were occasions when she had to operate as a Reconciler.

An **autocratic** dominant Prime Ministerial style can lead to loss of support and respect of colleagues when the party is unpopular; Sir Geoffrey Howe's resignation speech from Margaret Thatcher's Cabinet demonstrated this. A **collegiate** style of management with more equality between ministers is less likely to antagonise but can lead to charges of weakness as with John Major.

THE CABINET

The authority of the Prime Minister is based on the electorate, the party, Parliament and the Cabinet. As the supreme policy making body the Cabinet must be carried **politically** and **administratively**. The removal of Margaret Thatcher in 1990 demonstrated that relationships are not easy to maintain. The Prime Minister has responsibility for the following formal powers over the Cabinet:

- appointments, dismissals and reshuffles of ministers;
- structures and memberships of Cabinet committees;
- control of Cabinet agendas;
- management of Cabinet meetings;
- policy initiation and direction.

These formidable powers are supported by a Number Ten staff, a Policy Unit and various *ad hoc* arrangements of ministers, partial Cabinets (ministers from departments whose policy is under discussion) and Kitchen Cabinets (mixed groups of advisers of various kinds). In 1995 John Major's Kitchen Cabinet (the Number Twelve Committee) comprised a twenty strong committee of ministers, senior civil servants and party officials. Their task was to improve the presentation and coordination of government policy.

The Cabinet reshuffle of July 1995

This Cabinet reshuffle (held immediately after the Conservative leadership election) offered John Major the opportunity to **rebalance** the Cabinet to his own **left of centre** viewpoint. Michael Heseltine was promoted to Deputy Prime Minister with his own political and executive power and four ministers left the Cabinet: Jonathan Aitken, Jeremy Hanley, David Hunt and Douglas Hurd. Michael Portillo remained in the Cabinet but the failed challenger John Redwood was not brought back. This lead to further criticisms from the **Euro-sceptics** and **right** that the balance of the Cabinet had now shifted too far left and did not adequately reflect the views of the 111 MPs who did not vote for the Prime Minister in the election.

THE CIVIL SERVICE

A Prime Minister is assisted in the management of government and the core executive by the centralised civil service structure – in this Richard Crossman was correct. Power flows from the Prime Minister as First Lord of the Treasury down through a Permanent Secretary responsible for the Civil Service. Control of this **bureaucracy** theoretically guarantees the **implementation** of the Prime Minister's programme even though **neutrality** is one of the characteristic features of the officials. This bureaucracy will respond to whichever party is in power.

The charge of **politicisation** of the civil service made against Margaret Thatcher because she took a personal interest in the replacement of her permanent secretaries has not been substantiated. She may have advanced her favourites (*Hennessy 1989*), but the authoritative Royal Institute of Public Administration report of 1985 found no real evidence to substantiate charges of political interference. Clearly the fact that Margaret Thatcher was Prime Minister from 1979 to 1990 gave her the opportunity to replace a majority of her senior civil servants, but she had no direct control over the Senior Appointments Selection Committee even though she asked for greater freedom of choice (*Armstrong 1985*).

It is instructive to compare the political powers of an American President over the civil service with those of the Prime Minister. Since there is no politically neutral system of appointments to the American senior ranks, the service depends on political partisanship and patronage in a way that is not found in the British system – another reason why talk of the development of a Presidential Prime Minister is misleading.

THE PRIME MINISTER'S ENVIRONMENT

The Prime Minister's environment is increasingly complex. *Norton* (*1988*) suggests **three variables** within which he operates:

1 **The global economy** Furthest away from the Prime Minister and subject to least Prime Ministerial influence. Yet as a national leader the Prime Minister protects British interests in, for example, negotiations over European integration (1992/95) and in Economic Summit meetings (Canadian G7 talks 1995).

2 **The climate of expectation** Here the Prime Minister helps set a climate of public expectation (the Revolution of Rising Expectations) for constant improvement in living standards. The difficulty facing all governments is that they are now increasingly judged by the public and media as to how they respond to this pressure.

66 Revolution of Rising Expectations 99

Two policy areas illustrate the problem. The Conservative government's policy change in social welfare provision started by Margaret Thatcher and continued under John Major from universal provision to selective targeting represents a realisation that there are limits to the depth of the public purse (the fiscal crisis of the welfare state). In the late nineties there is also constant public expectation of personal tax cuts and some recovery in the housing market, as the electorate expect to regain the feelings of prosperity generated by a property owning democracy.

66 Fiscal crisis of the welfare state 99

3 **The proximate political situation** The immediate political environment around the Prime Minister over which the Prime Minister has most control includes the Cabinet, civil service and the machinery of government. This control and influence is facilitated by an informal **support system** known officially since 1976 as the Prime Minister's Office (*Jones 1980*). The Office (which never sleeps) comprises the following:

- A Private Office of civil servants or private secretaries responsible for different areas of policy, providing support to the Prime Minister.

- A Press Office headed by a Press Secretary – Bernard Ingham for Margaret Thatcher and Christopher Meyer for John Major – responsible for media management and presentation of government information.

- A Political Office coordinating the Prime Minister's political relationships to his constituency and party.

- A Policy Unit providing long term policy advice and analysis to the Prime Minister. From February 1995 headed by Norman Blackwell recruited by John Major from industry.

- Special advisers brought in by the Prime Minister covering different policy fields. Margaret Thatcher employed Sir Alan Walters for economic policy and the former diplomat, Sir Anthony Parsons, to advise on foreign affairs. The eventual clash between Sir Alan Walters and Margaret Thatcher's Chancellor, Nigel Lawson, lead to the latter's resignation from the government in 1989.

- Other units within the Prime Minister's Office include an Efficiency Unit established by Margaret Thatcher and a Number Twelve Committee (or Kitchen Cabinet – see p. 41) set up by John Major in January 1995 as an innovation in government. This twenty strong committee is seeking to improve the presentation and coordination of government policy and includes Cabinet Ministers, senior civil servants, party officials and the four advisers closest to the Prime Minister in its membership.

" Arguments for a Prime Minister's department "

In one sense, these informal groups act as a civil service department serving the Prime Minister but because of the complexity of coordinating the government machine, it is regularly suggested that a more formalised bureaucratic organisation be established.

All Prime Ministers to date have rejected these proposals preferring the informality of a system of secretaries and advisers. Former civil servants of the calibre of **Sir Kenneth Berril** have claimed that to improve coordination in the machinery of government, the Prime Minister's support staff needs enlargement even if the present system continues. To some extent John Major has done this with the establishment of the Number Twelve Committee.

FIELDS OF AUTHORITY

Around the nucleus of the Prime Minister's environment are three fields of authority within which he must successfully operate: Parliament, party and public opinion.

PARLIAMENT

" Parliamentary government "

The Prime Ministerial government thesis made much of a Prime Minister's control over Parliament – essentially the House of Commons. In the British system of parliamentary government the party that controls the House of Commons becomes the executive; the future of the two is bound together. Prime Ministers must of necessity secure a good working majority to ensure control and the passage of their legislation through the House. Margaret Thatcher was fortunate in achieving the high figure of 100 plus majorities from 1979 to 1990 over her opponents and we have seen how this impacted on her style of leadership. What is less well known is the **correlation** of **dissent** or **backbench rebellions** to those administrations with **good majorities**. *Norton (1994)* showed how Conservative backbench MPs were more rebellious during the eighties precisely because there was little fear of bringing down their government.

" Executive accountability "

Within the House of Commons, Prime Ministers will be judged on their performance at the Dispatch Box and in debates when speaking on the floor of the House. Their most opportune moments to impress are provided by **Prime Minister's Question Time** when they face the opposition and other critics. Traditionally held as a **device for maintaining executive accountability** to the legislature, most commentators now agree the institution has lost its focus (*Madgwick 1994*). Considerations of time, party advantage, publicity and (marginally) the televising of Parliament have served to reduce Question Time to a worthy spectacle, although it must be pointed out that an American President does not have to endure such a system.

Prime Ministers have the right to call for a **dissolution of Parliament** by making a formal recommendation to the monarch for a general election. As with all powers of the Prime Minister, there are opportunities and constraints working for and against them. Prime Ministers will obviously seek the opportune time when the party's popularity is at its highest to call the election and within the statutory five year limit (Representation of the Peoples Act 1949) will have a degree of manoeuvrability.

Occasionally the threat to call a dissolution is made by Prime Ministers to **silence backbench critics** in their own party (the doomsday scenario). Both Harold Wilson and James Callaghan threatened back benchers, and in a desperate attempt to secure **ratification of the Maastricht Treaty** in 1993, John Major let it be known that if he lost the vote he would regard it as a loss of confidence in his government and call a dissolution. Although he was successful on this occasion, the criticisms of his leadership continued until the Conservative election contest in June 1995.

" Timing general elections "

Opponents of the present dissolution power (specifically Tony Benn) wish to move to a **fixed term** system (as in Europe and America) when the date of the election is known. This would

- remove Prime Ministers' discretion in timing a general election and
- curtail their freedom to use the device as a control mechanism over backbenchers.

" The doomsday scenario "

This argument lacks conviction; realistically the result of a general election can go either way. In 1970 Harold Wilson's decision to call a general election produced a Conservative government with a 31 seat majority. The **doomsday scenario** would be little more successful to a desperate Prime Minister. Any dissolution called to silence backbench critics would split a political party and lead to electoral oblivion at the polls.

PARTY

66 Expulsion of
Euro-rebels 99

Party unity is essential to the survival of any Prime Minister. John Major showed during his struggle with the **Euro-sceptics** that he was prepared to discipline those who refused to support his leadership. In 1994 a number of Euro-rebels were expelled from the Conservative Party by the device of **withdrawal of the whip** (including Nicholas Budgen, Bill Cash, Teresa Gorman, Edward Leigh and Tony Marlow), which was not restored until 1995. This was either a sign of strength from John Major who finally decided to act to prevent further party schisms, or a desperate move from a beleaguered Prime Minister anxious to restore unity to a divided party. Whatever the final verdict, the event showed the dangers facing a Prime Minister experiencing **policy differences** with a sizeable section of his party. The 'Whipless Rebels' went on to form a party of their own within the Conservative Parliamentary Party and comprised the main supporters of John Redwood in his challenge to John Major in 1995.

The introduction of a more **democratic mechanism** for selecting the leader in 1965 changed the **relationship between Conservative Prime Ministers** and their **backbenchers**. Now they are dependent on the maintenance of good relations and up until the **rule change** in July 1995, could be challenged annually if there was enough backbench support for a leadership election contest. Both Edward Heath (1976) and Margaret Thatcher (1990) lost the leadership of the Conservative Party partly because they ceased to enjoy majority support and their aloof behaviour alienated their own backbenchers. As if conscious of their failures, John Major made strenuous efforts to contact personally a majority of backbench MPs in the Conservative leadership election of June 1995 with good results.

PUBLIC OPINION

Throughout 1995 John Major was continually more popular than the Conservative Party itself, showing that when it came to **voter preference and perception** of government competence, people were prepared to separate the Prime Minister from the party. Despite trailing in the opinion polls, Conservative Party ratings picked up and increased after the June/July leadership election and subsequent Cabinet reshuffle. Indeed, it was probably for **public opinion** purposes that the Cabinet was reshuffled to give the impression of a revived government with new policies.

66 Use of public relations
image makers 99

The **formation** of public opinion is helped by the **media** and presentation of politics in newspapers and television. Prime Ministers since the eighties have been made more aware of the importance of **presentational skills** in the attempt to win votes and influence the electorate. Party management of general election campaigns and publicity generally is assisted by public relations professionals or 'spin doctors' who attempt to maximise the favourable image of the Prime Minister and other leading politicians (*Coxall and Robins 1994*). Margaret Thatcher has herself commented on the assistance given by outside consultants in the preparation of a different, more friendly, public image (*Thatcher 1993*).

Prime Ministers have every opportunity for media exposure as chief executive and party leader. The media are always interested in their programme and this constant exposure serves to strengthen their role, authority, power and prestige. Conversely the media can **undermine** Prime Ministers by constant reference to their shortcomings, unpopularity or policy mistakes. John Major found his 'Back to Basics' policy was ridiculed in the press almost as soon as it was announced in 1993 because of ministerial impropriety and private indiscretions. The programme was abandoned as unworkable in 1994, and reflected poorly on the Prime Minister's image. Throughout the first half of 1995 John Major struggled hard to re-establish public popularity against adverse opinion polls, disappointing political events or 'banana skins' and attempts by some newspapers to de-stabilise him. Shortly after his appointment as Deputy Prime Minister (July 1995), Michael Heseltine complained that the media

66 Banana skins 99

were only interested in 'banana skins' as opposed to reporting government successes.

One of the tasks of John Major's new Kitchen Cabinet or Number Twelve Committee, was to steer the Prime Minister away from political trouble spots.

EXAMINATION QUESTIONS

1 Discuss the relationship between the office of Prime Minister and Parliament.
   (25)
   (ULEAC)

2 Consider the view that the most significant constraint upon British Prime Ministers is the power and influence of Cabinet colleagues. *(25)*
   (NEAB)

3 Assess the significance of the various factors which have contributed to the power of recent Prime Ministers. *(25)*
   (JMB)

ANSWERS TO EXAMINATION QUESTIONS

OUTLINE ANSWER TO QUESTION 1

This question asks for an understanding of the role of the Prime Minister in the legislature. It is bound up with the idea of legislative dominance by the majority party of the House of Commons – the Elective Dictatorship debate. The Prime Minister's relationship to Parliament requires a discussion of the following points:

- Necessity for a working majority in the House of Commons.
- Control of Commons timetable and procedure to reach legislative objective.
- Dissolution power to call a general election, and how real a threat to backbench critics.
- Patronage posts of approximately 100 government MPs (payroll vote) ensuring government majority in any divisions (votes on debates or legislation).
- Backbench dissent as a threat to the Prime Minister's government.
- Performance at Dispatch Box (Prime Minister's Question Time).
- Management of the party through the Whips' Office and public perceptions of the Prime Minister's ability (assisted by the media).

TUTOR'S ANSWER TO QUESTION 2

British Prime Ministers are subject to constraints from the Cabinet even though they have ultimate responsibility for the selection of its members. Such a view runs counter to the Prime Ministerial government idea that a Prime Minister can operate largely unchecked by the Cabinet. *Crossman (1963, 1977)* and *Benn (1980)* made much of the fact that executive power is now centralised in the Prime Minister's hands. Examples of policy initially bypassing the full Cabinet were Clement Attlee's decision to manufacture the nuclear bomb, Harold Macmillan's removal of a third of his government and, more recently, Margaret Thatcher's permission to allow the United States use of British airbases in their bombing of Libya. But the point is well put that in every example the Cabinet had to be told eventually.

The traditional view of Cabinet government is one of a Prime Minister *primus inter pares* (first among equals) with a collegiate as opposed to a monocratic style of governing (*Thain 1993*). This has always implied a good working relationship with Cabinet colleagues who are consulted at the highest level over policy making but are clearly not the equal of the Prime Minister.

Core executive theories place more emphasis on negotiated relationships in Cabinet as ministers are themselves policy centres and constraints on a Prime

Minister (*Rose 1984, Dunleavy and Husbands 1985, Dunleavy and Rhodes 1990*). As the chief executive the power and influence of the Prime Minister is never equal to Cabinet colleagues – they are appointed by the Prime Minister and can be removed. Their power and influence rest with backbenchers and the wider party, and it is very easy for a Prime Minister to loose touch with MPs. Edward Heath neglected back-bench opinion to his cost and Margaret Thatcher at the time of her removal behaved similarly.

In the Cabinet the Prime Minister will be restrained by sanction from other colleagues as and when necessary. Margaret Thatcher was persuaded to accept the settlement ending the Rhodesian civil war and the necessity of entry to the European Exchange Rate Mechanism against her will. John Major has faced difficulties from Cabinet colleagues over numerous issues, particularly Europe, and must accommodate the 'heavyweights' or 'bull elephants' capable of destabilising him: Heseltine, Clarke and Portillo.

Cabinet colleagues have a personal influence over a Prime Minister for a number of reasons apart from the obvious 'he is only one person' argument.

They are selected by the Prime Minister for political and administrative factors. They may be good administrators, but there is always the need to balance the Cabinet politically. As the supreme policy making body the Cabinet will usually contain a mix of ministers from all sections of the party. In the Cabinet reshuffle of July 1995 John Major may have tilted the balance towards left of centre with the promotion of Michael Heseltine to Deputy Prime Minister, but Michael Portillo and the new William Hague were still representative of the right. The important point here is that a Prime Minister will seek to keep representatives of all party factions in the Cabinet to avoid antagonising sections of the wider party and to keep an eye on possible future opponents.

By keeping potential opponents in the Cabinet a Prime Minister ensures they are bound by collective responsibility which prevents open opposition. Margaret Thatcher and Michael Heseltine were not politically close yet she kept him in the Cabinet (before his resignation over the Westland affair in 1986), possibly because he was too powerful to be dismissed.

Although it was claimed a Prime Minister had to be prepared to remove ministers from the Cabinet to emphasise changes in policy direction, it is clear that dismissals and reshuffles must be used with care (*Kavanagh 1991*). Administratively a Prime Minister will be conscious of the need to bring forward younger ministers to ensure periodic renewal of government personnel. Politically, dismissals are often counter-productive; Harold Macmillan's removal of a third of his Cabinet did little for his support in the electorate and Conservative Party in 1962. James Callaghan refused to reshuffle his Cabinet in 1979 for fear of creating enemies among those removed. Margaret Thatcher's removal of the 'wets' (left of centre Conservatives) heightened the impression that her management style was autocratic and disdainful of Cabinet colleagues. Her removal from the office of Prime Minister in 1990 can be seen as a continuation of disaffection with her leadership by the majority of the Cabinet.

When John Major faced his ultimate challenge in the Conservative leadership election of June 1995, his position was rather different to Margaret Thatcher's. He was fortunate that the majority of his Cabinet supported him, and he was re-elected. However, by promoting Michael Heseltine to Deputy Prime Minister with considerable executive and political powers of his own, he again gave the impression of a weak leader overshadowed by a more charismatic figure and a divided party.

STUDENT'S ANSWER TO QUESTION 3 WITH EXAMINER'S COMMENTS

66 Gets straight to the point of limitations 99

It is important to understand exactly what is meant by the 'powers' of Prime Ministers in order to satisfactorily answer the question. In this context, the functions of Prime Ministers can be equated with their powers. Although the functions cover a fairly wide area, there are limitations as to how far Prime Ministers can go.

Although in a democracy such as the UK, political power is supposedly derived from the electorate, the party which has formed the government can change its leader during the course of a term of office. This indicates that the sources of the Prime Minister's power, although based on elections, are derived mainly elsewhere.

The elections give a party a majority in the House of Commons, which gives that party power within the House. Although Prime Ministers are leaders of their party, they rely on party support to control the House. The party is an important source of authority, and Prime Ministers must keep their party united if their position is to be safe.

Another important source of authority is the Cabinet, the ruling body of the party headed by the Prime Minister. Although Prime Ministers have considerable power over the form and direction of the Cabinet, Cabinet support is vital if their authority is to be accepted. The level of Cabinet control versus Prime Ministerial control has been debated widely in the last few decades. Crossman and Benn both argue independently that there has been a vast reduction in the power of the Cabinet as opposed to the Prime Minister in the last fifty years. However, Margaret Thatcher's treatment of her Cabinet eventually led to her being challenged as leader, and losing the position of Prime Minister.

So the sources of the Prime Minister's authority are the electorate, Parliament and the party, and the Cabinet. In some situations, Cabinets are weak and dominated by the Prime Minister, at other times, the Cabinet can be a very strong body. In order to see the relationship between the various factors and the way that in different situations the balance can be completely different, it is necessary to look at Prime Ministers with different approaches, and the situations they find themselves in.

Margaret Thatcher was a leader in the 'chief executive' style. She was decisive, interventionist, and had specific aims. She liked to keep a close grip on the Cabinet, and use it and Parliament to further her ideologies. She was very ideological, and represented a movement in the Conservative Party called the New Right.

John Major follows a more 'chairman'-like approach. He focuses on consensus and keeping the party together. He was selected to prevent Michael Heseltine getting the job and there was nothing radical or exciting in his policies.

These different circumstances have been factors in how Prime Ministers choose to approach their roles. Margaret Thatcher was in a strong position with a large Commons majority for most of her time in office. John Major, on the other hand, was in a situation where even slight mistakes could have fatal consequences for his career.

The events surrounding the end of Margaret Thatcher's premiership, and the style adopted by John Major subsequently, indicate that the Cabinet is certainly the biggest source of Prime Ministers' power, and that we still have Cabinet government rather than Prime Ministerial government.

So, in order to have power, a Prime Minister's authority to use this power must be recognised primarily by the Cabinet and backbenchers of the party. With the support of these two groups a Prime Minister can control the Commons. No other factors have such an influence on the power of a Prime Minister.

> " This argument needs developing "

> " Some repetition here "

> " Good comparisons between Thatcher and Major "

> " Simplification of complex events "

❝ Quite a good essay focusing an Parliament and the Cabinet, but discussion of the media image of a Prime Minister is also important in this question. Greater attention could have been given to analysis of the new theoretical positions in the Prime Ministerial – Cabinet debate. Overall the answer is typical of a border-line C/B. ❞

REFERENCES IN THE TEXT

Armstrong, R 1985 Ministers, Politicians and Public Servants, *Public Money*

Benn, T 1980 The Case for a Constitutional Premiership, *Parliamentary Affairs*

Coxall, B and L Robins 1994 *Contemporary British politics*, London: Macmillan

Crossman, R 1963 Introduction. In W Bagehot *The English Constitution*, London: Fontana

Crossman, R 1977 *Diaries of a Cabinet Minister* **3**, London: Jonathan Cape

Dunleavy, P and C Husbands 1985 *British democracy at the crossroads*, Harlow: Longman

Dunleavy, P and R Rhodes 1990 Core executive studies in Britain, *Public Administration* **68** Spring

Heclo, H and A Wildavsky 1981 *The private government of public money*, London: Macmillan

Hennessy, P 1986 *Cabinet*, Oxford: Basil Blackwell

Hennessy, P 1989 *Whitehall*, London: Secker & Warburg

Jones, G 1980 The Prime Minister's aides. In A King (ed.) *The British Prime Minister*, London: Macmillan

Jones, G 1990 Mrs Thatcher and the power of the Prime Minister, *Contemporary Record* **3** April

Kavanagh, D 1991 Prime Ministerial power revisited, *Social Studies Review* March

King, A 1985 *The British Prime Minister*, London: Macmillan

Mackintosh, J 1962 *The British Cabinet*, London: Stevens

Madgwick, P 1994 *A new introduction to British politics*, Cheltenham: Stanley Thornes (Publishers)

Norton, P 1988 Prime Ministerial power, *Social Studies Review*, January

Norton, P 1994 Reform of the House of Commons. In B Jones (ed.) *Issues in British politics*, Manchester University Press

Rose, R 1984 *Do parties make a difference?* London: Macmillan

Thain, C 1993 The core executive. In W Wale (ed.) *Developments in politics* **4**, Ormskirk: Causeway Press Ltd.

Thatcher, M 1993 *Thatcher: the Downing Street years*, London: Harper Collins

Young, H 1994 Article in *The Guardian* 29 April

ORIGINS AND
STRUCTURES

CENTRAL FEATURES

THE WORK OF THE
CABINET

PROBLEMS AND REFORM

GETTING STARTED

The Cabinet (with the Prime Minister) is at the apex of the machinery of government as the central controlling body of the executive. Traditionally, the study of Cabinet government was approached through the perspective of public administration largely because the emphasis was on structures and their efficiency. However, the Cabinet has a dual purpose – it is both an administrative and political unit bringing together policy formulation and policy implementation at the highest level. For this reason political considerations are bound up in any analysis.

Study of the Cabinet cannot be isolated from the Prime Minister since the Prime Minister governs its existence, membership and deliberations, but the student should be prepared to answer questions on the institution alone.

Information in this chapter will enable you to answer questions on the following areas:

- The importance of the convention of Cabinet collective responsibility.

- The problems of Cabinet efficiency in policy making and coordination.

- Relationships with the Prime Minister and their effects on the structures of Cabinet.

- Constitutional and practical interpretations of the operation of Cabinet government.

ESSENTIAL PRINCIPLES

DEVELOPMENT OF THE CABINET

The origins of the modern Cabinet system (some think the concept originates from the Cabal named after the initials of Charles II's ministers – Clifford, Arlington, Buckingham, Ashley and Lauderdale) can be traced to the eighteenth century when the Hanoverian monarchs (George I, II and III) refused to attend its meetings. Gradually the Cabinet acquired the function of presenting policy advice to the monarch through a leading minister – eventually the Prime Minister. In the changed political climate of the nineteenth century *Bagehot* (*1867*) described the Cabinet and its ministers as 'the hyphen' or 'buckle' which joined 'the legislative part of the State to the executive part of the State'. By the close of that century traditional Cabinet government had emerged with a collegiate of ministers including a Prime Minister deciding policy at the highest level.

CONVENTIONAL PARAMETERS

The working of Cabinet government is based on **conventional practice** or rules which have evolved over time. Apart from the 1937 Ministers of the Crown Act (ensuring the payment of salaries), Cabinet Ministers and the Prime Minister manage to operate within constitutional parameters which do not have the backing of law; they are followed because it is politically expedient to do so. The major conventions or characteristics governing Cabinet operations are:

1 **Collective responsibility** Collective responsibility for policy decisions supported by all Cabinet members. In practice this now includes the whole executive – ministers of Cabinet and non-Cabinet rank.

2 **One party dominance** Selection of the executive from one political party. Cabinet members are chosen by the Prime Minister from the majority party in the House of Commons. Exceptions to this rule can occur if a coalition government is produced by the House of Commons or if crises (wars, economic slumps) necessitate the formation of a national government representing all shades of opinion.

3 **Accountability** Answerability or accountability of the Cabinet to the House of Commons and ultimately the electorate. There are two aspects to this:

   a) Sovereignty of Parliament has in the modern sense passed to the majority party in the Commons which implies the Cabinet and Prime Minister. Within Parliament therefore the Cabinet is responsible to a legislature dominated by itself.

   b) Although the executive dominates the House of Commons, there is provision for the removal of the Cabinet in the convention. If a government is defeated on a motion of no confidence, it must resign because it no longer commands the support of the House. Although first established in 1841, this **sanction** has only removed three administrations this century, the last being the 1979 Callaghan Labour government.

Party discipline prevents the government losing its majority in the House of Commons. In 1979 special circumstances deprived James Callaghan of his majority and ability to defeat the motion of no confidence.

Knowing that they rarely face defeat at the hands of the House, successive Prime Ministers have used the threat of a vote of no confidence to instil party loyalty into rebellious Commons backbenchers. *Bagehot* (*1867*) first observed that the Cabinet 'could dissolve the assembly which had appointed it' and although appointed by one Parliament, it could appeal to the next. John Major's threat to turn the ratification of the Maastricht Treaty into a vote of confidence issue in 1993 successfully demonstrated that a desperate Prime Minister can constitutionally risk a general election to achieve his objective.

❝ Threat to Parliament ❞

DESCRIBING THE CABINET

The Cabinet is the supreme executive committee of the government. It exists primarily to:

- Initiate and implement government policy.
- Coordinate the work of the administration.
- Settle disputes from lower down the ministerial hierarchy.
- Provide party political leadership to the Commons and the nation.

In a **narrow sense** it is a committee comprised of between 20 and 24 senior ministers who meet on a regular basis under the authority of the Prime Minister.

In a **broad sense** it is at the heart of what *Madgwick (1991)* calls the central executive territory which includes the Prime Minister and his office, the Cabinet Office, Cabinet and ministerial committees and senior officials and advisers.

MEMBERSHIP OF THE CABINET

Membership is conventionally restricted to the most senior politicians in the government. Within the Cabinet there are approximately twenty Secretaries of State responsible for the main departments. They are assisted (beyond the Cabinet) by Ministers of State and the more junior Parliamentary Under Secretaries. The ministerial support for Secretaries of State depends on the size of their respective departments – those combining a number of service or functional responsibilities (Defence and Environment are good examples) will have a greater establishment than smaller departments like Northern Ireland.

SIZE OF THE CABINET

The size of the Cabinet is governed by political and administrative considerations. Politically the heads of the main spending departments will be included as they contribute to and implement government policy as it affects their own area. Theoretically a Prime Minister will also **balance** the Cabinet to ensure all shades of party opinion have an outlet at the highest level. In practice both Margaret Thatcher after 1983 and John Major from 1995 tended to balance their Cabinets to the right and centre respectively. Administratively, before 1915 a Prime Minister could include the full ministerial establishment in the Cabinet. Today there are approximately 100 MPs in

66 Balance of opinions 99

Prime Minister	John Major	52
Deputy Prime Minister	Michael Heseltine	62
Lord Chancellor	Lord Mackay of Clashfern	67
Chancellor of Exchequer	Kenneth Clarke	55
Home Secretary	Michael Howard	53
Foreign Secretary	Malcolm Rifkind	49
President of Board of Trade	Ian Lang	55
Leader of the Commons	Antony Newton	57
Environment Secretary	John Gummer	55
Social Security Secretary	Peter Lilley	51
Chief Secretary to Treasury	William Waldegrave	48
Northern Ireland Secretary	Sir Patrick Mayhew	65
National Heritage Secretary	Virginia Bottomley	47
Education/Employment Secretary	Gillian Shephard	55
Defence Secretary	Michael Portillo	41
Party Chairman	Brian Mawhinney	54
Health Secretary	Stephen Dorrell	43
Lord Privy Seal	Viscount Cranborne	48
Transport Secretary	Sir George Young	53
Agriculture Minister	Douglas Hogg	50
Scottish Secretary	Michael Forsyth	40
Chancellor of Duchy of Lancaster	Roger Freeman	53
Welsh Secretary	William Hague	34

Fig. 5.1 The Conservative Cabinet of July 1995 and represented departments

the government (the so-called payroll vote) fulfilling various roles so making this impossible. Despite continuing **upward pressure** to expand the Cabinet in keeping with the growth of government responsibilities, Prime Ministers have managed to keep to an optimum or most efficient workable size. This has been achieved by a process of merger and amalgamation of smaller ministries into larger departments ensuring that all areas of government activity are still represented in the Cabinet.

Smaller Cabinets have the obvious advantage that they make it easier to reach decisions. *Gordon Walker* (*1970*), a former member of Harold Wilson's government, claimed correctly that a Cabinet larger than seventeen or eighteen ceased to be a council that could easily reach a collective view. Recent Prime Ministers with the exception of Edward Heath (1970–74) have found it impossible to accommodate political and administrative pressures within that number. Harold Wilson himself had 23 Cabinet Ministers (1964–70), Margaret Thatcher 22 (1979–90) and John Major 22 until July 1995.

After the Cabinet reshuffle of July 1995 the Cabinet reached 23 members with Michael Heseltine in his new post of Deputy Prime Minister and William Hague, Welsh Secretary, at 34 the youngest Conservative Cabinet member this century.

CENTRAL FEATURES

The whole operation of Cabinet government is underpinned by conventional practice. The most important convention is collective responsibility – without it the Cabinet as we know it could not function. Although the convention has faced considerable pressure for change, to which it has adapted, it still remains the underlying central principle of Cabinet government.

COLLECTIVE MINISTERIAL RESPONSIBILITY

66 Orthodox view 99

The classic description of collective ministerial responsibility was first given by *Lord Salisbury* (*1878*) in a statement much repeated but still operative: 'for all that passes in Cabinet, each member of it who does not resign is absolutely and irretrievably responsible, and has no right afterwards to say that he agreed in one case to a compromise, while in another he was persuaded by his colleagues'. In practice this has come to mean that public acceptance of government policies is a prerequisite for Cabinet membership. Within a Cabinet of twenty plus ministers there cannot (does not need to) be unanimity for all decisions, but publicly the appearance of unity or solidarity must be given. In its modern form, therefore, collective ministerial responsibility implies:

- Public agreement by all Cabinet members to all government policy decisions.
- Wherever possible the open avoidance of public criticism of government policy by serving Cabinet Ministers.
- A willingness to resign from the Cabinet if a member cannot reconcile private doubts over the direction of government policy with public pronouncements.

Operation of these principles (now part of the guidelines issued to all new ministers) occasionally leads to political controversy. This is likely to happen when a policy split divides a Cabinet resulting in:

- resignations
- media leaks or
- special arrangements.

Resignations

There are many factors working for or against a ministerial resignation for collective policy disputes in a Cabinet. Considerations of political ambition will for the most part keep ministers in a Cabinet. During the Wilson Cabinets of 1974–76 both Tony Benn and Michael Foot were critical of government foreign policy but did not resign. Acceptance of collective responsibility is so strong that resignations from Cabinets on these grounds are relatively rare.

Only five ministers resigned from Margaret Thatcher's governments during the period 1979 to 1990; Ian Gow (Treasury Minister of State); Michael Heseltine (Defence Secretary); Nigel Lawson (Chancellor of the Exchequer); Nicholas Ridley

(Trade and Industry Secretary); and Sir Geoffrey Howe (Deputy Prime Minister and Leader of the House of Commons). It is instructive that three of these resignations were from 'heavyweights' whose support was crucial for the survival of Margaret Thatcher. Once beyond the Cabinet, Michael Heseltine, Nigel Lawson and Sir Geoffrey Howe were free of the constraints imposed by collective responsibility – the need for secrecy or confidentiality, loyalty to the Prime Minister and support for policy they did not approve of. It is worth examining the events surrounding these three resignations because they provide us with an insight into how Margaret Thatcher ran her Cabinets.

66 Heseltine, Lawson, Howe 99

- **Michael Heseltine** Michael Heseltine disputed Margaret Thatcher's version of events surrounding the **Westland** Helicopter Affair (1985–86). Heseltine favoured a European bid to rescue the company and claimed that the Prime Minister acted unconstitutionally in not allowing him to argue his case in sufficient detail before Cabinet and Cabinet committees. Margaret Thatcher for her part evidently felt that Michael Heseltine was in breach of collective responsibility for failing to associate himself with the Cabinet-preferred option of a rescue bid by the American helicopter manufacturers Sikorsky (*Thatcher 1993*). It is interesting to speculate why Margaret Thatcher did not dismiss Michael Heseltine from the Cabinet before he finally resigned over the Westland Affair in January 1986. Michael Heseltine was too important a minister to lose and, as events were to prove in the subsequent 1990 Conservative leadership election contest, he very nearly became Prime Minister.

- **Nigel Lawson** Nigel Lawson's resignation as Chancellor of the Exchequer in 1989 highlighted another important aspect of collective responsibility, namely accountability for government policy as a collective. Margaret Thatcher is alleged to have preferred the policy advice of her personal economic adviser, Sir Alan Walters, over the matter of negotiation of the European Exchange Rate Mechanism to that of her Chancellor. Since Nigel Lawson was technically accountable to the House of Commons as the Cabinet Minister identified with economic and financial policy, he was placed in a difficult position. Resignation reconciled his conscience but was also a signal to Margaret Thatcher that he disapproved of the growing power in the relationship between a Prime Minister and special advisers.

- **Sir Geoffrey Howe** Sir Geoffrey Howe resigned because of disagreements with the Prime Minister over the best policy to adopt towards European integration. Clearly there were personal factors in his refusal to continue in Margaret Thatcher's government and these were visible in his emotional resignation speech to the House of Commons in late 1990. He had been publicly humiliated by Margaret Thatcher when she removed him from the important post of Foreign Secretary. Although he was compensated by the position of Deputy Prime Minister and Leader of the House of Commons, Sir Geoffrey Howe was never reconciled to this demotion. Although regarded as a political 'lightweight', his resignation speech was seen as a final devastating blow to the authority of Margaret Thatcher and signalled the beginning of the end of her premiership as opponents began to manoeuvre for her removal.

John Major's Cabinets since 1992 have been less troubled by resignations for collective responsibility reasons. This did not mean that the Cabinets were without policy conflict, but rather that, for reasons discussed earlier (see p. 52), the constraints keeping ministers in his Cabinets were greater than the impact of the policy disputes. This was evident during reported policy clashes over the possibility of adoption of the European Social Chapter during 1993 when a number of ministers were said to be on the point of resignation. In late 1994 Cabinet splits were reported over attitudes towards a proposed referendum on Europe. By 1995 divisions in the Cabinet and Conservative Party over Europe (Euro-enthusiasts versus Euro-sceptics) had been so publicly obvious (and therefore damaging of collective responsibility) as to force John Major to settle the issue by a Conservative leadership election contest in June/July 1995. In announcing the contest John Major said he wanted his critics to put up or shut up – one of the few public occasions when his emotions have been to the fore.

66 Euro splits 99

Media leaks

The conduct of the business of the Cabinet depends on **secrecy** – collective responsibility would break down without it. Ministers would not speak their minds in the privacy of the Cabinet room if they knew their respective positions on policy issues could be publicly identified. However, it is clearly impossible for a Cabinet of twenty plus ministers and all the attendant servicing documents to remain totally private. According to *Madgwick (1994)* approximately 200 people see Cabinet papers – except those relating to the most sensitive pieces of government information.

Cabinet secrecy (and collective responsibility) is breached by periodic deliberate approved 'leaking' of information to press and lobby correspondents. All governments suffer from unattributable leaking by ministers or Prime Ministers who use the media to publicise policy positions of respective parties 'off the record'. *Gordon Walker (1970)* first claimed that leaking was part of Cabinet conventional behaviour – that it functioned to reconcile the public fiction of unanimity in Cabinet with the reality of dispute in private. The former Conservative minister, *Alan Clark (1995)*, appeared to support this view when he claimed that selective leaking had become part of the machinery of government, because it proved so useful to ministers. In a detailed analysis of leaks *Castle (1995)* claimed there were more than 25 government leaks during 1994/95 without any culprits (civil servants, ministerial aids and others) being publicly identified. The most notable were:

❝ Value of leaks ❞

Leak	Date	Suspect
1 DTI cash	August 1994	Civil servant
2 ID cards	January 1995	Unknown
3 Joint Framework Document	February 1995	Pro-Unionist elements
4 Scott Inquiry	June 1995	Government
5 Education spending	September 1995	Department for Education and Employment
6 Lottery cash	October 1995	Department of National Heritage

Table 5.1 Government leaks 1994/5

The damaging impact of leaks on the conduct of government is probably overrated. The Cabinet Office, which is responsible for tracing culprits, appears complacent and as *Clark (1995)* points out, leaks do contribute to more open government allowing greater public debate of policy issues.

Cabinet secrecy is also breached by the **publication of memoirs or diaries** of former politicians when recollections of events in the Cabinet are placed in the public domain or prove embarrassing to government. The original *Crossman Diaries* published in 1977 proved embarrassing to the Harold Wilson Labour government, more for revelations about the minister/civil service relationship than for any specific reference to Cabinet policy. Richard Crossman's intention was to open the closed world of government and in this he succeeded. The **Radcliffe Committee** of 1976, set up specifically by Harold Wilson to review the publication of ministerial memoirs and their effects on collective responsibility, was unable to prevent publication of Crossman's uncleared diaries. This committee revised the rules governing future publications and heavily criticised Crossman for breaching confidentiality. Ministers were restricted to a fifteen year ban on the use of Cabinet papers (for the public this remains a 30 year ban) and had now to submit their manuscripts to the Cabinet Secretary for clearance against three tests of acceptability:

❝ Cabinet papers ❞

1 National security must not be breached.
2 International relations must not be damaged.
3 Confidences in the executive and administration must not be broken.

Former Ministers are free to write about their public life subject to these restrictions and the list is long. Apart from Richard Crossman, we have had recent memoirs from Tony Benn, Michael Foot, Lord Young, Edwina Currie, Norman Fowler and of course Margaret Thatcher herself.

Special arrangements

A final attempt to overcome an unresolved Cabinet policy dispute where resignations are to be avoided is the practice of **agreements to differ**. Theoretically impossible within the convention of collective responsibility which implies unanimity between colleagues, there have been two previous occasions when Prime Ministers have suspended collective responsibility in order to reconcile differing factions within their Cabinets.

- In 1932 Ramsay McDonald allowed ministers opposed to government tariff plans to dissent from the accepted line.
- Harold Wilson allowed those Labour ministers opposed to European Community membership to publicly campaign against his government's position in 1975.

Both these agreements were in a sense aberrations in government practice. Each Prime Minister was anxious to hold his government together and placed a different interpretation on the convention of collective responsibility.

THE WORK OF THE CABINET

As the senior committee of the executive, the Cabinet brings together departmental heads (Secretaries of State) and the Prime Minister to decide governmental policies and how they will be implemented. There are three broad areas of work at this level of government.

1 **Parliamentary and legislative matters**   The legislative programme discussed in Cabinet will be closely related to proposals contained in the party's manifesto but will need constant adaptation and change. The longer a government remains in office the more difficult it is to present a new programme to the electorate. From September 1995 John Major embarked on a series of 'meet the people' tours (in fact Conservative activists in the regions) in a consultation exercise to seek fresh legislative ideas for the closing years of the 1992 Parliament. New legislative proposals are either

Policy development

   (a) **completely new policies** produced in consultation with advisers, ministers, pressure groups and other interests, closing a legislative gap or perceived weakness in existing laws or

   (b) **adaptation or adjustments** to existing policies often brought to Cabinet level (with the agreement of the Prime Minister) by a minister supported by civil servants.

   The Cabinet will prioritise these legislative proposals and arrange for their introduction into the parliamentary timetable. Sometimes these discussions will involve the Prime Minister and relevant departmental ministers in a **partial Cabinet** as opposed to a full Cabinet.

2 **Foreign affairs**   The full Cabinet (or Cabinet Council (*Madgwick 1994*)) regularly discusses foreign policy. Important decisions have to be taken over the correct stance towards European integration and the European Union, both of which have caused on-going problems for the Conservative Party and John Major. Relations with the rest of the world and current issues of a routine or emergency nature also need Cabinet attention. During 1995 foreign affairs brought to Cabinet would have included the Framework Document producing a peace settlement in Northern Ireland and relationships to the Republic of Ireland; relations with NATO and the United Nations over the commitment of British forces to the Bosnian peace effort; and discussion with China over the future of the colony of Hong Kong.

3 **Co-ordination of government**   A major part of the work of the Cabinet involves oversight and coordination of government policy. All policy affects departments differently but some coherence is needed at the highest level if government is to reach its objectives. Any interdepartmental disputes over the allocation of resources will be referred to the Cabinet and Prime Minister for mediation and settlement, but neither can interfere in the internal working of a department. The relationship between the Prime Minister and Cabinet Ministers discussing co-ordination is one-sided. A Prime Minister can see matters in the round; ministers tend to be 'blinkered' by departmentalism – a tendency to view policy matters through the eyes of their departments (*Crossman 1979*).

CABINET MEETINGS

Traditionally the Cabinet meets on a Thursday for two or three hours of discussion and deliberation. Meetings follow a set pattern and are chaired by the Prime Minister assisted by the Cabinet Secretary. The agenda is circulated beforehand and the minutes are under the control of the Prime Minister and Cabinet Secretary respectively.

66 Cabinet record 99
The recording of Cabinet deliberation has given rise to claims of 'cosmetising' or interference with the record. Michael Heseltine in his dispute with Margaret Thatcher over the Westland Affair claimed that the minutes of one particular Cabinet meeting of December 1985 did not accurately reflect his views. The minutes of the Cabinet are important because the record of the Prime Minister's conclusions form the basis of the policy to be adopted in the administration and copies are forwarded to the respective ministers in their departments for implementation. Clearly any cosmetising of the minutes could have repercussions lower down the government hierarchy. Academic opinion appears to take the orthodox view that Prime Ministers do not see the minutes before they are issued (*King 1985* and *Seldon 1990*).

The conduct of proceedings in Cabinet varies according to the style and personality of the Prime Minister. Margaret Thatcher led from the front preferring decisiveness and direction in discussion to deliberation and debate. Her preference for discussions with inner Cabinets of trusted ministers, **bilateral meetings** with ministers and officials, use of Cabinet committees to bypass Cabinet and personal involvement in pushing policies (banning of trade union membership at GCHQ, the decision to abolish the GLC and metropolitan counties, introduction of the Community Charge or Poll Tax) were all cited as evidence for the Prime Ministerial government thesis. The replacement of Margaret Thatcher by John Major in 1990 marked a return to a more collegiate open style of running the Cabinet.

THE CABINET SECRETARIAT

The support system of Cabinet government is provided by the Cabinet Secretariat and a system of committees working in the Cabinet Office – the engine room of Cabinet (*Hennessy 1986*). The Secretariat is under the control of the Cabinet Secretary who acts as the Prime Minister's unofficial Chief Secretary. It was founded in 1916 by Lloyd George with the primary purpose of bringing order to the work of the Cabinet, which had managed with informal arrangements to that time. The Secretariat services the full Cabinet and committees, is responsible for the circulation of the minutes and generally manages Cabinet business ensuring that its decisions are implemented. Currently there are **six small secretariats**, focusing on the following specific areas of government work:

1 economic policy;
2 overseas and defence information;
3 European business;
4 home affairs;
5 science and technology policy;
6 security and intelligence matters.

CABINET COMMITTEES

The Cabinet Office oversees the operation of the Cabinet committee system which does much of the preparatory work of the full Cabinet. Until 1992 and John Major's
66 Types 99
open government initiative, the numbers and structures of the committees were covered by collective responsibility and Cabinet secrecy. However, it was generally known that there were two types of main committee and this has now been confirmed:

1 **Standing committees** cover the areas of main departmental work, for example overseas policy and defence, economic and domestic policy, legislation, public expenditure. In 1992 John Major had 27 of these committees including a number of subcommittees. Margaret Thatcher by contrast had 35 standing committees during her eleven years in office and her predecessor James Callaghan 25 (*Hennessy 1978*).

2 **Ad hoc committees** are formed for current specific purposes. Typical issues covered in the government of Margaret Thatcher included replacement of Polaris Missiles with Tridents, planning for teachers' and miners' strikes, and changes in local government structures. The most important of these committees is the '**Star**

Chamber', so called because it has the final word in any disputes about the allocation of funds to the main spending departments.

A large number of these committees are formally chaired by the Prime Minister or the Deputy Prime Minister. In a new development from July 1995 (the Cabinet reshuffle) Michael Heseltine as First Secretary of State and Deputy Prime Minister personally chairs nine Cabinet committees which gives him a power base to rival John Major. As the first official Deputy Prime Minister since R A Butler in the Macmillan government, Michael Heseltine works closely with John Major in an 'overlord' capacity coordinating policy through the Cabinet on behalf of the Prime Minister. John Major retains control of the membership, chairmanships and terms of reference for these committees in the traditional way which in turn enhances his power over the Cabinet. Committees sometimes work on subjects before full Cabinet deliberations, at other times they will consider policy matters passed down to relieve an otherwise 'overloaded' executive. Their authority is delegated from the full Cabinet which means in effect:

66 Overlord 99

(a) Their decisions bind the full Cabinet and the whole government.

(b) They do not have to refer back to the Cabinet for approval unless they cannot reach agreement.

The **main advantage** of the committee system is simply that it allows the full Cabinet to function. A **second advantage** concerns better coordination across departments for government policy. In their memberships, committees include ministers from other departments, civil servants and non-Cabinet ministers – all are associated with policy making and thus brought closer to the centre of government. The main drawback in the committee system is that it reinforces the Prime Minister's hold over the Cabinet and takes policy making power away from the full Cabinet, but that is inevitable.

PROBLEMS AND REFORM

As the Cabinet is both an administrative and political institution so the problems associated with it reflect political and organisational constraints. Politically there may be a lack of direction at the top of British government partly because Cabinet members do not have the time or lack the inclination to focus on the longer term (*Wass 1984*). This criticism appears to support the ideas of departmentalism noticed by *Headey (1974)* and confirmed by *Crossman (1979)* that ministers were too preoccupied with their departments' problems to worry about those collectively aired in Cabinet. If ministers were always preoccupied with their departments' concerns, then the traditional idea of Cabinet government as a body of twenty plus centralised ministers deciding policy was flawed. Even before the advent of Margaret Thatcher, the Cabinet was losing power to the Prime Minister. Policy decisions were increasingly being taken outside in the Cabinet committee system, in advisory groups and in bilateral meetings between the Prime Minister and other ministers.

66 Departmental view 99

POLICY CABINETS

As early as the 1940s commentators first noticed weaknesses in both the composition and coordinating abilities of the Cabinet. *Amery (1947)* argued that the Cabinet was ideally suited to management of the short term daily problems of government but departmental problems prevented ministers looking strategically forward. He suggested the establishment of a **small Policy Cabinet** made up of six 'super ministers' without departmental responsibilities. They would coordinate and direct policy without the problems normally associated with traditional Cabinet Secretaries.

THE OVERLORDS EXPERIMENT 1951–53

Winston Churchill, as Prime Minister in 1951, experimented with a system of co-ordinating ministers or **'Overlords'** in an attempt to bring strategic thinking into his Cabinet (see Figure 5.2). Three peers – Lords Leathers, Cherwell and Woolton – were given seats in the Cabinet with oversight of seven separate ministries, but without specific departmental responsibilities.

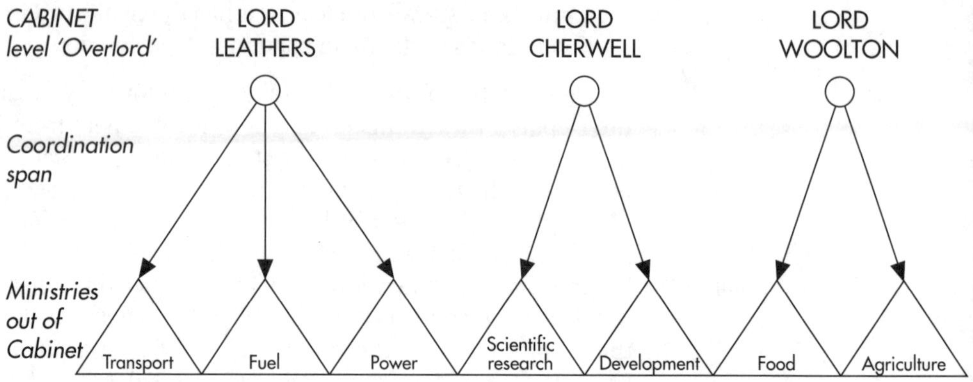

Fig.5.2 The 'Overlords' experiment
of 1951–53

The 'Overlords' experiment failed for a number of reasons. It was impractical to try to separate policy making from policy implementation. The ministers excluded from the Cabinet would not therefore have policy inputs. There were also problems in Cabinet responsibility. The peers were not technically answerable to the House of Commons yet had responsibility for a large number of departments. Functional ministers or representatives had to answer questions in the House yet did not sit in the Cabinet – a serious disadvantage which weakened the procedure.

LARGE VERSUS SMALLER CABINETS

The 'Overlords' experiment can be seen as an attempt by Churchill to reduce the size of his Cabinet to more manageable proportions. It was long recognised that large Cabinets were not effective in wartime and that smaller Cabinets did not function well in peacetime. The 1918 Haldane Committee on the machinery of government concluded that smaller Cabinets could be introduced as a long term reform but that there were practical difficulties.

66 **Coordination** 99

Without the complexity of 'super ministers', modern Prime Ministers have attempted to improve Cabinet co-ordination by:

- Using 'inner' or 'partial Cabinets' and bilateral meetings (especially Margaret Thatcher).

- Making changes to the structure of the administration by creating super departments. Most modern departments – Environment, Defence, Education/ Employment (since 1995) – represent enlarged, merged or super departments.

- Giving coordinating responsibility to a person of almost equal status – a new development since 1995 with Michael Heseltine as Deputy Prime Minister working closely with John Major.

THE DIFFICULTY OF REFORM

We have seen some of the problems relating to the efficiency of the Cabinet and it is difficult to see how the system could be improved. If in the traditional sense the Cabinet has joined what *Burch (1988)* calls the honorific part of the constitution, then this is an inevitable consequence of the growth in the powers of the Prime Minister. Policy shortcomings are not easily overcome either. The short lived Central Policy Review Staff (CPRS, 1971 to 1983) gave sometimes unpleasant advice to Prime Ministers but in the end was abolished by Margaret Thatcher because of duplication of work already done in the Cabinet Office or for political reasons. She preferred to make policy without constant reminders of the shortcomings in policy making. The idea of a traditional Cabinet making policy decisions on a collegiate basis is no longer an accurate description of events at the centre. But the Cabinet still fulfils useful functions under the convention of collective responsibility, including associating ministers with policy, coordinating the Cabinet committee system and as the leading political committee of the governing party.

EXAMINATION QUESTIONS

1 There is considerable difference between the constitutional model of Cabinet government and how the system operates in practice. Discuss. *(25)*
(NEAB)

2 (a) Define the convention of collective ministerial responsibility. *(20)*

   (b) How does it work in practice? *(20)*
(ULEAC)

3 The key issues are thrashed out in full Cabinet. How accurate is this comment on Cabinet government? Discuss. *(25)*
(NEAB)

ANSWERS TO EXAMINATION QUESTIONS

OUTLINE ANSWER TO QUESTION 2

The following points could be used in answer to this question:

(a) 1 Explain the importance of conventions in Cabinet government – give flexibility etc.

   2 Define collective responsibility (Lord Salisbury's definition) – classically Cabinet ministers are all held responsible.

   3 Explain why doctrine is still followed – unity in government, need to face criticism in House of Commons.

   4 Discuss the changing convention – ministers rarely resign today because of different way policy is decided.

(b) 1 Give examples of the working of the convention.

   2 Show how the classic principle has been relaxed – agreements to differ.

   3 Discuss why Prime Ministers allow relaxation of principle.

   4 Look at resignation of Howe, Heseltine and Lawson. Discuss their implications for the convention.

   5 Examine practice of leaks – how it affects convention, desirable/undesirable.

   6 Make some evaluation of the changed convention – is there any point keeping it? What purpose is it serving? Secrecy in government. How important to policy making.

TUTOR'S ANSWER TO QUESTION 1

The traditional view of Cabinet government was of a collective or collegiate committee at the highest point of government solely responsible for the initiation and implementation of policy. This Cabinet would be constitutionally answerable to Parliament under the convention of collective ministerial responsibility which implied a sanction over the executive if defeated on a motion of confidence in the House of Commons. The convention of collective responsibility also depended very much on Cabinet secrecy which gave the public impression of a united government fully supported by all its members. The modern view of Cabinet government entails a reinterpretation of many of these basic features emphasising that the work of the Cabinet has developed to one of coordination of policy and the machinery of government.

Constitutionally the Cabinet is still answerable to Parliament but as the working of government at this level depends on conventional practice, there have been considerable changes over the years. Now a government rarely resigns because of a defeat on a motion of no confidence in the House of Commons. James Callaghan's Labour government defeat in 1979 was a rare occurance in the modern sense because the party system invariably guarantees a working majority to the executive. Party loyalty (even from recalcitrant MPs if threatened by the Whips) usually ensures the government survives a vote of censure. John Major successfully risked the survival of his Cabinet by making the vote on ratification of the Maastricht Treaty in 1993 a vote of confidence in his leadership; the Euro-sceptics were forced to support him.

Answerability to Parliament is still an important conventional characteristic of Cabinet government, for individual ministers and the Prime Minister can face probing from a sometimes hostile House of Commons. However, it is now generally agreed that parliamentary sovereignty has given way to executive dominance of the House of Commons. This implies that the executive is answerable to a legislature dominated by itself, and can reinterpret the rules as it thinks fit. The Callaghan government of 1976–79 provided a good example of a weak executive in the parliamentary sense (it had a small majority which eventually disappeared through by-election defeats). Faced with these difficulties Callaghan chose to ignore many defeats in the Commons, reinterpreting the convention of resignation and remaining in office until the final censure of a vote of no confidence in late 1979.

Another area where there has been reinterpretation of traditional Cabinet principles relates to the size and function of the executive. According to *Madgwick (1991)* modern descriptions of the Cabinet (or Cabinet Council) should include in their broadest sense the Cabinet, Prime Minister, Cabinet Office, Cabinet committees, advisory staffs and ministerial committees because they are all involved in policy making. The classic narrow view of the Cabinet as a committee of senior ministers solely responsible for and making policy is clearly inaccurate. The expansion in government responsibilities this century and the corresponding growth in the administration have created a central executive territory that goes beyond the Cabinet room.

This expansion in the machinery of government has had implications for a) the structure of Cabinet and b) the doctrine of collective ministerial responsibility. Expansion in government responsibilities has been contained within Cabinets of manageable size of up to twenty ministers for as *Gordon Walker (1970)* correctly claimed, larger Cabinets find it difficult to secure a collective view. The work of the executive has been contained by the creation of super ministries through the amalgamation of smaller departments and by the continual use of Cabinet committees – both ad hoc and standing. Cabinet committees have come to have policy making powers which are delegated from the full Cabinet and whose decisions are binding on the whole government. These committees extend the power of the Prime Minister as they are under his authority and control (since the July 1995 Cabinet reshuffle Michael Heseltine, as Deputy Prime Minister, has had a trouble-shooting role chairing nine Cabinet committees) and make it possible to bypass the full Cabinet. But this is not a new development – traditionally during crises or wars important Cabinet decisions have been taken by small groups of ministers working with the Prime Minister, for example Margaret Thatcher ran the Falklands War in 1983/4 from the 'South Atlantic' Cabinet committee.

The spread of policy making from the full Cabinet downwards to Cabinet committees affects collective ministerial responsibility and makes it harder to keep all ministers publicly united behind government policy. If many binding policy decisions are taken in committees alone, certain Cabinet members will not be present at the initial stage but will be expected to publicly support the policy. Resignation within the convention of collective responsibility is available to ministers who feel they cannot reconcile their private policy difference with the Prime Minister. Although the constraints of a political career press hard on ministers preventing many resignations, Michael Heseltine, Nigel Lawson and Sir Geoffrey Howe had a fatal effect when they resigned from Margaret Thatcher's Cabinet. Recognised policy splits within Cabinet have on two occasions – 1932 (Tariff Reform) and 1975 (European Community) – led to special arrangements or 'agreements to differ'. These in themselves have contradicted the traditional view of a united Cabinet fully in support of government policy. On both occasions desperate Prime Ministers used the device to keep their Cabinets together. Since 1975 no government has had to resort to these arrangements although precedent has been set.

The modern practice of leaking confidential Cabinet information to the press has also affected collective responsibility. The convention depends on Cabinet secrecy and traditionally it was observed. Today unattributable leaks may be used by ministers to state their opposition to a policy they privately do not support even if they are publicly associated with it. Two writers – the former Labour minister *Patrick Gordon Walker* (*1970*) and *Alan Clark* (*1995*), a minister in Margaret Thatcher's government – have both testified to the usefulness of unattributable leaks. Leaks from the civil service can also be deeply embarrassing to ministers bound by collective responsibility. Michael Heseltine was compromised by Clive Ponting's leaks during the Falklands War and Gillian Shephard was exposed to criticism after the leak of her briefs to a Special Strategy Cabinet in September 1995.

Part of the work of the Cabinet is coordination of government policy at the highest level. As policy making has spread from the Cabinet, the coordination function assumes greater importance. Traditionally the Cabinet Secretariat served the whole Cabinet as a recording and transmitting agency, but with the growth in the development of the power of the Prime Minister it has increasingly come to appear more like the Prime Minister's department. The Prime Minister has the overview of government business so necessary for co-ordination and although ministers are associated with other policy through their committee work, they do not have the time or outlooks to gain a strategic forward view.

Amery (*1947*) and *Crossman* (*1979*) have both commented on the departmental view of Cabinet Ministers preventing long term policy interpretation. Amery suggested a small Policy Cabinet of 'super ministers' to overcome the problem and Crossman wanted more democracy in the relationship between ministers and the Prime Minister. Churchill's 'Overlords experiment' was also an attempt to move away from Cabinets burdened with departmental responsibilities. The failure of the Policy Cabinet idea points to the impracticality of separating policy initiation from policy implementation – the two are inseparable.

Finally, there have been a number of reforms in the machinery of Cabinet government designed to produce greater efficiency in policy making. The CPRS (Central Policy Review Staff) was one experiment designed to improve the quality of policy advice to ministers and the Prime Minister. Initially the establishment of the Cabinet Secretariat by Lloyd George in 1916 introduced a welcome organisation into what had previously been a haphazard system. The long term problems in the Cabinet remain, however, primarily because it is both a political and administrative unit. In its modern form it is different from classic descriptions but it is still functioning well as the supreme executive committee of government.

STUDENT'S ANSWER TO QUESTION 3 WITH EXAMINER'S COMMENTS

The conventional view of the Cabinet system holds that power over policy resides with the whole Cabinet and this is the view proposed by the statement in the question. Cabinet Ministers are able to set the framework within which policies arise and develop and they also oversee and broadly control resulting policy activity. This view implies that all issues of significant importance are brought before Cabinet whereupon they are fully debated and result in policies agreed collectively by top members of government. Upon this hinges the convention of collective responsibility whereby policy once agreed is expected to be supported by all members of the government. This clearly requires all key matters to have been debated properly beforehand.

  Two crucial questions present themselves when this view is studied closely: Firstly, what constitutes a 'key' policy issue? And secondly, does the Cabinet have the capacity and competence to act in the fully collective manner proposed above? Different interpretations of these questions with different answers have led to alternative views of power relations within the executive. Those who hold these views argue that Cabinet has neither the capacity nor the competence to handle the range of business presented to it. In fact Cabinet does not generally exercise

❝❝ Good introduction ❞❞

oversight, nor usually manage to establish a clear framework of values and policy aims within which more detailed policy can be developed. If ever this is clear it is at the moment with pronounced divisions across a whole spectrum of policy issues, represented most obviously by John Redwood's challenge to the Prime Minister, which was symbolic of the party's more right wing members' dissatisfaction with the failure of the leadership to deal with squabbling within the government. Also, Cabinet meets only once a week for about two to three hours. It is thus doubtful whether thorough and informed discussion can take place on a variety of salient topics especially when the ministers involved will be knowledgeable only in the area of their department.

Another proposition is that power lies in the hands of ministers in Cabinet committees. These are an extension of Cabinet and are empowered to reach decisions in their own right without reference to it – 'even though a decision may not reach the Cabinet itself, the decision will be fully considered and the final judgement will be sufficiently authoritative to ensure that the government as a whole can be expected to accept responsibility for it' ('Questions of procedure for Ministers'). So in the modern situation, the term Cabinet encompasses both Cabinet and its committees.

The third view holds that power lies in the hands of the Cabinet Secretariat who organise and handle business when it enters the Cabinet system. Six secretariats currently exist within the Cabinet Office under the supervision of the Secretary of the Cabinet. These cover economic policy, home affairs, overseas and defence, European matters, science and technology, and intelligence and security. The major responsibility for the handling of business is taken by the 40 or so senior officials who are contained within the first three secretariats. They are responsible for ensuring that papers for Cabinet and its committees are available on time, circulating these papers, drafting handling briefs for the chairmen of Cabinet and committees, drawing up the agenda in consultation with committee chairmen and recording and circulating the minutes and conclusions of meetings.

Another popular argument is that the Prime Minister ultimately wields the most significant powers. However, the notion of Prime Ministerial government can easily be overstated and much depends upon the extent to which the formal powers of the Prime Minister are applied in practice. One of the key powers of the Prime Minister is the theoretically unlimited power to hire and fire fellow ministers. Another important set of powers which lie in the hands of the Prime Minister are those concerning the machinery of Cabinet government, i.e. the setting up of Cabinet committees and determining who sits on them and even the items which are sent to them.

The last view is that power lies in the hands of groups of ministers outside the formal committee system. Important informal political activity takes place beyond the confines of the formal machinery of politics and must be considered when approaching any kind of policy making organisation. Within the Cabinet system much discussion takes place and many decisions are shaped in informal

❝ Identify academic views ❞

66 Evidence 99

meetings of both ministers and officials. Under Mrs Thatcher meetings were usually on a one-to-one basis or very small informal groups. Such meetings involved initiation and clarification of policy details. One of the most important links is between the Treasury and the Prime Minister's office. With an increasing emphasis on decreasing public spending this alliance has been central to the operation of Cabinet government.

In conclusion then, it seems that the conventional view as purported by the statement in the question is simplistic to say the least. It leaves out many factors in the policy initiation and decision processes. Clearly some exercise a greater amount of influence than others and no one of the proposed statements is right at the exclusion of the others concerning where power really lies in the Cabinet system.

66 A thorough answer with a fairly good description of the mechanism of policy making within the Cabinet. I would have liked to see more references to academic sources to back up the points made. Worthy of a B grade. 99

REFERENCES IN THE TEXT

Amery, L S 1947 *Thoughts on the constitution*, Oxford University Press

Bagehot, W 1964, first published 1867 *The English constitution*, Watt

Burch, M 1988 The British Cabinet: a residual executive, *Parliamentary Affairs* **46**

Castle, S 1995 Whitehall leaks turn into a tidal wave, *Independent On Sunday* 22 October

Clark, A 1995 Don't plug the leaks – they give debate a chance, *Mail On Sunday* 17 September

Crossman, R 1979 *The Crossman diaries*, London: Methuen

Gordon Walker, P 1970 *The Cabinet*, London: Collins

Headey, B 1974 *British Cabinet Ministers*, London: Allen and Unwin

Hennessy, P 1978 How Mr Callaghan runs things, *The Times* 21 July

Hennessy, P 1986 *Cabinet*, Oxford: Blackwell

King, A 1985 *The British Prime Minister*, London: Macmillan

Madgwick, P 1991 *British government: the central executive territory*, Hemel Hempstead: Phillip Allan

Madgwick, P 1994 *A new introduction to British politics*, Cheltenham: Stanley Thornes

Salisbury, Lord 1878 House of Lords 8 April, Parliamentary debate. Quoted in P Madgwick *New introduction to British politics* 1994, Cheltenham: Stanley Thornes

Seldon, A 1990 The Cabinet Office and co-ordination, *Public Administration*, Spring

Thatcher, M 1993 *The Downing Street years*, London: Harper Collins

Wass, Sir D 1984 *Government and the governed*, London: Routledge and Kegan Paul

CHAPTER

6

PARLIAMENT

PERSPECTIVES ON PARLIAMENT

THE HOUSE OF COMMONS

MEMBERS OF PARLIAMENT

THE HOUSE OF LORDS

GETTING STARTED

The British Parliament (the Queen, the House of Commons and the House of Lords) has long been subject to academic debate about its effectiveness in terms of both legislation and control over the executive. Although reforms have been introduced – the departmental select committee system since 1979 – the parliamentary legislative system is effectively still dominated by the executive. This raises questions about the role of Parliament – should it be an adjunct to government policy making or should it have an existence of its own evaluating proposals on their merits? The corresponding role of Members of Parliament is also subsumed under these considerations, as is the importance of the House of Lords as a reviewing chamber.

Questions on this part of the syllabus focus on the following areas:

- The effectiveness of Parliament in controlling the executive.
- The role of the House of Commons in legislation, scrutiny and debate.
- Members of Parliament as representatives.
- The House of Lords as a second chamber.
- Parliamentary reform of the Commons and Lords.

Useful definitions

- **Bicameral legislature** – a two House legislature comprising the House of Lords and the House of Commons. Theoretically the House of Lords is superior as the Upper House. Politically the House of Commons has superiority because of its electoral accountability.

- **Golden Age of Parliament** – a reference to the mid nineteenth-century situation when the House of Commons had more independence from the executive because the party system had yet to fully develop.

- **Government by committee** – the passing of legislative initiative to committees of the House of Commons thereby weakening the government's control over the House.

ESSENTIAL PRINCIPLES

Theoretical views of Parliament focus essentially on the House of Commons as it plays a more important role in legislation than the House of Lords. There are three basic models centring around the historical, reformist and legal aspects of Parliament.

LEGAL INSTITUTIONAL MODEL

For a brief period in the nineteenth century (the so-called Golden Age 1832–68) parliamentary strength over the executive was at its maximum. Sovereignty resided in a House of Commons that was able to change governments, force the removal of ministers and decide legislation on its merits. The House of Commons was able to do this because the party system and affiliations of MPs had yet to crystallise around a government/opposition axis. By the twentieth century the stranglehold over Parliament by the party machine meant in effect that MPs lost their independent status and became subject to party political control.

This model accepts the constitutional position of a legal system subordinated to Parliament. The judiciary apply or interpret the law; they do not get drawn into arguments about the efficacy or otherwise of legislation. Parliament has a limited impact on policy making, largely because the party system guarantees the government a working majority which in turn implies executive control over legislation.

It is accepted therefore that the role of Parliament has changed in the modern period – the legislature is weak, the government strong. Parliamentary strength will only return with a coalition government in the Commons (achieved through electoral reform or under the existing system); this would make the executive more dependent again on the legislature.

WESTMINSTER MODEL

From this perspective it is recognised that Parliament has never played a major policy making role. According to *Adonis* (*1990*) the House of Commons has never sought to usurp the functions of government but plays a marginal role. **Positively** this embraces:

- Being a debating forum for government and opposition.
- Keeping the party battle in focus for the media and the public.

Negatively the Commons is weak because:

- Government controls debate and the legislative timetable.
- Scrutiny of legislation by standing committee is largely ineffective.
- Investigative work of government by specialist committees is not productive.
- Political partisanship dominates procedure in the House of Commons reducing checks on the executive to party controversy.

This rather negative view of the House of Commons is now regarded as **orthodox** simply because a government with a good majority will always prefer executive power over the parliamentary.

TRANSFORMATIVE MODEL

According to some writers, Parliament since the eighties has redefined its powers and reasserted its role as a check on the executive (*Norton 1981*). Parliament does therefore impact on executive policy making even if in small ways. Changes in the operation of the House of Commons include:

- There is now more **backbench dissent** resulting in oppositional behaviour from government MPs willing to defy their leadership. This was particularly evident during the government of Margaret Thatcher but has continued under John Major.
- The new **departmental select committees** (since 1979) have extended scrutiny

over the executive raising public awareness of policy weaknesses which have in some cases been corrected.

- Votes on **conscience issues** have had increased significance as MPs are given **free votes** away from party dictates. The list of issues is long ranging from capital punishment, abortion laws, divorce, house conveyancing, to Sunday shopping and televising of Parliament.

THE HOUSE OF COMMONS

The House of Commons has assumed primacy in the British parliamentary system as the sole elected national assembly representing the wishes of the people – a criterion regarded as essential for democratic government. Although technically the Lower House in a bicameral legislature, the Commons is more important than the House of Lords in current parliamentary practice.

PERSONNEL AND PROCEDURES

There are now 658 (since the 1995 session) Members of Parliament representing constituencies in England, Wales, Scotland and Northern Ireland. Each constituency returns one MP elected on the simple majority system under a party label. Now it is virtually impossible to get into Parliament without the support of a political party; the days of the independent Member have long gone. Once in the House, party strictures are strong. Except for the creation of the Social Democratic Party in 1981 when 27 Labour and one Conservative MP left their respective parties to join the SDP, only three MPs have 'crossed the floor' of the Commons to join the other party in recent times. In 1976 Reginald Prentice, a Labour Cabinet Minister, was rejected by his local Labour Party (Newham North East) and eventually joined the Conservative Party.

In October 1995 Alan Howarth, Conservative MP for Stratford-upon-Avon, defected to the Labour Party because of policy differences with his government. In his resignation letter he complained that the government had moved too far to the right, whereas he had hoped for a return to One Nation Conservatism. In December 1995 the prominent Conservative MP, Emma Nicholson, defected to the Liberal Democrats citing a variety of factors in her decision including social policy, attitudes to Europe and weak leadership by a government that no longer cared. In February 1996 Peter Thurnham resigned the Conservative Whip as a result of the Scott Inquiry and then continued to sit as an independent Conservative.

The Speaker

The Speaker is the chairperson of the House of Commons with a long list of responsibilities including:

- chairing debates;
- controlling procedure;
- managing the business of the House;
- representing the House on official and informal occasions.

66 Impartiality 99

Speakers do not vote in divisions except to break a deadlock when they cast a tie-breaker vote usually (by tradition) supportive of the government of the day. Selected for a new Parliament (or after death or retirement of their predecessor), the convention of the House is for the majority party to nominate a successor after discussion with the other parties. When Miss Betty Boothroyd (Labour) replaced Bernard Weatherill (Conservative) in 1992 she had the distinction of being the first female House of Commons Speaker after securing a majority of 372 votes in an open election.

Whips and party discipline

Party discipline is essential to the life of the Commons – without it the House could not satisfactorily conduct its business. To this end the major parties choose a number of MPs as Party Whips whose function is to maintain discipline amongst their MPs. *Silk (1995)* likens their role more to that of **personnel managers** rather than draconian figures disciplining their backbenchers. Each party selects a Chief Whip (on the government side he arranges the business of the House) who cooperate with each other to ensure the smooth running of legislation through the 'usual channels'.

Party Whips also act as the 'eyes and ears' of the party leaders carrying back information on the opinions and morale of the backbenchers. In order to control attendance in divisions (when the House votes on a proposal – legislative or debate) government and opposition Party Whips issue **the whip** which is an instruction to attend for a division. If the government has a small majority (John Major's Conservative overall majority was 21 after the 1992 general election and two after the defections of Alan Howarth, Emma Nicholson and Peter Thurnham) it is likely that it will do its utmost to win divisions. However since the collapse of the Labour government of James Callaghan in 1979 after losing a vote of no confidence, governments tend to **ignore defeats** in the Commons unless they affect a crucial part of their programme, as in the case of the passage of the Maastricht ratification process 1992–93.

Dissident MPs

❝ Types of whip ❞

The whip is divided according to importance of the instruction to attend: the **one line whip** requests attendance; **two line whips** insist on attendance unless the MP is paired (cancelled out) with a member on the opposite side; the most serious is the **three line whip** where attendance is mandatory. The ratification of the Maastricht Treaty highlighted divisions within the Conservative Party where rebellious (dissident) MPs ignored any type of whip and voted against their government on a number of occasions. This in turn lead John Major to:

- Use the threat of a dissolution of Parliament (and hence a general election) in the form of making a final defeat on the Maastricht Bill into a motion of no confidence in the government in July 1993.

- Expel eight Conservative Euro-rebel MPs from the Parliamentary Party in November 1994 by withdrawing the whip in punishment for refusal to support the government over the vote on increases to the European Union budget.

The withdrawal of the whip from the 'whipless rebels' (Richard Shepherd, John Wilkinson, Tony Marlow, Teresa Gorman, Nicolas Budgen, Sir Teddy Taylor, Michael Cartliss and Christopher Gill) technically lead to the loss of John Major's majority in the Commons and the formation of a Euro-sceptical party within the Parliamentary Conservative Party. This small group of Conservative MPs attracted intense media attention during the six months they were in the 'wilderness' (the whip was restored in April 1995) and later went on to support John Redwood's unsuccessful attempt to replace John Major in the July Conservative leadership election contest that year.

❝ Backbench dissent ❞

Paradoxically, dissent by government backbenchers originally highlighted by *Norton (1980)*, during the long Conservative administration of Margaret Thatcher and continuing under John Major, has had ramifications on the role of Parliament. Because of large Conservative majorities the official Labour opposition has been less effective than opponents on the government side. And independent behaviour by MPs is generally regarded as returning power back to the floor of the House of Commons. However, as *Madgwick (1994)* notes, the object of protests against legislation by government backbenchers is to secure influence over it, not to bring about eventual defeat in a general election. Such influence was well demonstrated in November 1995 when the Lord Chancellor, Lord McKay, was forced to withdraw his Family Homes and Domestic Violence Bill. In a series of meetings Conservative backbenchers let it be known they would oppose the bill unless certain changes in property rights for women were made; if this was done, they would support the bill.

FUNCTIONS OF THE HOUSE OF COMMONS

It is generally accepted that the House of Commons has five or six functions depending on the emphasis between the formal and real powers of Parliament (*Norton 1981*).

1 The function of legitimation is the overarching agreement given to the executive to govern by the House of Commons from which it draws its **legitimacy to rule**. The Commons also gives legitimisation to the laws passed by the government – without this approval there can be no legislation. Clearly a government that loses control over the House (a lost majority) cannot claim any legitimacy from the Commons and must tender its resignation.

2 British government is representative and responsible *(Birch 1964)*, which implies a **representative** tie to the electorate through the Commons. MPs **indirectly**

represent all the constituents in their area whether they supported the MPs or not. Since government ministers are recruited from MPs by the Prime Minister, a career in the House of Commons is usually a prerequisite for high office. Ministers are therefore trained in parliamentary procedure and carry their representativeness into government.

3   As a forum of national debate the House of Commons is fulfilling an informative and educative role. There are many opportunities for the House to debate government policy including:

- Queen's speech;
- opposition days;
- emergency debates;
- finance bill;
- confidence debate;
- debates on bills.

As governments usually win the vote after debates (divisions), and much of what is said is party political point scoring, critics tend to focus on their negative impact. Whilst it is true that the Commons is a 'talking shop', *Norton (1981)* makes the point that Parliaments are exactly that. The value of debate is in exposing weaknesses in the performance of government ministers, which the electorate will evaluate in general elections.

The last main functions of the House of Commons – **legislation** and **scrutiny** – are possibly the most important functions of a Parliament and demand more extensive analysis.

LEGISLATION

66 MPs and legislation 99

The legislative activity of the House of Commons involves the whole House overseeing the passage of bills, giving sanction to the government's programme. Except in the case of private members' bills, MPs do not in the strict sense have **legislative initiative**, rather they concentrate within their respective parties on influencing the content of legislation. Because most legislation originates with the government, which has a majority on standing committees dealing with it, the broad direction of policy is unlikely to be affected greatly by any amendments proposed by opposition MPs.

Types of legislation

The bills which come before the House of Commons are either **private** or **public** (see Figure 6.1). The former relate to a specific interest; the latter affect the community at large.

PUBLIC BILLS – Affect public as a whole   PRIVATE BILLS – Affect private interests

1)	GOVERNMENT BILLS	Most legislation affecting public		For example, LOCAL GOVERNMENT by-laws giving special powers to a local authority
2)	PRIVATE MEMBERS' BILLS	Mainly controversial topics (capital punishment, abortion, law etc.)		

1) Introduced by government
2) Introduced by backbench MPs

Fig. 6.1 Types of legislation

Government bills

Most public bills are sponsored by the executive. **Government bills** have the greatest chance of reaching the legislative statute book because they are prioritised by government control of the Commons timetable. Some of the government's legislative intentions will be spelt out in the Queen's Speech, which is delivered to Parliament each November at the opening of a new session. Other legislative proposals will be laid before the electorate in the governing party's manifesto, which forms a loose **mandate** for office once in power. Governments also acquire public legislative powers through statutory instruments (SIs) which follow a different route from ordinary bills.

Private members' bills

Procedure

A small percentage of parliamentary time is allocated to private members' bills which do not usually reach the statute book for lack of government support. As public bills they will often tackle social or moral issues which governments prefer to leave for fear of electoral ramifications. Occasionally they will highlight an area of growing public concern where the government will act after the failure of the private member's bill. MPs successful in the ballot to introduce a bill (other ways include the ten minute rule after the day's proceedings, or Standing Order 58, by giving notice to the Speaker) are often approached by outside interests anxious to promote legislation of their own. In early 1995 the Labour MP John McFall was persuaded by the League Against Cruel Sports to introduce his Wild Mammals (Protection) Bill which was in effect written by the League. Although the bill failed it did secure publicity for the case against hare coursing and other blood sports which is part of the objective of the private members' bill activity. The subsequent revision of this Bill introduced by the Labour MP Alan Meale, enabled it to pass both Houses of Parliament by February 1996 as The Wild Mammals (Protection) Act (see p. 123).

Private bills

Private bills form a small part of the legislative output of Parliament. Governments are generally not in favour of granting special powers to public bodies like local authorities because this impinges on the concept of parliamentary sovereignty and makes it harder to control legislation. For this reason private bills go through an elaborate and expensive process of being 'proved' by special committees of both Houses of Parliament, before embarking on their different stages. Typical powers granted to local authorities under this type of bill include regulatory laws to control the activities of local markets, small business and other activities. *Silk (1995)* gives numerous examples including the Birmingham City Council Act 1985 which allowed motor racing on public roads in the city.

Legislative stages

To become law, bills must pass through legislative stages in both the House of Commons and the House of Lords (see Figure 6.2). Bills that begin in the Lords (less politically contentious) end in the Commons and those starting in the Commons end in the Lords. The final stage, the royal assent, is a formality; the monarch does not personally sign bills (the Clerk to the Parliaments affixes the royal assent in Norman French). The last monarch to refuse assent was Queen Anne in 1707, and Queen Victoria in 1854 was the last to sign in person.

Of these respective stages, the committee stage is possibly the most important from the point of view of the opposition who can table amendments to bills more effectively at this stage. Bills go before **standing committees** (committees of debate organised along party lines) where they are examined clause by clause.

Amendments will be considered and sometimes accepted by the government if they improve the effectiveness of the bill, but not if they alter policy considered important or attempt to wreck it. Wrecking amendments, together with effective management of the timetable, are a major reason why government managers bring in **Time motions** the time motions of the **guillotine** or **kangaroo.** Both restrict the amount of time spent in debate and in consideration of a bill and are frequently criticised by opposition parties as being undemocratic. Certainly, as *Madgwick (1994)* notes, the use of guillotine motions has increased in recent years, particularly where bills are fought 'line by line' through committee. Executive control of the legislative timetable for bills also ensures that the vast majority of accepted amendments made to general legislation in standing committees are government sponsored with opposition and backbench amendments hardly succeeding.

Comment on the legislative process

The effectiveness of the House of Commons is related to any policy influence that can be brought to bear over government controlled legislation. Because the functions of

STAGE	WHERE TAKEN	COMMENTS
First reading	Floor of House	Formal introduction; no debate
Second reading	Floor of House	Debate on principle of Bill
Committee	Standing committee in Commons	Clauses examined; amendments can be made
Report	Floor of House	Bill reported back to House; amendment possible
Third reading	Floor of House	Final approval; no amendments in Commons
Lords or Commons Amendments	Floor of House	Consideration of amendments by other House
Royal assent		Bill becomes Act of Parliament

Fig. 6.2 Stages of parliamentary legislation

the modern Commons are subsumed under party control – in effect majority government – the legislative role is weak. This is particularly evident from the following criticisms.

1 **The legislative stage** is too lengthy, complex and time consuming (*Norton 1995*). As MPs insist on their rights to debate principles and details of controversial bills – both in standing committee and on the floor of the House – attempts to reform procedure have yet to succeed.

2 **Parliament has little input** in the pre-legislative stage. Bills coming into the Commons are at an advanced stage of formulation thus reducing MPs' influence. Suggestions for improvement include the placing of committee stage at the beginning of the legislative process where the wider implications of a bill can be examined (*Norton 1995*).

3 **Structurally standing committees** are not able to offer a convincing check on executive legislative powers. As presently arranged, they are formed to consider bills under heads A, B, C, D etc., then disbanded after their work. This ad hoc nature and dispersal prevents the accumulation of member expertise which would assist public policy scrutiny.

4 **Only a fraction** of statutory instruments (SIs) made under Acts of Parliament are examined by the Commons Select Committee on Statutory Instruments. Now approximately 3000 to 4000 SIs are produced each year giving additional powers to the executive. The vast majority are formally 'laid before Parliament' and are signed into law – 'nodded through' – with little or no debate (*Booker 1995*).

SCRUTINY

Scrutiny of the work of the executive is possibly the most effective area of the House of Commons business, in the sense that it focuses on the politically sensitive aspect of **policy implementation** rather than **policy initiation**.

Scrutiny of government takes two forms:

1 Spontaneous contemporary examination through questions to ministers.

2 Procedural investigation of administrative activity through departmental select committees. Select committees are the more effective check on policy, or have

most influence because they traditionally operate on non partisan (non-party political) grounds from a parliamentary perspective.

Questions to ministers

Question Time was traditionally held up as the parliamentary institution which enshrined ministerial accountability to the House of Commons. Now less is expected of the procedure which has been absorbed by the party political battle. Notice must be given (at least two days) of questions to ministers (including the Prime Minister) to allow time for the preparation of answers. Answers will be **oral** (if the question is starred) or given as a **written** reply in Hansard, the official House of Commons record. The strengths and weaknesses of Question Time are well documented (see Figure 6.3).

ADVANTAGES	DISADVANTAGES
1 Directly confrontational (government v. opposition) 2 Attracts media attention 3 Easy to follow 4 Can reveal **gaps** in government knowledge 5 Supplementary questions can surprise ministers	1 Time not adequate for many questions 2 Ministers can avoid straight answers 3 Prime Ministerial Question Time degenerates into party political battle 4 MPs who want more detail prefer written questions which get written answers

Fig.6.3 Strengths and weaknesses of Question Time

The Nolan Committee on Standards in Public Life 1994

The activity of two Conservative backbench MPs – David Tredinnick and Graham Riddick – in accepting payments in return for placing questions to ministers in 1994, prompted the government to set up the Nolan Committee into public standards. Prior to the activities of these two MPs there had been serious questions raised over the activities of Members and their financial links to outside sources. Although Parliament established a voluntary **Register of Members' Interests** in 1975, there were many unrecorded cases of MPs receiving gifts, payments or commissions for raising matters pertaining to those particular interests. As a result the Select Committee on Members' Interests recommended in 1992 that the House of Commons tighten up its rules on disclosure of the financial relationships of MPs.

The Nolan Report into Standards in Public Life was therefore the third attempt to tighten up financial and commercial relationships between MPs and outside interests. Nolan's main recommendations were:

1 The establishment of a Parliamentary Commissioner for Standards (implemented 1995).
2 The Register of MPs' Interests should be tightened up.
3 MPs should not work for lobby firms that had more than one client.
4 MPs should disclose outside earnings relating to their parliamentary work (implemented 1995).

This last proposal formed the main obstacle to acceptance for many Conservative MPs with the result that John Major placed the whole issue into an all-party select committee. This committee's recommendation to declare for public scrutiny all MPs' outside earnings relating to their parliamentary role was passed after a **free vote** in the Commons in November 1995. The result deeply embarrassed John Major, because his recommendation (through Tony Newton, Leader of the House and Committee Chairman) was to reject Nolan's recommendations for full disclosure. Since November 1995 MPs have had to declare their earnings to the new Parliamentary Commissioner for Standards and these have been made public since April 1996.

Departmental select committees

The most effective form of scrutiny of the work of the executive has always come from the **investigative** or **select committees** of the House of Commons. These were first established in the nineteenth century (the oldest committee is Public Accounts dating from 1861) and have become a regular feature of parliamentary life since that time. Various piecemeal reforms were carried out to committees (in the 1950s and 1960s) until 1979 when the then Leader of the House of Commons, Norman St. John Stevas, implemented the decision by the House to extend the system to cover government departments (the **St. John Stevas reforms**). The new departmental select committees (DSCs) were the first attempt to regularise the scrutiny system with committees that could examine 'the expenditure, administration and policy' of the main government departments (1979 Report of the House of Commons Procedure Committee).

Initially fourteen departmental committees were established. By 1995 this had risen to seventeen and included a new committee on Northern Ireland (see Figure 6.4).

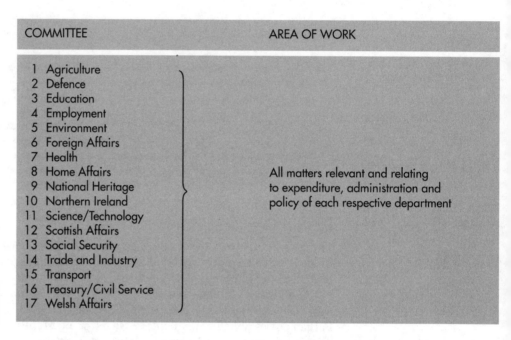

COMMITTEE	AREA OF WORK
1 Agriculture 2 Defence 3 Education 4 Employment 5 Environment 6 Foreign Affairs 7 Health 8 Home Affairs 9 National Heritage 10 Northern Ireland 11 Science/Technology 12 Scottish Affairs 13 Social Security 14 Trade and Industry 15 Transport 16 Treasury/Civil Service 17 Welsh Affairs	All matters relevant and relating to expenditure, administration and policy of each respective department

Fig. 6.4 Departmental select committees of the House of Commons from 1994

 ❝ Powers ❞

Committees have substantial powers given to them by Parliament and can call for **'persons, papers and records'**. They publish unanimous reports of their deliberations (which the government replies to) and, unlike standing committees, operate in a non-partisan parliamentary way. Committees have attracted their share of **criticism**. They cannot compel MPs, ministers and other witnesses to attend. Some, like Arthur Scargill (NUM President) and Edwina Currie MP (over Salmonella in Eggs Affair 1989) attended after numerous initial refusals. Civil servants only attend with express permission of their permanent or deputy secretaries and then they are governed by the 'Osmotherly Rules' regulating their conduct (*Shell 1993*). Access to information is restricted, committees have no express powers to examine departmental records, nor to compel witnesses to answer their questions. This was graphically demonstrated by the stonewalling actions of the Maxwell brothers in refusing to answer questions before the Social Services Committee in 1992. A final difficulty is the fact that the government is not obliged to act on a committee's recommendations – although it makes a response. Such behaviour limits any **policy influence** committees may have over the executive. (*Norton 1994*) talks of the marginal influence of DSCs on government policy although generally he believes this has had positive results.

❝ Advantages ❞

There is little doubt that select committees have improved the scrutiny function of the House of Commons over the executive. According to *Norton* (*1994*) the following improvements are a direct result of the work of the committee system.

1 The House of Commons is better informed about government work through MPs' specialised critical activity in select committees.

2 Committees have had a deterrent effect on the behaviour of government in the knowledge that their affairs are publicly scrutinised.

3 There is now more openness in government as a direct result of committees examining ministers in public and placing more information into the public domain than previously.

4   Groups and outside interests are given more access to policy makers by being called before or submitting evidence to committees.

5   Although difficult to quantify, the reports of select committees may have greater policy influence than is obvious. Many recommendations are later adopted by the government and proposals may find their way into improvements in policy.

Occasionally proposals are made to increase the effectiveness of select committees still further – increased budgets, longer sitting days, greater links with the floor of the House of Commons (*Norton 1994*).

Government by committee

Executives in parliamentary systems are generally reluctant to see increased powers given to scrutiny committees for fear of losing policy initiatives to what in effect becomes **government by committee**. Reformers sometimes compare the weakness of the British select committee system to the strengths of American congressional committees. This is not particularly useful for constitutional reasons – the US federal system and separation of power allow the existence of powerful legislative and investigative committees as a check on an otherwise overpowerful President. The British Prime Minister and executive operate within a parliamentary system answerable to a House of Commons.

COMMONS REFORM

66 **Reform of Parliament Group** 99

Attitudes to reform of the House of Commons depend very much on the position adopted with regard to the orthodox role of the House. Various approaches have been well publicised since the activities of the academic Reform of Parliament Group from the 1970s. Simplistically there are two opposing views to reform, one weak the other strong.

1   **The weak view**   Generally identified in the writings of *Crick* (*1970*) who claimed that Parliament's role was educational and supportive of constituents. The policy making function rests with the executive and the House of Commons should concentrate on scrutiny and criticism. Any **reforms** should be **internal**, relating to improving procedure and MPs' effectiveness.

2   **The strong view**   Associated with the work of *Walkland* (*1979*), who argued for an ending of the adversary party political battle which denigrates Parliament. Two-party dominance of the House of Commons will only end with electoral reform. There should therefore be an emphasis on **external reform**; changing the electoral system would produce a genuine multi-party House of Commons able to control government.

Evaluation

The choice facing reformers revolves around a weak Parliament and strong executive (the present situation), or a reformed stronger Parliament and weak executive. Only the future will tell.

MEMBERS OF PARLIAMENT

The public image of the House of Commons is closely bound up with the behaviour of Members of Parliament. Before the televising of the House of Commons in 1989, people's perception of the House owed much to sound broadcasts (started in 1975) and newspaper coverage. The general impression given was of a disorderly place absorbed in a party political battle with MPs of radically different ideologies arguing about legislation and government policy. Televising of the House has produced a change in parliamentary behaviour – MPs appear **less confrontational** in debate, there is less 'ya booing' or heckling as they seek to create favourable impressions with the electorate (*Adonis 1990*). Structurally (because of the government–opposition seating arrangements) the classic impression given of the House of Commons

66 **Modern view** 99

was of a place where representatives of the working class (Labour) faced representatives of the middle and upper classes (Conservative and Liberals (Democrats)) in an adversarial contest. Such a picture is now less relevant and no longer an accurate description of events.

THEORIES OF MEMBERS OF PARLIAMENT

There are two basic theories of representation used to account for Members of
Parliament.

1 **Representative or Burkean theory** According to this view MPs are representatives of their constituents and owe their constituents their better judgement in
any decisions relating to their behaviour in the Commons. They **do not slavishly
follow** their constituents' dictates but consider opinions in an overall evaluation
before casting their vote. These ideas have their origins in the writings of the
Whig philosopher and eighteenth century MP *Edmund Burke* (*1729–97*). Burke
was no democrat – he preferred aristocratic rule (because aristocrats were trust-
ful) and was opposed to the extension of the franchise to women and the labouring
classes.

   Burke's ideas have become influential because of his emphasis on the freedom
of MPs from restraining ties of their electorate. Yet in the modern House of
Commons MPs are tied to party machines (except in 'free votes') so it could be
argued that Burke's philosophic notion of pure representation has never been
achieved.

2 **Delegate theory** The delegate theory of MPs has more recent origins and can
be traced to early this century with the extension of the franchise and the creation
of the Labour Party. Essentially this view recognises a stronger electoral tie
between MPs and their constituents. Since their constituents elect them to
Parliament, they should (like a delegate) **subordinate** their **personal views** and
vote according to their constituents' dictates, or the party constitution. Left wing
Labour MPs put more emphasis on this perspective largely because of the tradition of mandated (instructed) delegates to the Labour Party Annual Conference
and associated trade union conferences. There is also a philosophic left wing connection to the idea that the Labour MPs should endeavour to keep to the socialist
principles established in their constitution. The attempt by the Labour left to
ensure the permanent mandatory reselection of MPs can be seen against this
background.

Comment on representative theories

Clearly British MPs lean more to the Burkean or representative view of representation. Labour, Conservative and Liberal Democrats are not mandated in the true sense
of the word as delegates for their constituents. Indeed, there are those on the right
who regard the delegate theory as positively harmful to the orthodox idea of a 'free'
representation. This contrasts with the philosophic position of members of the US
Congress who are part delegate and part representative because of the federal nature
of US representation at local, state and national level.

SOCIAL BACKGROUND OF MPs

MPs are predominantly male, middle aged and middle class (three Ms). Apart from
the under-representation of the working class in their ranks, women and members
from the ethnic minorities also have less chance of becoming MPs. Two reasons are
advanced for this situation.

1 Parties tend to select so-called 'safe' candidates for parliamentary elections. There
is a generally held belief supported by research that black candidates (*Sewell
1993*) and women (*Baxter 1993*) and members of the working class are seen as
liabilities by the electorate and are therefore not selected by the mainstream parties.

2 Working class representatives, women and ethnic minority group members tend
not to present themselves as candidates for fear of selection failure and this reinforces the low numbers succeeding.

Comment on social background

Parliament has never socially mirrored the nation or 'selectorate' that it represents
(*Rush 1987*). This does not imply a conspiracy to under-represent the majority for

❝ Minorities and MPs ❞

indirect representatives have in that sense always been elitist. However, there is now a general feeling that women and ethnic minority communities should have more MPs and the major political parties are moving in this direction. The Labour Party introduced rule changes that allowed all-women shortlists in safe Labour seats (EMILY's List) from 1993 until 1996. Following a ruling by an industrial tribunal that it was illegal to discriminate in this way, the party abandoned the practice in early 1996. Under the scheme half the candidates in 'winnable' or safe Labour seats and half of those in retiring seats had to be women. The party's attitude to the selection of black candidates is changing since the election of four ethnic minority MPs in the 1987 general election.

CLASS BACKGROUND OF MPs

The House of Commons is a middle class institution – most MPs are drawn from professions with university education an important criteria. Examination of the occupational background of successful parliamentary candidates in the 1992 general election showed business and private sector professionals dominating the Conservative Party whilst public sector teachers and lecturers dominated the Labour Party (*Butler and Kavanagh 1992*).

This development, which has been tracked since the 1945 Parliament, has two implications.

1 The class background of all MPs has **converged** towards the middle class. The Conservative Party is no longer dominated by the upper class and the Parliamentary Labour Party has few MPs of working class origin.

2 The **social gap** between the electorate and MPs is now greater for the Labour Party and its working class base than the Conservative Party and its middle class base.

FUNCTIONS OF MPs

According to *Adonis (1990)* MPs' functions can be subsumed under the following heads:

1 **Party loyalist/activist** The majority of MPs are loyal to the party that puts them into Parliament.

2 **Constituency representative** Constituency work takes vast amounts of MPs' time. Surgeries, local public relations and correspondence from constituents have increased pressure on MPs.

3 **Member of the Commons** The main work of MPs includes debates, committee work, divisions and general legislative activity, embracing private members' bills. In carrying out their role (which each MP interprets independently) they face pressures from their party, constituents and parliamentary work, all of which lead to questions of their effectiveness and how it could be improved.

THE EFFECTIVENESS OF MPs

The effectiveness of MPs is often judged against their performance in the House of Commons which in turn relates to pay and conditions of service. Conditions of work in the Commons are frequently criticised as inadequate in terms of office space, secretarial support and working environment. MPs work long hours and need more support services if they are to carry out their roles effectively. Considerable confusion surrounds the **financial reward** for this work with the standard response that MPs are underpaid by professional middle class standards. It is always invidious to focus on actual salaries and allowances (the politics of envy) and because of the time lag between writing and reading a book figures will always be outdated. The former Conservative minister *Alan Clark* writing in 1995 claimed that MPs' total remuneration reached £120,000 including tax free secretarial and cost of living allowances. After the Nolan proposals on disclosure of outside earnings, there was discussion on raising the basic salary of MPs to a £60,000 indexed rate excluding allowances. Were

❝ Salaries ❞

this to happen, MPs could no longer claim that lack of financial remuneration was hindering their effectiveness as legislators, although by international standards they are not overpaid.

AMATEUR OR PROFESSIONAL MPs

The recommendations of the Nolan Committee on Standards in Public Life finally accepted by the House of Commons in late 1995 have brought back into focus the question of MPs' status and external earnings. Many Conservative MPs were resentful of the disclosure rules on earnings which have now been accepted because they maintain consultancies and outside lobby contacts which bring substantial financial rewards. Such MPs support the idea that they should have outside contacts to enrich their experiences, and should not be forced to **become closeted full time parliamentary professionals**.

The counter view that MPs should concentrate on their parliamentary work is propagated mainly by those with fewer outside contacts – primarily Labour and Liberal Democrats. They claim that Parliament should be **the sole occupation** of MPs and that those without outside employment are able to discharge their duties properly. *Norton (1994)* identified a growing trend among the newer MPs to regard Parliament as a main professional career. The difficulty for such MPs is the counter argument that if they lose their seats at a general election they will have no occupation to return to. Many lawyers and other professionals maintain their alternative occupations for just such an eventuality.

THE HOUSE OF LORDS

66 Executive relationship 99

There have been many attempts to reform the House of Lords, all of which have failed. From this it can be concluded that there is a broad nature of agreement between all the main parties that the Lords should continue in existence playing its major role as a second chamber criticising the executive (*Brazier 1991*). Even though the composition of the House has been questioned, there appears little controversy over its role and functions. As presently organised the Lords does not threaten executive dominance of the legislature and no present or future government wants to see the House rival its power over the Commons. Those who want reform generally feel the Lords should be more effective in its legislative role and more democratically accountable in its representative function.

THE POWERS OF THE HOUSE OF LORDS

The powers of the House of Lords are subject to the operation of the Parliament Acts 1911 and 1949. The first Act removed powers over financial bills. The second Act restricted delaying power to one year (effectively one parliamentary session). It is important to clarify this position.

In practice the House has worked out its relationship to the executive in the Commons through an arrangement referred to as **Lord Salisbury's Convention**. The fear facing the newly elected Labour government of 1945 was that the Conservative dominated Lords would frustrate the wishes of the electorate by delaying legislation for two years under the 1911 Parliament Act. Accommodation was reached with the Conservative Leader of the Lords in 1945 that the House would not seek to prevent the passage of legislation contained in a party's election manifesto. In effect, therefore, bills in a government's manifesto have the authority of an electoral mandate and are not opposed outright by the Lords. The House does retain the right to propose amendments to bills, however, but these are rarely pressed if the government insists on its legislative detail unaltered.

Clearly this power to amend and delay bills from the Lower House can be beneficial in forcing ministers to reconsider legislation. In 1994 Home Secretary Michael Howard was persuaded to reconsider plans for reform of the police service, but the Lords backed down during the 1992–93 session on the Railways Privatisation Bill (*Shell 1993*).

In operating their legislative powers peers tend to behave with circumspection as if direct challenges to the executive can lead to reform proposals of the House on the grounds of preventing popular legislation. The power to delay bills under the 1949

Parliament Act (passed by a Labour government anxious to further restrict the Lords) is rarely used because the Commons can subsequently pass bills to royal assent without the Lords if the latter attempt rejection. In recent times the only bill delayed was the 1991 War Crimes Act which became operative in 1993.

CONSTITUTIONAL SAFEGUARD

The powers and functions of the House of Lords are inseparable in that how it behaves or functions is governed by its power. It has a major role as a **constitutional safeguard** against arbitrary conduct by a government in the Commons. It can prevent absolutely any bills to extend the life of Parliament beyond the statutory five year term. This last **absolute veto** provides the greatest single argument for retaining the Lords, for if it was abolished this function would have either to pass to the Commons or to the courts which do not have power over the executive.

66 Absolute powers *99*

DELIBERATION AND SCRUTINY

The first televising of the House of Lords in 1985 brought publicity to the debating qualities of members of the upper House. Although of high standard debates rarely affect anything of major significance (*Adonis 1990*). Paradoxically, debates illustrate the representative composition of the House for a large number of life peers have wide interests and experience of life even though many are past retirement age. Again, the much criticised hereditary peers also have younger members in their ranks – some of the newer life peers are also younger.

The scrutiny function of the Lords follows much the same process as the Commons and as all bills have to pass both Houses before the royal assent, any amendments made by the House will need:

1   agreement by the Commons,

2   rejection by the Commons or

3   substitution of a Lords amendment by a Commons amendment.

Usually the House backs down in the face of concerted Commons (government) pressure and accepts the agreed version of a Bill which then goes for royal assent.

The Lords has established scrutiny select committees on **European Community legislation** and **statutory instruments** which operate on a similar pattern to those found in the House of Commons in addition to its standing legislative committees. The scrutiny function is completed by Question Time which has less significance than its Commons counterpart. Peers can ask oral or starred questions of the government spokespersons and also receive written answers. One measure of the **revival** of the House since the early eighties is the increase in the number of questions now being asked (*Adonis 1990*).

COMPOSITION

There are four categories of membership of the House of Lords:

- Bishops   26
- Hereditary peers   772
- Life peers   390
- Law Lords (current)   12

     Total at March 1995   1200

Since the admission of **life peers** in 1958 (Life Peerage Act), breaking the hereditary stranglehold over the House, the political imbalance between the Conservative leaning **hereditary peers** and the rest has been moderated. Although those who take the Conservative whip outnumber the other parties, three factors moderate this prospect:

1   A considerable number of peers (up to 300) do not take a party whip and prefer to sit as **crossbenchers**.

2 Lord Denham, a former Conservative Chief Whip in the Lords, once complained that it was difficult to muster all his supporters in a division because the majority of Conservative hereditary peers were inactive. **Backwoodsmen** – the Conservative in-built majority – will apparently attend for matters affecting the Monarchy, Land and the Constitution; otherwise they prefer to stay away.

3 Attendance figures to the Lords have increased to an average of 300 (*Norton 1993*), making it more likely that the Labour and Liberal Democratic parties can rely on their memberships in divisions. Life peers (many Labour and Liberal Democratic, but also Conservative; since 1983 few hereditary peers have been created of any party) tend to be more active and see their legislative role in the House as their major occupation.

REFORM OF THE LORDS

The last serious attempt to reform the House of Lords came with the Parliament (No 2) Bill of 1968/69. The essential provisions in this bill (which could form a blueprint for future reform) were:

- Distinguish between voting peers and non-voting peers (mainly hereditary).
- Voting or appointed life peers would carry out most of the work.
- Non-voting peers would gradually diminish in strength.
- Governments to have a ten per cent in-built majority in voting arrangements.
- Delaying power reduced to six months.

This bill was lost for the same reasons that prevent serious reform of the Lords today: a failure to reach agreement between all parties. Conservative opponents felt it would destroy the ancient relationship between the hereditary peerage and the legislature. And Labour opponents argued that it would entrench privilege. Both attitudes are still prevalent in current arguments. In February 1996 Tony Blair announced that a future Labour government would remove hereditary peers from the Lords because of their irrelevance in a modern democracy.

Reform proposals

Those who support the status quo believe the House has experienced a **revival** during the eighties and is now seen as the real opposition to a Conservative government controlling the Commons.

Opponents of the present system either feel the House of Lords should be abolished (not very practical), or that the House should be reformed along the lines of the last attempt in 1968. The problem in turning to an **elected democratic chamber** guaranteeing representativeness is that it could rival the House of Commons in its claim to legitimacy (*Rush 1994*). Governments of whatever persuasion are unlikely to agree to this, leaving the Lords as it has always been – necessary to the working of Parliament.

EXAMINATION QUESTIONS

1 Can the House of Lords be justified in a modern democracy?   *(25)*
(UODLE)

2 How well does the House of Commons perform its main functions?   *(25)*
(NEAB)

3 Which do you consider to be the most important duties of a backbench Member of Parliament?   *(25)*
(UODLE)

ANSWERS TO EXAMINATION QUESTIONS

OUTLINE ANSWER TO QUESTION 2

This question demands a thorough understanding of the role of the House of Commons against the background of executive dominance. It is important to show the positive attributes of the House although current debate focuses on the shortcomings. An examination of the different perspectives on Parliament would be useful followed by careful discussion of the legislative, deliberative and scrutiny function of the Commons. The legislative role of Members of Parliament needs evaluation including their performance in departmental select committees. Finally, there should be an analysis of reform proposals of the Commons set against the orthodox role of the modern House.

TUTOR'S ANSWER TO QUESTION 1

Clearly the existence of the House of Lords can be justified in a modern democracy, for although it is possible to have a unicameral legislature (as in Sweden and Denmark) the advantages of a bicameral system outweigh the drawbacks. The House of Lords is fulfilling a number of important roles – not the least the reviewing of legislation that passes quickly through the Commons. It also has a judicial role as the highest Court of Appeal and acts as a final safeguard against an arbitrary government extending its life beyond the statutory five year limit.

It is possible to argue from a representative point of view that the composition of the House of Lords is out of step with practices followed in modern democracies. The fact that the majority of hereditary peers (772) are by nature unelected gives them no constituency to represent nor mandate to partake in legislation and law making. From the perspective of the democratic House of Commons this would be an accurate comment, but it does not take us very far. The hereditary element in the House of Lords has other virtues. Because they are removed from constituency pressures, party discipline can be more relaxed in the Lords. Peers have more time to deliberate and scrutinise government proposals which as of necessity must come before the Upper House also before laws are made. Some hereditary peers are young, active and take a full part in the proceedings of the House.

Whatever drawbacks exist with the hereditary arrangement (and one must surely be the preponderance of 'backwoodsmen' – inactive hereditaries – who take the Conservative whip) the existence of life peers admitted since 1958 helps to redress the political balance. Of the 390 life peers, many have distinguished themselves in various walks of public life before membership and this experience greatly contributes to the quality of debates in the House.

In fulfilling its legislative function the Lords assists the House of Commons by revising bills that may have received cursory approval in that House. This is to be welcomed even if under the 1949 Parliament Act the Lords can delay legislation for up to a year (one parliamentary session). This does not frustrate the policies of a democratically elected government in the Commons because of three safeguards. Firstly, the existence of Lord Salisbury's Convention (1945) prevents the Lords from opposing legislation that has a popular mandate by inclusion in the government's election manifesto. Secondly, the fact that a government in the Commons can override Lords amendments after two parliamentary sessions and secure the royal assent, removes the Upper House veto. And finally, under the provisions of the 1911 Parliament Act the Lords lost its veto over financial legislation. The passage of the 1911 Act (caused by the Lords' rejection of the Liberal government's People's Budget of 1909 which was subsequently tested in two general elections in 1910) demonstrated that ultimate sovereign power resides in the Commons. It is unlikely therefore that this challenge will be repeated.

The value of the House of Lords to the constitution can be clearly shown in its other work. It helps to legitimate the government by sharing the legislative role with the House of Commons. Its select committee work, both on European legislation and statutory instruments, is admired for its quality as are its debates (*Phillip Norton*). In terms of scrutiny of legislation, the Lords have acted as the real opposition to a Conservative government in power continuously since 1979. There have been many examples where the Lords have forced changes in legislation or a second 'rethink' by the government during these years – opposition to the abolition of the Greater London Council, charging for school transport and the Poll Tax are some examples.

Finally, although the House of Lords is justified, it may need reform. Critics fall into two categories: those who wish to abolish it (generally on the left of the political spectrum) because it is associated with an elitist privileged class system, and those who feel its performance and accountability can be improved by moving towards a democratic footing. The so-called 'second chamber' paradox of an elected Upper House has to be considered – a democratic House of Lords will possibly rival the popularly elected House of Commons causing more difficulties. A possible way forward was demonstrated in the proposals of the Labour government Parliament (No. 2) Bill of 1968/69. This would have reformed both the powers and the composition of the House with safeguards for a government majority. As an appointed House it would not have challenged the electoral legitimacy of the Commons. A possible option is to leave the Lords as it is – supporters of the status quo feel there is little to be gained by changing it.

STUDENT'S ANSWER TO QUESTION 3 WITH EXAMINER'S COMMENTS

66 Weak opening 99

The debate as to where MPs' responsibility lies is an old one. MPs feel pressures from a wide range of both moral and political obligations; sometimes these responsibilities are reconcilable, other times they are not. There are two main, diametrically opposed ideologies about the basic relationship between MPs and their constituents. These are the Burkean, or representative theory, and the delegate theory.

The basic premise of the Burkean theory is that Parliament is the deliberative assembly of the nation, with one interest – that of the whole. MPs are elected as representatives of their constituents, but are not expected to follow their constituents' dictates. Under this viewpoint, MPs are expected to follow their judgement in the interests of the nation, and not be bound by the narrow interests of their constituents.

The delegate theory is based on the idea that parliament is a body for reaching agreement and getting your case heard. The MPs' function is that of servants to their constituents. They must reflect their constituents' opinions and argue their constituents' case in Parliament, so that reasonable compromise can be reached between conflicting interests.

This country tends to adopt a more Burkean approach to the responsibility of MPs, with opinion varying over party boundaries. The Conservative Party are strongly Burkean in their views on this subject, whilst the Labour Party, with its history of trade union power, follow a more delegative point of view. This can also be seen in their mandatory reselection policies of 1979–90.

66 Simplified point 99

There are drawbacks with each approach. At the extremes of representative theory, the Members of Parliament would become too removed from their constituencies, their debates and decisions divorced from a real life context. With the delegate theory, there is the danger of breakdown of relations – too many conflicting points of view, and no-one able to mediate properly because of strong ties to constituents' wishes.

It can be seen, therefore, that a process of compromise between these two viewpoints could offer a solution. However, we have not yet considered other pressures on MPs, or other, slightly differing arguments as to the location of responsibility.

Disraeli said 'Damn your principles! Stick to your party.' He was advocating what is known as the Doctrine of the Mandate, which suggests that electors vote for a package of ideologies and policies put forward in a manifesto. The electorate gives the victorious party a mandate to rule. This being the case, MPs serve their constituents best by supporting their party. This viewpoint is very strong in British politics, particularly within the Conservative Party.

Labour MPs have slightly different pressure on them. For the Labour Party, the Party Conference is, in theory, a policy making body, unlike the Tory Conference. It has been argued by democratic socialists such as Tony Benn that Conference policy should determine Labour MPs' responsibilities. In real terms over the last few years, however, the importance of the Conference in this respect is diminishing due to the support that more radical views often get, which can affect a party's attempts at election winning.

Even with a Burkean approach to MPs' responsibility, it must always be remembered by MPs that it is their local party that selects them, provides back-up and support at election times, and provides them with a base to operate from. MPs must remain in touch with their local parties if they wish to keep this support, and with the electorate more widely if they wish to be re-elected. Total subservience to the party would destroy the role of constituency MPs, and neither the Burkean theory nor the Doctrine of the Mandate are completely accepted by the public. MPs are expected to listen sympathetically to their constituents, and to do what they can to help those with needs or genuine grievances. Not to do this would almost certainly incur the wrath of the constituents and endanger an MP's chances of re-election.

66 More detail needed 99

It can be seen from these points that MPs have a wide range of pressures on them, from a responsibility to the general good of the whole nation to party loyalty, to their constituents' needs. These different layers of responsibility have, in the past, led to conflict and difficult decisions. The Conservative backbenchers' rebellion over increased payments to Europe provides examples of these kinds of conflict. They were expected by their party to give support, although many had severe personal misgivings about the bill and its worth to the nation as a whole. Some were fully supported and encouraged by their constituents to resist the bill, despite threats from the government to withdraw the whip if party loyalty did not triumph over either conscience or constituents' wishes. In a situation like this none of the theories and arguments above provide a complete answer.

Having provided the ideological and practical background to the question, it would seem that the most satisfactory answer would be to say that it is part of the job of backbench Members of Parliament to seek to reconcile the various demands on their loyalty. It is a task of balancing

> all the differing opinions, needs and demands as best as possible. To do this, MPs need to be free of claustrophobic restraints on their conscience. The demands of constituents or parties should never be able to rule absolutely. It is the task of all MPs to use their judgement in weighing all the factors. This is perhaps one of the most difficult and demanding parts of the job of MPs. It is the part which requires probably the most careful consideration, as there is no easy answer. Where pressures on MPs conflict, they are forced to make difficult decisions. Perhaps this freedom to decide is one of the most sacred parts of our political system.

❝❝ This essay could have done with a little more clarity. There is little discussion of the legislative role although the reference to underlying theory is sound. Probably a D grade because of the weaknesses. ❞❞

REFERENCES IN THE TEXT

Adonis, A 1990 *Parliament today*, Manchester University Press

Baxter, S 1993 The Nimbies in the Labour Party, *New Statesman and Society* 26 November

Birch, A H 1964 *Representative and responsible government*, London: Allen and Unwin

Booker, C 1995 So does this place count any longer, *Daily Mail* 18 October

Brazier, R 1991 *Constitutional reform*, Oxford: Clarendon

Butler, D and D Kavanagh 1992 *The British general election of 1992*, London: Macmillan

Clark, A 1995 The enormous price we pay for democracy, *The Mail on Sunday* November 12

Crick, B 1970 *The reform of Parliament*, London: Weidenfeld & Nicolson

Madgwick, P 1994 *A new introduction to British politics*, Cheltenham: Stanley Thornes (Publishers) Ltd

Norton, P 1980 *Dissension in the House of Commons*, Oxford University Press

Norton, P 1981 *The Commons in perspective*, Oxford: Martin Robertson

Norton, P 1993 *Does Parliament matter?* Hemel Hempstead: Harvester Wheatsheaf

Norton, P 1994 Select committees in the House of Commons: watchdogs or poodles? *Politics Review* **4** November

Norton, P 1995 Standing committees in the House of Commons, *Politics Review* **4** April

Rush, M 1987 The selectorate revisited. In L. Robins (ed.) *Political Institutions in Britain*, Harlow: Longman

Rush, M 1994 The House of Lords, end it or mend it? In W Wale (ed.) *Developments in politics* Vol. 5, Ormskirk: Causeway Press Ltd

Sewell, T 1993 *Black tribunes: black political participation in Britain*, London: Lawrence & Wishart

Shell, D 1993 Departmental select committees, *Politics Review* **2** April

Silk, P 1995 *How Parliament works* 3rd edn, Harlow: Longman

Walkland, S A 1979 *The House of Commons in the twentieth century*, Oxford University Press

POLITICAL PARTIES

PARTIES IN DEMOCRACIES

PARTY SYSTEMS

CONSERVATISM AND THE CONSERVATIVE PARTY

SOCIALISM AND THE LABOUR PARTY

LIBERAL DEMOCRATS

MINOR PARTIES

GETTING STARTED

The mid nineties have seen considerable change in the main British political parties if not in the party system. The Labour Party (or 'New' Labour) has responded to a long period in opposition – since 1979 – by ideological and organisational reforms. Tony Blair's emphasis on 'modernist' ideas and his success in changing Clause IV of the Labour constitution (mid 1995), once regarded as a central platform in the party's commitment to socialism, could be seen as preparation for the next general election and as an appeal to the voter.

John Major's achievement in holding the different factions of the Conservative Party together after the unsuccessful leadership challenge by the New Right candidate, John Redwood, in July 1995 reasserted his authority over the party. But Michael Heseltine's elevation to the new post of Deputy Prime Minister recognises John Major's dependence on a powerful colleague, both within Cabinet and the party.

Questions on this part of the syllabus tend to focus on the traditional aspects of political parties: structures, organisations and philosophies. In particular:

- The position of the respective leaders and their relationships to the party organisation.
- Comparisons of Conservative, Socialist and Liberal Democratic philosophies.
- The question of internal party democracy.
- The distribution of power within the parties.
- Discussion of the two party/multi-party perspectives.

PARTIES IN DEMOCRACIES

ESSENTIAL PRINCIPLES

Political parties are an essential ingredient in democratic society. They can be described as voluntary organisations designed to aggregate people of like minded interests concerned to produce policies which they hope will be implemented once they achieve governmental power. Their most important functions are:

66 Functions 99

- **Representation** In placing themselves before the electorate, parties hope to secure enough votes to form governments. Since the state does not organise parties in a democracy, this function would not be carried out otherwise. By organising the vote, parties are helping the representative process – they will represent the views of electors who support them either in government or in opposition. In terms of structure, a major problem in representative parties has been the creation of bureaucracies at the top since the majority cannot actively organise the party. The classic writer *Michells* (*1949*) first drew attention to what he called '**the Iron Law of Oligarchy'**, whereby representative power inevitably falls into the hands of a party elite. The three main political parties in Britain – Conservatives, Labour and Liberal Democratic – are to some extent lead by a parliamentary elite, although all have developed more democratic structures since *Michells* wrote.

- **Participation** Parties are important vehicles for political participation bringing people into politics. Political activity for the majority appears limited to casting a vote for a party in local or national elections. The minority are politically active, attending meetings, helping to get out the vote or participating as politicians. Although **political apathy** is low in Britain measured by turnout in general elections (between 70 per cent to 80 per cent average (*Butler and Kavanagh 1992*)), **political involvement** in terms of party membership, attendance at political meetings and helping to run political parties is also low. *Parry, Moyser and Day* (*1992*) estimate that seven per cent of the electorate, only 2.3 million people, are members of political parties.

  There are three generally accepted reasons put forward as explanations of apolitical behaviour:

1 **Apathy** – political participation is regarded as a futile process bearing no relationship to the disinterested.

2 **Cynicism** – cynical views of the political process relate to the feeling that politicians and the political process are corrupt.

3 **Alienation** – political alienation is a situation where individuals see no connection between their lives and the government. In their classic study of the civil culture *Almond and Verba* (*1963*) found greater degrees of political alienation in Britain, Germany and Italy than the United States.

PARTY TYPES

66 Typologies 99

Political parties can be classified sociologically into two broad general types: **mass** parties with a broad base or **elitist** with a narrow support base (see Figure 8.1). The former are found in Western democratic countries, the latter were typical of the parties in the former Soviet Union and Eastern Bloc countries.

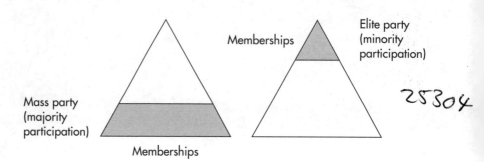

Fig. **8.1** Mass parties and elite parties

25304

The essential point about the diagrams in Figure 8.1 is that there is said to be a healthier relationship between the leaders and the citizens in a mass party with larger memberships, and more chance of achieving **bottom up** policies when that party comes to power. Elite parties represent an active minority governing electorates on behalf of themselves or supposedly in the interests of the mass (the old style Communist Party of the Soviet Union). Such an arrangement would produce **top down** policies, with little citizen involvement.

According to *Duverger (1966)* political parties can be subdivided according to membership into three categories:

1 **Caucus party** – membership based on a limited elite or caucus (small grouping) who hold the strings of political power. The nineteenth-century Conservative and Liberal parties were of this category.

2 **Cell or militia party** – based on a cell or militia structure, highly centralised and disciplined. Usually found in parties engaged in revolutionary activity. The Irish Republic Army were organised along cell lines before the Northern Irish cease-fire and peace process of 1994 to 1996.

3 **Mass membership party** – based on large fee paying memberships either directly or indirectly related through affiliated organisations. The Labour Party's affiliated membership arises from trade unions affiliated to the party and individual members paying the political levy. The Conservative Party has no affiliated members.

PARTY SYSTEMS

" Party competition "

Democratic political systems depend on the existence of a number of parties competing for power. It is hard to characterise the British political system as either **one party**, **two party** or **multi-party**; party competition has passed through periods of adversarial politics into consensus and back again. A common feature of all democratic systems is a struggle for political power along one, two or any number of dimensions. Consensus and cleavage are an integral part of this competition *(Lipset 1963)*.

A ONE PARTY SYSTEM

Britain does not have a one party system in the orthodox sense of a single party holding all the political power in a state. The long period of Conservative government in the mid nineties has raised the spectre of **one party dominance** in a dominant party system which constantly returned a single party to office even though there are other large competing parties in existence. On closer examination it is obvious that two factors contribute to this situation:

1 The weakness of the opposition parties. Because the Labour and Liberal Democratic Parties oppose each other as well as the Conservative Party, their parliamentary strength is dissipated, allowing the Conservatives to remain in office.

2 The simple majority electoral system used in the United Kingdom favours the larger parties at the expense of the smaller. The opposition vote was greater at 58 per cent in the 1992 general election, yet the Conservatives formed their fourth consecutive administration on a 41.9 per cent share of the vote. But the peculiarities of this system mean that no government (Conservative or Labour) has achieved more than 50 per cent of the popular vote since 1951.

A TWO PARTY SYSTEM

The traditional description of the British party system has always emphasised the importance of two parties competing for the power of government. Historically, party competition has for the most part been between two factions; first the Whigs and Tories (eighteenth and nineteenth centuries), then the Liberals and Conservatives (early twentieth century) and finally Conservatives and Labour (late twentieth century). But because this party system is never static we cannot predict with certainty that this pattern will remain in the future. It is possible that **political cleavage** always finds an outlet in two dimensions; certainly *Ingle (1993)* found this pattern occurring over 300 years of British history. It is also sometimes claimed that the British people prefer an either/or choice between two parties alone leaving little room for centre parties. A system of two party dominance does prevent the emergence to power of extremist parties because the majority of the electorate, or the **median voters** (those with equal numbers to the left and right in a political continuum), are at the centre ground.

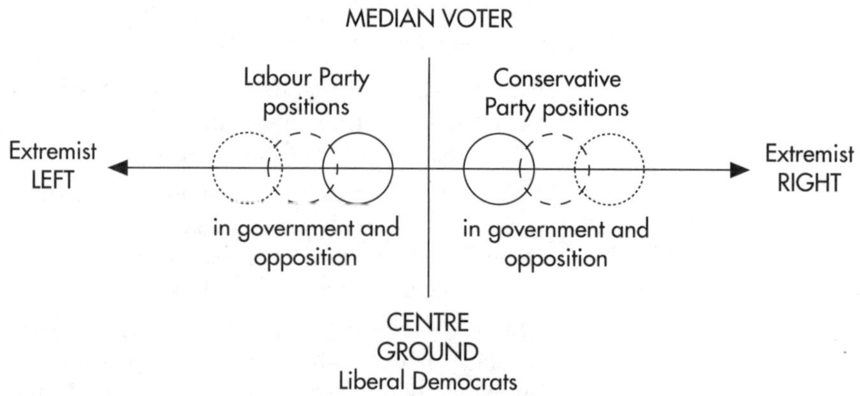

MEDIAN VOTER

Fig. 8.2 The two party political continuum and median voter

66 Political squeeze 99

Figure 8.2 shows how centre parties are squeezed by the two main parties. This occurs electorally as the Conservative and Labour Parties take votes from the Liberal Democrats, and ideologically as Conservatives and Socialists adopt centre policies they feel they can make their own. Environmental issues are a good case in point. For long they were championed by the Liberal Democrats, only to be picked up by the Conservatives in government and Labour in opposition.

Advantages of two party competition

The two main advantages of a two party system are:

1 **Strong responsible government**. The system virtually guarantees the winning party a good majority in the House of Commons. This in turn ensures the majority party is responsible to the wishes of the electorate.

2 **Alternation in government**. A two party system with an official opposition waiting to take power is a better guarantee of democracy because it enables alternative policies to be placed before the electorate. Although the Conservatives had remained in continuous office since 1979, there was the electoral probability that the Labour Party or a combination of Labour/Liberal Democrats would replace them in the future. Under the **pendulum theory** of party competition (popularised by *McKenzie 1963*) the regular alternation in power of an 'in' and 'out' party is a sign of a healthy democracy. The problem with the long run of Conservative dominance in the eighties and nineties is the danger of the Labour Party being associated in the minds of the electorate with the image of a natural party of opposition against the Conservative Party image of a natural party of government (*Crewe 1992*).

66 Alternation of parties 99

Disadvantages of two party competition

Two disadvantages of two party competition relate to:

■ **An economic model** A major tendency with modern governments is to exploit the political market place for their own ends. The governing party can manipulate the economy so as to produce policies which the electorate find attractive. If a government is able to continually satisfy median voters (the 'feelgood' factor), it increases its chances of remaining in office. This partially explains the success of Margaret Thatcher's three consecutive general election victories of 1979, 1983 and 1987, and was a factor in the previous long run of Conservative victories from 1951 to 1964.

■ **An adversarial model** The two party system favours the outlooks of adversary politics. Under this model political debate is channelled through two aggressively competing avenues – a **left spectrum** versus a **right spectrum**. The first serious analysis of these effects was carried out by *Finer (1975)*. He showed how the system of government/opposition made the parties more polar than they otherwise would be. Party leaders are encouraged to make ideological commitments to the extremist wings of their respective parties giving the impression of radical policies to the electorate. Once in power, governing parties tend to reverse many of the policies of their predecessors irrespective of their merits. Political debate between major parties concentrates on differences between them, on **destructive** rather than **constructive** criticism (*Ball 1987*) Part of the appeal of the Liberal Democrats has always been that they seek to capture the essence of consensus – that the majority of the electorate do not cluster at the extremist end of the political spectrum.

A MULTI-PARTY SYSTEM

From an electoral point of view (but not parliamentary) Britain has a multi-party system. There are always three or more parties competing for electoral support, which in turn gives greater choice to the voter: Conservatives, Labour, Liberal Democrats, Scottish Nationalists, Welsh Nationalists and Northern Irish parties. However, this choice appears to have little impact on who governs, largely because of the simple majority electoral system. It could therefore be argued that since minor parties have little chance of gaining power (even the Liberal Democrats 1992 17.8 per cent share of the vote only gained them 20 MPs), those who support these parties are effectively

66 Disenfranchised voters 99

disenfranchised unless party labels on MPs are disregarded from a total representative point of view. *Dearlove and Saunders* (*1991*) emphasise the importance of the electoral system in translating voter choice into party systems. Because the electoral system favours the two main parties, they distinguish between the **two party system** in Parliament, the **dominant party** system of the executive and the **multi-party** system of elections.

The British multi-party system does not in normal circumstances translate into House of Commons arithmetic. In the European model, weak governments are dependent on alliances in strong Parliaments. Except for a brief period in the late seventies, when the Labour minority government of James Callaghan were dependent on the then Liberal Party for office (the Lib-Lab Pact), the British electoral system prevents this happening. We do not therefore possess a multi-party system in the true sense of the words.

CONSERVATISM AND THE CONSERVATIVE PARTY

Political commentators describe the modern Conservative Party as the most successful of any party to have operated in the British political system. If the main indicator of political success is the ability to win elections and form governments, taking the period 1900 to 1996 the Conservatives alone/or with allies have been in power over two thirds of that time. The reasons for this success relate to the following features:

1 **Pragmatism** – The Conservative Party has always prided itself on being pragmatic – of adjusting policies to suit political circumstances. For this reason the party is often portrayed as being less ideological than the Labour Party and Liberal Democratic Parties. The ideas of Margaret Thatcher are developed below (see p. 104).

2 **Flexibility** – Although the nineteenth-century Conservative (Tory) Party was fiercely upper class or aristocratic, it always allowed members of the middle class into its ranks. This flexibility gave the party an edge when it came to accommodating to new social groupings in the twentieth century. The social background of modern Conservative MPs is therefore little different to that of their opponents. Indeed, it could be said that John Major's background was more 'ordinary' than Tony Blair's.

3 **Adjustment** – The Conservatives were quick to adjust to the electoral changes brought about by the expansion of the franchise in the late nineteenth and early twentieth centuries. As a result, they have successfully combatted the electoral challenge of Socialism and held on to a sizeable share of the working class vote.

These features find their way into modern Conservative ideology.

CONSERVATIVE IDEOLOGY

The philosophical basis of Conservatism lies in the idea of individualism – that individuals are responsible for their own existence and standard of life. The task of government is therefore limited to protecting the citizens in the state, not the correction of any inequalities that exist in society. As individuals are created with different abilities, so there will always be those who acquire more wealth and property than the rest. Government should protect the acquisition of this private property since it forms the basis of a free society.

66 Individualism 99

Conservatives are therefore suspicious of political philosophies that aim to level people down or restrict the freedom of individuals to create wealth. **Human nature** is inevitably flawed – people do not necessarily improve their condition over time and there is no blueprint for a perfect or future society. Applied to the institutions of the state, this philosophical creed teaches caution and revolutionary change. Intellectually the ideas of *Edmund Burke (1729–97)* did much to establish the notion that revolutionary change threatened the status quo and was to be resisted. Burkianism has influenced modern Conservative thinking.

Modern Conservatism takes much from the leader of the party because the leader characterises its policies which in turn underpin the philosophy. There are two current strands in Conservative thought that can be identified:

1 **One Nation Conservatism** One Nation Conservatism has its origins in the work of Benjamin Disraeli, Conservative Prime Minister and leader of the party from the mid 1800s. Disraeli created Conservative Central Office in 1870 with the express purpose of bringing together the separate elements in the party which would now focus on securing the vote from a growing industrial electorate. One Nation Conservatives built the party into a national party in the nineteenth century by successfully confronting the Liberal challenge for the working class vote; Disraeli wanted Conservatism to move away from narrow aristocratic sectional interests.

These ideas were again emphasised throughout the first eighty years of the twentieth century as Conservative Prime Ministers came to embrace progressive policies which assisted the working classes (*Whiteley et al. 1994*). Prime Ministers Winston Churchill (1951–55), Anthony Eden (1955–57), Harold Macmillan (1957–63), Alec Douglas-Home (1963–64) and Edward Heath (1970–74) all in their own ways advocated a mixed economy and welfare state ideas in economic management, education, housing and social welfare. When Margaret Thatcher replaced Edward Heath as Conservative leader in 1976 (she did not become Prime Minister until 1979), the ideas of One Nation Conservatism were held responsible for the policy failures of the seventies and a new strand in Conservative thinking was identified.

2 **New Right or Liberal Conservatism** Part of the attraction of One Nation Conservatism had always been the lack of philosophical dogma in comparison with the creed of Socialism. For Conservatives there was no blueprint for a future society or a written party constitution restricting activity. But this freedom had allowed **Conservative leaders to interpret their philosophy**. Now the policies of failure (Edward Heath's government) forced the new leader Margaret Thatcher to turn to the ideas of Liberal Conservatism. In doing this Margaret Thatcher was not introducing ideology into Conservative Party politics as some have claimed (*Ingle 1993*); ideology had always existed in the party. As circumstances changed, so the leadership would emphasise one strand of thinking against others. By the 1980s Conservatives were trying to recapture a radicalism that would distance them from the **consensus policies** of One Nation Conservatives (or 'Wets' as they so disparagingly came to be called) and the ideas of Socialism.

66 Ideology 99

New Right Conservative thinking (or Thatcherism) embraced a number of radical policies. To some it was an attack on the social democratic ideas embraced by both One Nation Conservatives and the Labour Party (*Gamble 1990*). To others it was a general set of political principles embracing council house sales, privatisation, trade union legislation and monetarism (*Kellner 1988*). Margaret Thatcher was influenced in these New Right policies by a variety of thinkers opposed to collectivism and the power of the state including *Alfred Sherman, Milton Friedman, Sir Keith Joseph* and *Freidrich Hayek*. Economically her monetarist policies owed much to the ideas of her economic adviser, Professor Alan Walters. Part of the objective was to reduce state interference in the affairs of the individual, cut government spending, reduce taxation, target welfare spending on the poor and encourage the development of 'popular capitalism'; the property enfranchisement of working class people living in council owned property.

Despite Margaret Thatcher's success in pursuing these policies (she won three consecutive general elections), the Conservative Party removed her from office in 1990 for a variety of reasons (electoral unpopularity, Poll Tax problems, rising unemployment, opposition from within the Cabinet, problems with European relationships, and backbench dissent in the House of Commons).

CONSERVATIVE PARTY ORGANISATION

The Conservative Party organisation can be described as **unitary** or **autocratic** in that power flows from the top down with authority concentrated in the leader's hands. In terms of structure there are three components in the party but little internal democracy (*Kelly 1995*). The three parts are:

1   The Parliamentary Party comprising MPs.
2   Conservative Central Office, including the professional staff of full time officials.
3   The National Union of Conservative Associations, bringing together activists and coordinating the various local associations.

Structures

This organisation has its origins in the advisory structures of the nineteenth century organised to provide the leadership with support. Central Office and the National Union are very much subordinated to the parliamentary leadership and the Prime Minister. In an effort to improve coordination of the extra-parliamentary machine, a Conservative Board of Management was established in 1993 with members from the three components of the party.

THE PLACE OF THE LEADER

The standard work on the distribution of power in the Conservative and Labour Parties was *McKenzie's British Political Parties*, first published in 1955. Writing of the Conservative leader, he said that the leader leads and the party follows – as long as the leader is successful at winning elections. Although, therefore, leaders are in an unrivalled position of superiority in the party (deciding policy, choosing Cabinet colleagues and Party Chairman) they are vulnerable to electoral failures. Their security of office is problematical and they can now be challenged in office.

"" Electoral system ""

Since 1965 the leader has been **elected by ballot** of the Conservative Parliamentary Party. Edward Heath was first chosen by this method in 1965, to be followed by Margaret Thatcher in 1975 and John Major in 1990. Prior to 1965 the leader 'emerged' after consultation with leading Conservatives. The more democratic leadership method (less so than Labour and Liberal Democrats who enfranchised all party members in leadership elections) was a recognition of the need to be seen to be more democratic in the face of criticisms surrounding the selection of Lord Home (Sir Alec Douglas Home) as Conservative leader in 1963 under the old method.

Challenges to Conservative leaders

The change to an electoral system reduced the authority of the Conservative leader who was now dependent on the opinions of backbench MPs in an open contest. Both Edward Heath and Margaret Thatcher were elevated to the Prime Ministership by the backbenchers and subsequently removed by them. In **July 1995 John Major faced the most serious challenge to his leadership** from the Cabinet member, John Redwood.

John Major	218
John Redwood	89
Abstentions	8
Spoiled ballots	12
Non voters	2
Total Conservative MPs eligible to vote	329

Fig. 8.3 The Conservative leadership election result, July 1995

Analysis of the Conservative election of July 1995

- John Major gained a convincing 2:1 win over his challenger John Redwood.
- The threat of a further leadership challenge (under the contest rules a leader can face an annual challenge) was lifted from 1995 until the next general election.
- John Major was saved embarrassment by the decision of the heavyweight Michael Heseltine not to enter the contest, leaving his supporters the opportunity of backing the Prime Minister.
- Before the election Michael Heseltine was offered and accepted the post of Number Two in the Cabinet as Deputy Prime Minister with sweeping executive powers.

THE ANNUAL CONFERENCE

The power of the Conservative Party Annual Conference has traditionally received less attention than the power of the Labour Party Annual Conference because of its lack of formal power over policy making and the party leadership. The emphasis has always been on publicising loyalty to the Conservative leadership in a party where power flows from the top down (*Ingle 1989*). Recent research by *Kelly* (*1994*) has shown that the importance of the Conservative Annual Conference has to be seen against a background of regional and sectional conferences where policy criticisms are raised. Certainly since 1965 the party leader has attended the whole conference, giving an appearance of policy input from the rank and file who draw leadership attention to issues of current concern to ordinary members.

GROUPS WITHIN THE CONSERVATIVE PARTY

There are a bewildering number of groups within the modern Conservative Party each representing a faction or ideological position. The most obvious splits occur across the European dimension (Euro-sceptics and Euro-enthusiasts) followed by the One Nation or progressive Conservatives and those of the New Right. The Conservative election challenger in 1995, John Redwood, was a joint contender with Michael Portillo for the leadership of the New Right, and after his defeat established his own think tank, the Conservative 2000 Foundation, to propagate his ideas in the party. Factions on the left of the party include The Bow Group, The One Nation Group and The Tory Reform Group. On the right of the party are groups associated with the defence of free market principles and the ideas of Margaret Thatcher: The No Turning Back Group, Conservative Way Forward and the Euro-sceptical Bruges Group.

SOCIALISM AND THE LABOUR PARTY

Although the Labour Party has had fewer electoral successes than the Conservative Party, it did succeed in eclipsing the Liberal Party in the early part of this century as the second force in British politics. Because of its origins as an extra-parliamentary party, the Labour Party has

- paid more attention to internal democracy in its organisational structure;
- divided policy formulation between the Annual Party Conference and the leadership;
- appeared more divided than the Conservative Party because of its commitment to a political creed (socialism) which has produced a variety of interpretations.

For these and other reasons the task of governing what is a **federal party** structure is more difficult for a leader preparing the party for government again.

LABOUR IDEOLOGY

Philosophically the Labour Party has its roots in socialism. The problem for those deciphering socialism and its significance for the modern Labour Party is to interpret the different strands that made it up. When the Labour Party was founded in 1900, four constituent elements were instrumental in its make-up, but only one (the Social Democratic Federation) had a strong ideology. The four elements were:

1   **the trade unions** who wanted working class representation in parliament;
2   **the Social Democratic Federation** which admired the teachings of Karl Marx;
3   **the Fabian Society** of gradualist philosophers and writers;
4   **the Independent Labour Party** which had championed the election of working class MPs away from the Liberal banner.

66 **Collectivism** 99

These disparate groups produced a version of moderate evolutionary socialism with which they hoped to transform capitalist society. Intellectually they supported the ideas of a fairer and more just society, to be achieved through parliamentary adjustment of capitalism. Human nature, they claimed, was collectivist rather than individualist and could reach perfection. It was possible to set out plans for a better, more humane future society where working class people's lives would be freed from the drudgery of capitalism. To reach a better society, the state would have to intervene and run industry for the collective good.

In 1918 the Labour Party committed itself to a written constitution which future socialist governments would implement. The most important feature of this constitution was Clause IV which committed the Labour Party to nationalisation or common ownership of the means of production, distribution and exchange. This clause and the first 1918 constitution would survive unchanged until 1995 when they were replaced by a more moderate second constitution, with a modified Clause IV without the commitment to nationalisation.

Ideological debates

Throughout the history of the Labour Party there has been debate over the nationalisation issue as a token of the commitment to socialism. The general division between the left and right of the party has always existed as each tried to eclipse the other. We can regard the left as having a stronger commitment to **fundamentalist** socialism (hence **fundamentalists**) mirrored in their blueprint for a future socialist society: anti-capitalist, decentralised, state ownership and equality between the classes. Those opposed to what they regarded as extremist socialism – an electoral liability in their eyes – sought to modify the commitment to socialism by **revising** (hence **revisionists**) Clause IV. During the post war years the fundamentalists were lead by Aneurin Bevan, later Tony Benn and Ken Livingstone; the revisionists by Hugh Gaitskell, Anthony Crosland and Prime Ministers Harold Wilson and James Callaghan. Later Neil Kinnock, John Smith and Tony Blair lead the Labour Party from the revisionist right. Neil Kinnock successfully defeated the left (expelling the Trotskyist Militant Tendency in the early eighties) and Tony Blair finally completed the modernisation (or revisionism) of the party constitution by late 1995.

Why the revisionists (modernisers) triumphed

There has always been tension between the fundamentalist and revisionist wings of the Labour Party (by 1995 the two wings were renamed traditionalists and modernisers) (*Kelly 1995*). The modernisers have generally centred on the Parliamentary Labour Party whilst the traditionalists have their strength in the extra-parliamentary elements – constituencies and affiliated organisations. As the parliamentary wing of the party has always sought to present itself as the alternative party of government, it has closely followed the wishes of the electorate in adapting policies to it. One reason why modernisers fought so hard to remove the old Clause IV was that they correctly perceived that from the 1960s nationalisation as an issue became an electoral liability for Labour (*Jones 1994*).

Traditionalists by contrast had emphasised the protest side of Labour politics. In their view the Labour Party should not lose sight of its roots in the urban working class and trade unions. Nationalisation and public ownership (rather than moderniser public control) were crucial ways to redress the class balance between rich and poor. During the years in opposition to Margaret Thatcher's centralisation policies over local government, **New Urban Socialists** like Ken Livingstone argued that the Labour Party should rebuild socialism from the localist position to convince voters

66 **Left** 99 that Labour policies could work (*Gyford 1985*). The activities of Left Labour

controlled councils would prove as much of an embarrassment to the Labour leadership of Neil Kinnock as to the government of Margaret Thatcher.

LABOUR PARTY ORGANISATION

The organisation of the Labour Party is **federalist** in the sense that political power and policy making are divided between the leader, the Annual Conference, constituencies and trade unions. The origins of the party outside Parliament are reflected in this structure. A central point of debate in Labour Party politics has always been the degree to which the extra-parliamentary organisation controls the parliamentary wing. As a reformist party anxious to implement policies which would change the status quo, the Labour Party had radical inputs from its memberships, plus a written constitution partially beyond the control of its parliamentary leadership. This did not matter when Labour was in opposition, but once it started to form governments it was inevitable that the parliamentary leadership would want a free hand to govern.

McKenzie (*1963*) first addressed this problem. In his examination of the power relationships in the Labour Party, he reached the controversial conclusion that because of the convention of governing (Cabinet responsibility) final authority rested with the Labour leadership, not with the Annual Conference. Certainly Labour leaders since the sixties behaved as though this was a correct interpretation. Hugh Gaitskell (party leader 1955–63) battled with the Annual Conference over Clause IV; Harold Wilson and James Callaghan both ignored the more extreme Conference resolutions (on, for example, the abolition of the House of Lords). McKenzie's thesis was therefore helpful to the right wing parliamentary leaders of the Labour Party, particularly the assertion that once in office the restraints on a Labour Prime Minister from the Annual Conference and National Executive Committee (NEC) fell away. In effect, therefore, a Labour Prime Minister was as strong constitutionally as a Conservative Prime Minister. Although this theory was challenged by *Minkin* (*1980*) who reasserted the traditional authority of the Annual Conference, it would have a profound effect on the party's internal structural reforms.

66 **Power in party** 99

Structural changes

The ideological disputes mentioned above also had their counterparts in the internal organisation of the party. Accepting McKenzie's ideas, the Labour left (led by Tony Benn) campaigned for greater internal democracy in the party (the Campaign for Labour Party Democracy) on the grounds that stronger controls were needed over the leadership to ensure the implementation of socialist policies through a Labour government. Responding to these changes through a **Special Conference in 1981** the party decided on the following reforms:

- Election of the leader and deputy leader to be democratised to the whole party rather than Members of Parliament.
- MPs to face mandatory reselection on an annual basis (changed in 1990 to periodic reselection only on request of local party).

An attempt to remove control over the party manifesto from the hands of the leader was not implemented but the adoption of these changes was instrumental in the split from Labour of the so-called 'Gang of Four' who proceeded to set up the rival Social Democratic Party (Roy Jenkins, Shirley Williams, David Owen and William Rodgers).

Modifications

The second successive electoral defeat for the Labour Party in 1983 prompted the party leadership to reassert its authority over the left and prepare further organisational changes that had an impact on the leaders, MPs, the Party Conference, the power of the trade unions and party constituencies.

THE LABOUR LEADER

The traditional method of selecting a Labour Party leader until 1981 had been by a ballot of MPs, largely similar to the Conservative process. In democratising the procedure the party set up an **Electoral College** with an initial vote split: 40 per cent trade unions, 30 per cent Parliamentary Party and 30 per cent constituency parties. After the selection of Margaret Beckett as deputy leader in 1992, the 1993 Annual Conference altered the proportionate share of the vote to **one third** for each constituent part, which had the effect of reducing the power of the trade unions in the

❝ OMOV ❞

selection process. The introduction of the **one member one vote** principle (OMOV) removed the trade union bloc vote in leadership elections. Now seven million individual trade unionists could vote on an equal footing with Labour MPs, Euro MPs and constituency members of the Labour Party. This new system was effectively used for the first time in 1994 with the selection of Tony Blair as new Labour leader and John Prescott as his deputy.

Evaluation of the power of the Labour leader

By democratising completely the election of the Labour leader the party has demonstrated an unintentional unity between its various constituent parts – the Parliamentary Party, the constituencies and the trade unions. Tony Blair has pushed

❝ New Labour ❞

on with his plans for **ethical socialism**, and the modernisation of the (New) Labour Party. He was successful at the 1995 Labour Annual Conference in uniting the party behind his reforms and is planning further reductions in trade union conference power determined to demonstrate that (New) Labour are not the servants of organised labour. Paradoxically, he did resort to pre-conference behind the scenes negotiations with trade union leaders to head off hostile reactions to his refusal to commit the party to a stated minimum wage – a technique used by old style Labour leaders and union 'bosses' to manage Conference (*Coxall and Robins 1994*).

GROUPS WITHIN THE LABOUR PARTY

The Labour Party has its share of groups or factions reflecting divisions along a left continuum (hard, centre or soft) now translated as modernisers and traditionalists. Typical of those on the far left is Labour Briefing which is critical of the current leadership and was linked with the Target Labour Government Group of the early 1980s. Another hard left group is the Campaign Group opposed to the current modernising tendencies of the Labour leadership. Right wing groups include Labour 2000 founded in late 1995 which presses for more modernising policies and accepts many of the Conservative reforms on unemployment and competitive tendering.

LIBERAL DEMOCRATS

The Liberal Democrat Party was formed out of a merger of the new Social Democratic Party and the traditional Liberal Party in 1988. Prior to this merger the Liberal Party had represented the **third force** in British politics after its last period in office in 1922. A number of reasons are advanced for the Liberal decline since that time. They include:

- **A failure to adapt** to changing social, political and economic situations.
- **The Labour Party** proved more attractive to the working class vote.
- **A series of damaging splits** destroyed the parliamentary strength of the party.

Although the Liberals (Liberal Democrats) have suffered exclusion from political power since the 1920s (because of the electoral system), they have always had minority representation at Westminster (winning 20 seats in the 1992 general election) and a healthier presence in local government. Part of their attraction in local government has always been their philosophic emphasis on people's rights, local participation and decentralisation of political power.

IDEOLOGY

❝ Liberalism ❞

The modern ideas of the Liberal Democrats – belief in a free market, but a state controlled economy, civil rights and a written constitution, environmental protection, devolution of political power, a reformed parliamentary and electoral system – can be traced to the old Liberal Party ideology. This was made up of a coalition of beliefs ranging from an individualistic attachment to *laissez-faire* economics and a suspicion of state power, to a trust in democratic politics with reformed parliamentary institutions.

MINOR PARTIES

There are a considerable number of minor parties in Britain including the politically serious Celtic parties (Scottish and Welsh Nationalists), Northern Irish and Green Party. Other parties exist on the political **'fringe'** or **extremes** – the Fascist, Communist and Marxist Parties. Some belong to the 'fun' side of politics – Monster Raving Loony Party – where they participate in elections to publicise their causes. Others are religious organisations like the Natural Law Party seeking to attract attention to their version of the truth.

All minor parties suffer from the effects of the 'first past the post' electoral system as do the Liberal Democrats. Obviously the Scottish National Party and Plaid Cymru (Welsh Nationalists) are in a league of their own attracting sizeable support within their own countries. The SNP is now less supportive of any devolution proposals produced by the Labour and Liberal Democratic Parties and the Scottish Constitutional Convention, and favours independence for Scotland. Plaid Cymru are now more united around the issue of the survival of the Welsh language than on a separate state for Wales.

EXAMINATION QUESTIONS

1 To what extent have changes in the organisation of the Parliamentary Labour Party affected internal party democracy? *(25)*
(ULEAC)

2 What are the main functions performed by parties in the British political system? *(25)*
(UCLES)

3 Compare the influence of Conservative and Labour leaders within their respective parties. *(25)*
(NEAB)

ANSWERS TO EXAMINATION QUESTIONS

OUTLINE ANSWER TO QUESTION 3

This essay demands an understanding of the power relationships in both the Conservative and Labour Parties and the respective roles of the leaders. An answer could discuss the following:

pressure from a written constitution.

1 A comparison of the two party structures to illustrate the place of the leader.

2 Compare the constitutional position of the Labour leader to that of the Conservative leader.

3 Discuss the *McKenzie* thesis and counter it with *Lewis Minkin.*

Under pressure from more separate areas.
Cons. – more autocratic

4 Examine the selection process of the respective leaders. Labour is more democratic, but does that give Tony Blair more or less power than John Major?

5 Look at the machinery for the removal of the respective leaders. Is a Conservative leader more vulnerable to removal?

6 Analyse the respective leaders' roles to their Annual Conference. Remember the policy making power of the Labour Conference, but also note the increased attention given to Conservative Conference by the leader.

7 Make some evaluation yourself based on the academic evidence as a conclusion.

TUTOR'S ANSWER TO QUESTION 2

Political parties perform a number of functions within the British political system. Possibly the most important function is representation, followed by participation, articulation, communication, electoral choice and the process of governing.

Parties are voluntary organisations that represent the views of the electorate to the government. By providing party manifestos they set out to the voter their policy plans should their MPs be elected. Most democratic states operate a system of indirect democracy whereby Members of Parliament represent all the electorate's wishes, irrespective of which party supported them. As a representative the party MP is not tied to any particular interest – a problem that has in the past affected the Labour Party. But the duty of the representative (working through the party) is to carry the concerns of the electorate into the public policy arena. Parties are therefore playing a valuable role here; if, as *Stephen Ingle* has suggested, we imagine a political system without parties then we will be more aware of this function.

Parties help the participative function of democracy in a number of ways. They encourage people to participate in local and national politics either as passive helpers or active members. Again, without the activity of political parties it would be difficult to find people willing to participate in politics at all. Even in a developed political democracy like Britain, political apathy between general elections is high. Those that are encouraged to join find the party provides a vehicle for political recruitment to office. In local councils the political parties provide the members that run the machine, independent candidates having all but disappeared at this level. Participation in local politics is often a recruiting and training ground for national political office, therefore its importance cannot be over stressed.

In a democracy it is difficult for individuals to articulate their demands to policy makers. Joining a political party gives this opportunity. Although *Robert McKenzie* claimed correctly that more people were engaged in pressure group activity than political parties, the two complement each other. If pressure group activity has taken members away from political parties, many others will see the political importance of their actions and return to influence the parties.

The communication function of political parties revolves around the internal structures and memberships. Although the modern Conservative and Labour Parties may suffer from what *Robert Michells* called 'the Iron Law of Oligarchy', whereby an unrepresentative oligarchy or elite evidently control the party, eventually the leadership of political parties must be responsive to their membership's views. There have been recent trends towards internal democratisation in both the Conservative and Labour Parties making the leaderships more aware of rank and file interests. Party leaders who ignore party opinion, whether in Parliament or the wider party, often find themselves challenged.

It is fairly obvious that without the political parties there would be little electoral choice for the electorate. By placing themselves before the electorate, governing and opposition parties hope to secure re-election/election with a mandate from the people to govern. The difficulty in the British system centres around the electoral mechanism of first past the post, which offers a real either/or choice to the voters which results in one of two main parties winning. The British system therefore gives more electoral choice to supporters of the two main parties (Conservative and Labour) and less choice to those who support the Liberal Democrats or other minor parties. Electorally, the voter has a wide choice; legislatively, two main parties dominate Parliament in either a two party or dominant party parliamentary system.

The governing function is also essential to democratic politics. Parties provide the mechanism whereby legislatures can function. Majority parties in the British system are usually guaranteed control over the House of Commons; one virtue of the present electoral system is the avoidance of weak governments. When in office the party is able to implement its programme. The electorate are aware of the consequences of a Conservative or Labour administration. Although the electoral system usually produces alternation in government and therefore healthy renewal, if the electorate so choose one party can be dominant with long runs in office. At the present time the Conservative Party are in the seventeenth year of successive government leading some to criticise the system. Until or when the electorate decide, the Conservative Party will continue to take the governing function to itself.

STUDENT'S ANSWER TO QUESTION 1 WITH EXAMINER'S COMMENTS

66 Gets to the point **99**

Like all of the major political parties, Labour holds an Annual Conference. It is here that intra-party democracy is exercised at its fullest. Here the membership of the party decide the policy of the party and elect and hold the party leaders responsible for their actions.

In Labour's case, the Conference is the supreme policy making body as opposed to the Conservatives, whose Conference offers advice only. With the Labour conference any motion approved by a two-thirds majority vote automatically becomes part of the party programme. Conference in whole or in part elects 27 of the 29 members of the National Executive Committee: the trade union section, the constituency section, the women's section and the socialist societies section. In addition, the leader and the deputy leader of the party sit as of right on the NEC.

Critics and advocates of intra-party democracy claim that Conference is there to instruct the Parliamentary Labour Party. An early resolution (1907) said that MPs should carry out the programme but the method and timing should be left to the Parliamentary Party.

One view is that within the Labour Party there are different centres of authority, namely Conference, the NEC and the PLP. These must work together, and in practice have done so. Only in 1960, when Conference voted for unilateral disarmament, did the party leader openly defy the authority of Conference and successfully battle to reverse the vote the next year. The Conservative Party leader, on the other hand, represents a clear form of authority, with powers of appointment and dismissal and a great deal of influence over policy itself.

66 Good detail on the left **99**

Into the seventies the left of the party began to exert increasingly more influence and calls were made for more attention to be paid to grass roots opinions. Proposed reforms included the election of the party leader by an electoral college, representing all sections of the party, not exclusively MPs; the mandatory reselection of MPs between elections, which later was carried through, assuring that MPs were both receptive to local party opinion and represented their constituency effectively; and the NEC's control of the party's election manifesto. The first two changes came in 1981 and 1982. They increased the leverage of the extra-parliamentary elements and reduced the autonomy of Labour MPs, a significant shift in the power structure of the party. This swing towards the left was brought about by a number of factors, one of the most significant being its failure in office. The current swing to the right seems to have been brought about by its failure in opposition in contrast. Mrs Thatcher's three election victories and John Major's one have led to the rejection of many elements of socialism within the Labour Party, or at least the leadership. Labour's immediate reaction to its third election defeat was to review its policies via the establishment of a number of policy groups who submitted their proposals to the NEC, whose final statement was submitted for discussion before the issues were voted on at the 1989 Conference. At the same time Labour ran a 'Labour Listens' campaign, which aimed to identify the greatest consensus of the voters which could be used in the policy review process. This demonstrates Labour's attention to democracy despite its shifts away from the left.

The main constitutional change agreed at the 1987 Conference altered the way that Labour candidates are selected and reselected. Prior to the Conference Labour candidates tended to be chosen by the most committed left wing activists. Labour has also made it possible to join the party nationally, with provisional membership being confirmed later by the relevant constituency party (January 1989).

More recently, under the leadership of John Smith the block vote at Conference was abolished in favour of one member one vote. This is a step away from intra-party democracy with more emphasis on the individual rather than accepting that politics is a group process and shared interests are best discussed and voted on accordingly. (The vote was taken at the 1992 Conference.)

66 **Show how** 99

The current leader, Tony Blair, has gone much further than any other leader in 'modernising' the party. He sits firmly on the right of the party and many of his policy ideas are practically indistinguishable from those of the current government. His approach has been met with much criticism by the left of the party. With the party leader currently riding high in the opinion polls, internal public criticism of him has been muted.

Labour looks as if it has put internal party democracy on hold for now, but whilst it may make more use of consultation if it wins the next election, a number of structural changes will ensure the party leadership can carry through pretty much whatever it wants. It seems certain anyway that if Labour gain office in 1996-7, they will have to deal with deep divisions that have been concealed under Mr Blair's New Labour populism.

66 A good competent answer showing a grasp of current facts. I would have liked to see more links between the ideology of the party and its organisation. Typical of a C grade. 99

REFERENCES IN THE TEXT

Almond, G and S Verba 1963 *The civic culture*, Princeton University Press

Ball, A 1987 *British political parties*, London: Macmillan

Butler, D and D Kavanagh 1992 *The British general election of 1992*, London: Macmillan

Coxall, B and L Robins 1994 *Contemporary British politics*, London: Macmillan

Crewe, I 1992 Why did Labour lose (yet again), *Politics Review* September

Dearlove, J and P Saunders 1991 *Introduction to British politics*, Cambridge: Polity Press

Duverger, M 1966 *The idea of politics*, London: Methuen

Finer, S E 1975 *Adversary politics and electoral reform*, London: Anthony Wigram

Gamble, A 1990 *Britain in decline*, London: Macmillan

Gyford, J 1985 *The politics of local socialism*, London: Allen and Unwin

Ingle, S 1989 *The British party system*, Oxford: Blackwell

Ingle, S 1993 Political parties in the nineties *Talking Politics*, **6** Autumn

Jones, B 1994 *Political issues in Britain today*, Manchester University Press

Kellner, P 1988 *The Independent* 15 February

Kelly, R 1994 British political parties: organisation, leadership and democracy. In W Wale (ed.) *Developments in politics*, **5**, Ormskirk: Causeway Press

Kelly, R 1995 Labour's leadership contest and internal organisation, *Politics Review*, February

Lipset, S M 1963 *Political man*, London: Mercury Books

McKenzie, R 1963 *British political parties*, Oxford: Heinemann

Michells, R 1949 *Political parties*, Glencoe USA: The Free Press

Minkin, L 1980 *The Labour Party Conference*, Manchester University Press

Parry, G, G Moyser and N Day 1992 *Political participation and democracy in Britain*, Cambridge University Press

Whiteley, P, P Seyd and J Richardson 1994 *True blues: the politics of Conservative Party membership*, Oxford University Press

PRESSURE GROUPS

THEORETICAL
APPROACHES

CLASSIFICATIONS AND
COMPARISONS

INFLUENCING POLICY
MAKERS

GROUPS AND
DEMOCRACY

GETTING STARTED

Pressure groups are a well established feature of the British political system. They complement political party organisation and play an important part in the representation process guaranteeing participation in policy making to a wide number of interests. Because they are considered essential to the working of a democratic state, discussion of groups inevitably involves an examination of some theoretical approaches to political systems This is one area where you must keep up to date with the changes in issues reaching the **public agenda** through the influence of groups. For example, a selection of issues of group concern in late 1995/6 included constitutional reform, export of live animals, opposition to field sports, individual rights, road building protests, environmental protection and anti-nuclear activity.

Questions on this part of the syllabus demand a knowledge of the reasons for the change in group activity in addition to detailed discussion of the influence of interests.

The main themes of questions set in this area are:

- Examination of the part played by pressure groups in the policy making process.

- The relationships prevailing between pressure groups and democracy.

- Changes in the long term developments of pressure groups and why these occur.

- The declining influence of pressure groups in British politics generally.

Useful definitions

- **Functionalism** – a sociological concept that pictures a society made up of constituent parts functioning together.

- **Lobbying** – the process whereby influence is applied to legislators behind the scenes of Parliament or the civil service.

- **Political culture** – a description of the system of beliefs and values that underpin the working of democratic society.

THEORETICAL APPROACHES

❝ The main concept of the democratic state ❞

ESSENTIAL PRINCIPLES

The analysis of pressure groups is approached from the general perspective of **pluralism**. This is an attempt to conceptualise a democratic political system as a constellation or grouping of separate interests impacting on each other. Within the construct there will be **equal** influence with policy makers in a two way process of inputs and outputs.

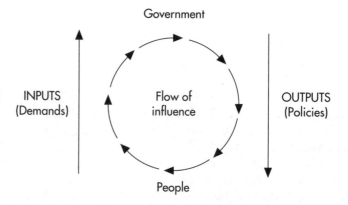

Fig. 9.1 A systems model of politics

Within this perspective we can identify **five interrelated models** of group activity:

1 group politics;
2 collective action;
3 sectional;
4 neo-corporatist;
5 neo-liberal.

GROUP POLITICS

❝ Political culture ❞

A pure pluralist approach, this emphasises the importance of group behaviour for influence with policy makers. Large numbers of groups exist within a political culture, which is constantly changing. Governments listen to the views of all individual groups but inevitably larger, more powerful groups have more influence. Some check on this system exists as group pressures are counteracted by others – **countervailing power** (see Figure 9.2).

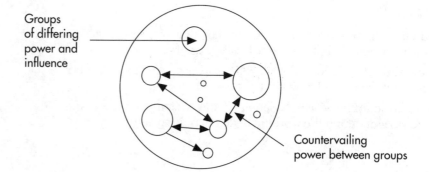

Fig.9.2 A group politics view of the state

COLLECTIVE ACTION

This model is similar to the above except it emphasises why people join groups. People have policy influence collectively, not as individuals, and will join groups if the benefits gained from membership are greater than the costs. The problem for some exclusive groups is that **improvements** in policies go to **all** the public, not selectively to group members, but this is inevitable in democracies.

SECTIONAL

66 Elite pluralism 99

Here groups are seen as influencing the policy agenda for their own ends. Sometimes referred to as elite pluralism because one section, or a **combination** of powerful **interests**, concentrates on advancing their interests at the expense of the wider community. The leaderships of these organisations also benefit more than the memberships.

NEO-CORPORATIST

66 Tripartism 99

Pure corporatism existed in political states where industrial interests (business and labour organisations) combined in policy formulation with the government, as in Germany and Italy in the thirties and forties. A variation on this arrangement was said to exist during the Labour governments of Harold Wilson and James Callaghan when the **Trades Union Congress** and **Confederation of British Industry** worked closely over industrial policy in a tripartite (three way) relationship (see Figure 9.3).

66 The Tripartite relationship 99

Labour
governments

1

Policy
dialogue

2   3

Business
organisations
CBI

Labour
organisations
TUC

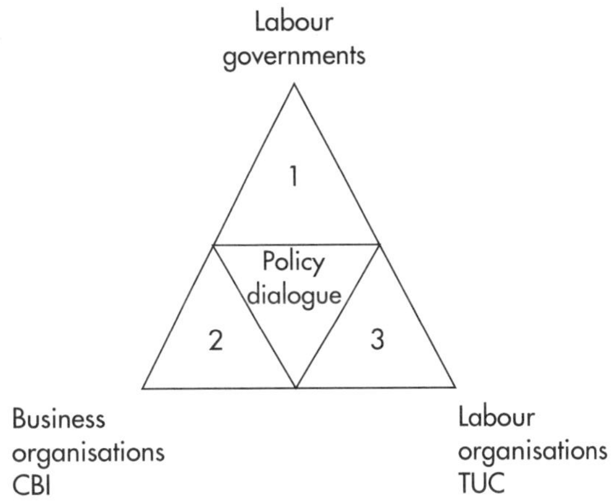

Fig. 9.3 A neo-corporatist view of the state

NEO-LIBERAL

66 Low priority to groups 99

This view places parliamentary representation above the importance of groups which are tolerated in the political system. Associated with Margaret Thatcher's Conservative governments of 1979 to 1990 when trade unions were excluded from close governmental relationships in industrial policy for **ideological** reasons. This government preferred to keep open a two way dialogue with business interests in a dual relationship.

Evaluation of theoretical approaches

All theoretical approaches have a contribution to make to our understanding of group politics. Pluralism is clearly the overriding perspective derived from classic American writers who tended to adopt a functionalist view of the democratic state (*Easton 1953*, *Dahl 1961*).

66 John Major, Tony Blair 99

Of the models within pluralism, the neo-corporatist view is now historical and is unlikely to be repeated with any future Labour governments. Under Tony Blair's leadership the New Labour Party has begun the process of distancing itself from the trade unions. John Major has continued a Conservative policy of neutrality or **holding the ring** towards groups which are regarded as too sectional for the public interest but cannot be ignored.

CLASSIFICATIONS AND COMPARISONS

DEFINITIONS

A pressure group (or interest group) is a **voluntary organisation** that exists to influence public policy at any level of government. There is little point in arguing about terminology; all groups represent some interests and most interests are concerned to promote themselves to policy makers. Comparisons are usually made with political parties for both are involved in the representation and participation process of

66 Comparing parties and groups 99

democracy, although the classic writer *McKenzie* (1963) felt that groups were more important in this respect. There are two important differences between a pressure group and a political party:

1 **Existence**   Groups exist for more **specific** purposes than a political party. A party is **all-embracing** in its policy making, appealing to the general public. A group, usually having fewer resources, will be preoccupied with one area of public policy although this will have wider implications. The League Against Cruel Sports is an established organisation (71 years old) fighting to extend the protection of laws over domestic animals to wildlife. Although a **single issue** group in this sense, its activities stretch beyond opposition to the hunting of wildlife to include conservation of species and ownership of over 2,000 acres of sanctuary land.

    For a political party to be so narrowly focused is clearly an electoral liability; the organisation is seeking to maximise its appeal. Both the Labour and Liberal Democratic Parties have suffered in the past from voter identification (helped by the media) with narrow or **sectional** interests. The Liberal Democrats are electorally strong in English local government, being the second party behind Labour since the 1995 local elections, and have been identified in the past as the party of community politics. The Labour Party (which began life as a form of organised labour pressure group) has in the 85 years of its existence been closely identified with trade unions and radical causes. The transition to a party of government has not been easy.

2 **Objectives**   Pressure groups and political parties can be further differentiated in terms of their objectives. Groups are seeking **influence** with policy makers, parties exist to acquire and hold political **power**. For a political party the most frustrating aspect of opposition is the inability to achieve its policies whilst presenting itself as a government in waiting. A pressure group does not concern itself with elections and political campaigns (except to influence the parties' policies) and will operate with whichever party is in power. During the eighties the Green lobby had remarkable success in changing party attitudes to the environment and this was reflected in the party manifestos at the 1992 general election.

CLASSIFYING GROUPS

66 Simple types 99

Early attempts to analyse pressure group activity produced confusing classifications. There are two basic types of group: **sectional** and **cause**. Sectional groups exist to protect one section of the population; in this sense they are **partial** to their memberships (*Duverger 1966*). They are found mainly in the economic sphere of society representing the interests of professionals, organised labour, civic and other groups (see Figure 9.4).

Cause groups exist to advance (**promote**) an idea, set of values or beliefs. They are not exclusive and draw their memberships from a wide sympathetic public. Typical groups in this category would operate in the areas of the environment, welfare, animal rights and civil liberties (see Figure 9.5).

---

1 Industrial Commercial

    Institute of Directors
    Building Societies Association

2 Employee Labour Organisations

    Trades Union Congress
    Unison

3 Professional

    Royal Institute of British Architects
    The Law Society

4 Civic

    County Councils Association

5 Other

    Royal Automobile Club

Fig. 9.4 Examples of sectional groups

1   Environment
        World Wide Fund for Nature
        Greenpeace

2   Welfare
        National Society for Prevention of Cruelty to Children
        Age Concern

3   Animal Rights
        League Against Cruel Sports
        Royal Society for Prevention of Cruelty to Animals

4   Civil Liberties
        Liberty
        Charter 88

Fig. 9.5 Example of cause groups

Resources

Although the two categories of sectional and cause overlap and **hybrid groups** belong equally to both, there are fairly clear distinctions between them. In terms of **resources** sectional groups have the financial edge because of fee paying subscriptions from memberships. Organisations like trade unions are usually well resourced with large centralised head office staffs offering a range of services to their members. Smaller, less powerful cause groups have to rely on public donations and fewer staff but can sometimes be equally effective. The single issue group CLEAR (Campaign for Lead Free Air, 1981–83), founded with a grant from business, was successful in convincing policy makers of the need to reduce lead in petrol.

Influence

66 **Why government listens** 99

In terms of **influence**, groups are further distinguished by the possession of **insider** or **outsider** status (*Grant 1993*). Insider groups have most influence with government because they offer expertise essential to the implementation of policy. According to *Finer (1968)*, much of this influence is traded in an anonymous empire of officials and contacts with group representatives. Studies of the National Farmers Union have shown how the agricultural industry secured preferential policies by being on the inside (*Self and Storing 1962*).

Outsider groups are usually less influential with government as they offer little **expertise** or **trade off** in return for policy influence. The Campaign For Nuclear Disarmament, a major protest group in the sixties and seventies, never entered the 'closed' world of influence. For ideological reasons the objectives of this group would never be compatible with the defence and nuclear policies of a Conservative government. Indeed, CND was regarded as a Labour pressure group partly because of the pacifism still remaining in that party and because Socialists took an active part in unilateral peace campaigns.

Although CND remains an 'ideological' outsider, there are examples of groups gradually acquiring insider status as they become more acceptable to government. Certain cause groups – The Howard League For Penal Reform is one example – have achieved **respectability** and will be in regular contact with policy makers where their interests are affected. In a study of change in pressure group politics, *Baggot (1992)* showed a gradual trend by government to consult with outsider groups more frequently than in the past, removing to some extent the disadvantages facing these types of group.

Membership and representation

66 **Competition for memberships** 99

Sectional and cause groups have different memberships although clearly they are not mutually exclusive. Considerable numbers of motorists are members of the motoring organisations (Automobile Association, Royal Automobile Club), but will be involved in other employment or professional groups in their daily lives. Groups will seek to maximise their strengths wherever possible, occasionally enticing members from other rival organisations. Apart from the increased financial resources larger memberships bring, numbers are important to groups for two reasons:

1 The amount of **leverage** or influence over policy makers is usually greater with larger memberships.

2 Membership is the key to **representativeness** – the ability to show the government that a group speaks for as many of the people as it claims to represent.

The strength of many professional groups is based on the notion that they represent their total profession. Sociologically, the old professions of law and medicine (Law Society, British Medical Association) have more influence with policy makers than the newer profession of teaching which is divided between various groups (Association of Teachers and Lecturers, National Union of Teachers. Professional Association of Teachers, Association of Masters and Mistresses).

Many cause groups seeking influence can claim larger **potential** than **actual** memberships. In the campaign to 'clean up' public broadcasting and violence in the media, the National Viewers and Listeners Association (founded by Mary Whitehouse) could claim to represent a large silent majority of dissatisfied viewers and listeners, in its consultations with the BBC. Similar claims could be made by the British Field Sports Society (see Figure 9.6) in its fight against John McFall's Wild Mammals Protection Bill of March 1995.

66 Vocal minority, silent majority 99

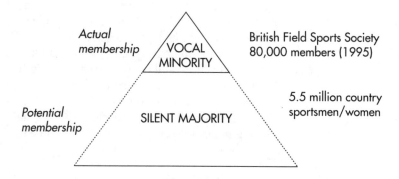

Fig. 9.6 Group representativeness. The example of the British Field Sports Society

---

THE POLICY DEBATE

Influencing the public policy debate demands different strategies and techniques depending on the type of group involved. Before a group can move to influence government opinion, it must first concentrate on **raising awareness** with the public. According to *McCulloch* (*1988*) an issue attention cycle must be negotiated before governments act on a problem. Once a matter is placed in the **public agenda**, groups will endeavour to keep it there until policy is enacted, changed or protected.

CAMPAIGNING

66 Most noise equals least success 99

Many insider groups use **quiet** campaigns behind the scenes with government ministers and officials, which rarely attract media or public attention. Cause groups are traditionally associated with protests and demonstrations in attempts to get their message across – often a sign of desperation and a signal that they have little insider influence. The Campaign for Nuclear Disarmament raised public awareness of the dangers of nuclear war despite years of public demonstrations. Some groups had more influence on public policy because their ideas were more compatible with government. Improvements in the environment fall into this category.

66 Protest violence 99

The passing of the Criminal Justice and Public Order Act 1994 gave the police additional powers to control public protests and demonstrations: the new charge of aggravated trespass could be used particularly against road protesters and hunt saboteurs. Extensive media coverage of demonstrations throughout 1995 against the road building programme, the export of live animals and other emotive issues, again brought into focus the problem of anti-parliamentary activity. **Direct action** protests and demonstrations can result in unintentional violence, or anti-political activity. By their very nature they are a challenge to parliamentary representation and the established machinery of protest.

ACCESS POINTS

There are various access or influence points in the political system (after public opinion) which provide an opening for pressure groups to affect policy making. The most important are:

- European Union;
- executive and administration;
- local government;
- Parliament;
- political parties.

European Union

The European Union and its institutions (The Council of Ministers, European Parliament and European Commission) are increasingly targeted by national pressure groups attempting to influence legislation affecting their interests. Often this **lobbying** will be directed at British ministers, MPs and civil servants in a consultation process before laws are made or after it is discovered that **EU Directives** are impacting on their interests. Three examples of British interests which have been affected by European legislation are:

66 Impact of European Union 99

1 agriculture;
2 road haulage;
3 fisheries and fishing.

In agriculture, the National Farmers Union have shown their negotiating strength by securing reasonable treatment in the allocation of grants from the Common Agricultural Policy. The road haulage industry was less than successful in resisting the imposition from Europe of the extra costs of tachometers to vehicles restricting journey times in the interests of health and safety. British fishing has suffered natural decline reflected in negotiations with Europe. European fishing quotas have been resented by a weak industry that regards the granting of access to British waters as a betrayal of their interests.

Executive and administration

Pressure groups are able to exert direct influence on government through contacts with ministers and officials. Although we have seen that insider groups have the advantage in the **consultation process**, many outsider groups will be contacted should the government so wish. **Generalised contacts** between group representatives and ministers occur in the numerous standing advisory committees (over 1000 in 1995) set up by government in most policy areas. Groups will also be represented, by government invitation, in the work carried out by royal commissions, tribunals and inquiries.

66 Advisory committees 99

It is now accepted practice for government to consult with group representatives in an affected policy area before contemplating legislation. This **institutionalised** arrangement works because:

66 Advantages of consultation 99

1 groups have the opportunity to influence legislation and
2 government gains the cooperation and expertise of interests essential to the successful implementation of policy.

Without this contact or dialogue, policy would be unworkable and the **expertise** possessed by some groups could be used against the government. Margaret Thatcher was able to resist the National Union of Mineworkers **sanction** in the strikes of 1983, but her successor John Major had less success with education. The introduction of tests for school pupils under the National Curriculum was initially opposed by the teaching unions who refused to cooperate with the scheme. After a prolonged dispute, the Department For Education agreed to modify the procedures and John Patten, the minister responsible, was replaced by the more conciliatory Gillian Shephard.

The closest contact between a government and groups occurs in the **clientele relationship** established in the policy communities of the civil service (or Whitehall).

Officials in each main spending department (Education, Health, Social Security, Agriculture, Home Office) regularly consult their 'client' group representatives, whose opinions, expertise and contacts are essential for the smooth implementation of policy (see Figure 9.7).

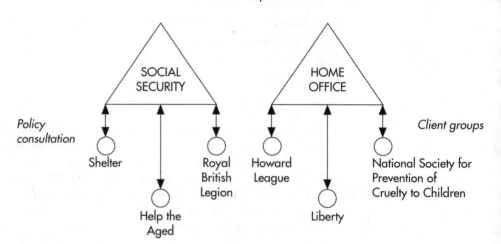

Fig. 9.7 A clientele relationship

Local government

66 **Dependence on central government** 99

In the United Kingdom, local authorities (counties and district councils) are the main providers of localised services. Two features make them very dependent on central government:

1   Most of their financial resource comes from the centre.
2   Their statutory powers are derived from Parliament.

This has implications for pressure groups at the local level – their activity will be directed at the way authorities implement central policies. Of the many contentious issues found in local and community politics, **land use** probably arouses the most interest, and will serve as a good example of the activity of such groups.

The former Environment Minister Nicholas Ridley once referred to the NIMBY syndrome (Not In My Back Yard) as signifying the opposition to development found in the British countryside. People opposed to developments quickly form local **direct action** groups and are prepared to take on planners, central government inspectors, local officials and councillors. Typical areas where groups are active include:

■   The road programme – building of bypasses around villages removes heavy traffic but destroys important farming land.

■   Waste disposal – sites are needed for the disposal of domestic and industrial waste, but few people welcome them.

■   Major national construction projects – these are needed for the economy but resisted because they affect the character of local communities.

66 **Local action groups** 99

In 1970 the Wing Airport Resistance Association (WARA) showed how successful local action groups can be. By skilful lobbying locally and nationally, they were able to convince the government that the siting of the proposed Third London Airport (TLA) in a green field site in Buckinghamshire was uneconomic.

The construction of the Channel Tunnel throughout 1993 and 1994 aroused considerable group interest. Kent villages threatened by blight from the first proposed Channel route successfully lobbied Members of Parliament from their own constituencies. The final route for the rail link avoided these communities but was imposed on others, a classic illustration of the land use dilemma.

Parliament

Both Houses of Parliament (House of Commons and House of Lords) are targeted by groups seeking to influence **legislation**. Groups can employ the services of professional lobby organisations but traditionally make direct approaches themselves. This is particularly evident in the procedure surrounding the introduction of **private**

members' bills, when interests target Members of Parliament with prearranged legislative detail. John McFall's unsuccessful Wild Mammals (Protection) Bill (1995) was written by the League Against Cruel Sports. Changes made to this bill (removing the hunting clauses) allowed it to be brought forward by Alan Meale in January 1996. The subsequent bill passed both Houses of Parliament and was enacted as the Wild Mammals (Protection) Act receiving Royal assent in February 1996. Austin Mitchell's Home Buyers Bill, enacted in 1984, was produced largely by the Consumers' Association intent on breaking the Law Society's monopoly of house conveyancing. Both bills illustrate that it is easier to change the particulars (**the politics of detail**) rather than the overall policy direction (**the politics of issues**) which is set by a government.

❝❝ Peers, MPs and members of Congress ❞❞

Although not as legislatively strong as members of the American Congress, British Members of Parliament and peers can speak in debates, table amendments to bills, raise questions with ministers, take part in committee proceedings and generally advance the cause of groups. For every issue or cause, sympathetic Members of Parliament or peers will be found supporting and advancing or opposing and obstructing the matter, a clear example of countervailing pressure.

Political parties

Certain pressure groups have close relationships with political parties and most groups attempt to influence party policy if they can. The most publicised links exist between the Labour Party and the trade unions and the Conservative Party and business. The Liberal Democrats try to avoid open identification with any one section, for fear of damaging their centrist image.

❝❝ Union and business links ❞❞

Heavy financial dependence on the trade unions has been electorally disadvantageous to Labour in all previous general elections and the party is seeking to modify this. After the Nolan Committee Inquiry into Standards in Public Life (1995) Tony Blair made it clear that he would seek a new financial relationship with the unions. The removal of the sponsorship link whereby individual unions help the electoral expenses of candidates would:

1 demonstrate publicly that the Labour Party is not controlled by extra-parliamentary unions;

2 keep the main financial link through donations from unions and other sources;

3 put pressure on the Conservative Party and their financial sources;

4 keep the trade unions at arm's length over policy matters.

Although the Labour – union connection receives most publicity in terms of **policy influence**, it is equally important to note that business organisations have substantial 'behind the scenes' influence over the Conservative Party. Financially, both major parties are dependent on donations from their respective interests and although they govern for the democratic majority, they tend to focus on their own group constituencies.

GROUPS AND DEMOCRACY

SECTIONAL AND COMMUNITY INTEREST

Pressure groups are an essential ingredient in democratic politics complementing the activity of political parties in a pluralist society. If citizens have rights to be heard by government and participate in policy making, then pressure groups help this process (*Finer 1968*).

❝❝ Problem of group control ❞❞

The problem for government is striking the right balance between granting access to sectional representation and protecting the interests of the community, assuming the two are different. There are two basic positions on this dilemma:

■ The equilibrium theory describes pressure groups as a valuable asset to society. In a **pure pluralist** system the interests of the minority (the section) are balanced or held in equilibrium against the majority (the public) interest.

■ The conspiracy theory, or **elite pluralism**, claims pressure groups are a danger to democratic society. Powerful interests dominate the lobbying process and secure favourable policies from government.

Both the above positions oversimplify the world of pressure group politics. The public interest is difficult to define and there will be occasions when it will coincide with the sectional since groups cover the vast majority of the population in some form or another. Clearly some groups are more influential with government than others but there is a tendency for a balance to be reestablished. Organised labour was influential with the governments of Harold Wilson and James Callaghan and business interests with the governments of Margaret Thatcher and John Major.

CHANGING GROUP INFLUENCE

Public sector groups – teachers, nurses, the police, doctors – and trade unions generally have **lost influence** with recent Conservative governments mainly for ideological reasons, whilst financial and business interests have enjoyed close contacts.

66 New cause groups 99

Alienation from the traditional party and group system (especially by the young) is said to be a contributory factor in the rise of new social movements intent on challenging the economic and social order (*Hallsworth 1994*). Some of these groups represent new interests; Alarm UK was founded in 1995 by Emma Must to coordinate the activity of 300 local road action groups. Others are a reworking of the traditional, rather than radical departures from the old interests.

It is possible to see a parallel between the activities of protest movements of the sixties and seventies, when the emotive issues were the Vietnam War, nuclear weapons and minority rights, and the new cause groups. Rising affluence and declining class identities (*Inglehart 1977*), coupled with the break-up of the Soviet Union and ending of the Cold War, may have refocused issues for new generations. In 1995/6 groups at the forefront of protest were concentrating on animal rights, roadbuilding, wildlife protection, atmospheric pollution and citizens' rights among others.

EXAMINATION QUESTIONS

1 What makes a pressure group successful? *(25)*
(UODLE)

2 To what extent is' the role of pressure groups in policy making changing? *(25)*
(ULEAC)

3 To what extent do pressure groups strengthen or undermine the democratic process in Britain? *(25)*
(NEAB)

4 What access do pressure groups have to policy making in Britain? *(25)*
(UODLE)

ANSWERS TO EXAMINATION QUESTIONS

OUTLINE ANSWERS

Question 1

The answer to this question is fairly straightforward and could take the following form.

1 A discussion of 'successful'. How do groups measure success?

2 A general description of the different types of group (sectional and cause).

3 Examination of the representativeness of certain groups.

4 A consideration of insider/outsider status and how this reflects on influence.

5 Discussion of expertise, leverage and sanction and how this relates to success or failure of groups.

Question 2

This question focuses on the specific policy making role of groups and demands an understanding of parliamentary processes. Material for the answer could include:

1 A discussion of the access points between groups, the executive and administration.

2 How groups influence legislative detail, particularly through private members' bills.

3 The tendency for insider groups to form clientele relationships with government departments.

4 Discussion of the formalised consultation process that now occurs as standard practice between groups and government.

5 The removal of certain public sector and trade union groups from close policy influence since the eighties.

TUTOR'S ANSWER TO QUESTION 4

Pressure groups are usually granted access to policy making by governments in a democratic state. This process fits the classic description of the pluralist systems model of politics and is beneficial to both sides (*Easton 1953*). Government knows its policies will be acceptable to the groups most affected by its policies in that area. Groups are more willing to 'play by the rules' in assisting the implementation of policy if they have an influence over its design.

A number of access or influence points in the political system must be negotiated before groups secure influence. These can be divided into external and internal environments. The main external environment is public opinion, including the public agenda. For an issue to reach policy makers and the public agenda, it must pass through the issue attention cycle according to *McCulloch* (*1988*). Public interest must be aroused for this to happen as governments are ignorant of many problems until brought to their attention.

Obviously the media play a vital part in influencing public opinion, hence the attention placed on campaigning by sectional groups. Public support is important for the success or failure of a group's objectives. It was instrumental in slowing down the pit closures under the Coal Mine Closure Plan in 1992. The protests against the export of veal calves and other livestock secured a high degree of public sympathy in early 1995 after extensive media coverage.

The most important internal access points from the group aspect are the executive and administration followed by Parliament, the European Union, political parties and local government.

Groups are aware that it is important to influence policy making at the centre. This implies contacts between ministers and officials at the policy formulation stage. Central government policy is decided by the Prime Minister and Cabinet together, but they are advised by other ministers and officials. Insider sectional groups (accepted largely because they have expertise to trade off for influence) have most contact at this level, in what *Finer* (*1968*) called the anonymous empire. The National Farmers Union is a good example of a group that has secured access to policy making at the highest level. Other producer groups have been less successful; fishermen have never been close to the centre. During the Labour governments of Harold Wilson and James Callaghan, the Trades Union Congress secured influence over industrial policy in a tripartite arrangement now regarded as a form of neo-corporatism.

Administratively, most influence is channelled through regular consultation between officials and group representatives in numerous advisory committees, royal commissions and inquiries. A clientele relationship also exists between groups and respective spending departments. At this level interests are able to share their expertise with government which is reflected in many policy changes.

Legislative or parliamentary access is now crucially important as an access point for groups. Although the executive have control over overall policy (the politics of issues), it is at the discussion stage of the parliamentary process of legislation that group interests can be effectively heard and acted upon (the politics of detail). Since the introduction of large majorities for Conservative governments since 1979, it is often claimed that the most effective opposition is found on the back benches of the House of Commons and House of Lords. For this reason groups have renewed their interests in targeting peers and Members of Parliament at the legislative stage.

Peers can table amendments to important bills and bring about improvements in legislation on behalf of groups – improved access to public buildings for the disabled is one example. Members of Parliament receive draft bills from pressure groups if successful in the procedure for private members' bills (John McFall's Wild Mammals Protection Bill of 1995 and Alan Meale's Wild Mammals (Protection) Bill of 1996). The informal contacts between groups and Members of Parliament (trade unions and the Labour Party and business and the Conservative Party) also provide an opportunity for parliamentary publicity of interests. It is at this level that countervailing pressure will become obvious as opponents face supporters of interests seeking to influence legislation.

Britain's membership of the European Union has added another tier of law making to the national parliaments. This implies that pressure groups must now seek policy influence with the institutions of Europe if they are to continue to advance their interests. Influence can be applied directly by lobbying European Members of Parliament, the European Court and the European Commission, or indirectly by contacting federations of groups working in Europe. *Grant* (*1993*) gives the example of the outsider Motorcycle Action Group, campaigning for fewer restrictions on their members, joining the Federation of European Motorcyclists.

Political parties have always been a major access point for pressure groups anxious to see their interests protected or advanced by the governing party. The closest publicised policy link between interests and government existed under the tripartite arrangements (mentioned above) of the seventies when the Trade Union and Labour Party Liaison Committee produced industrial laws for the Labour government. Such arrangements were not continued with the Conservative governments of Margaret Thatcher and John Major, although both parties remained dependent on organised labour or business.

The financial links between business and the Conservative Party and the trade unions and the Labour Party do not guarantee policy influence over the parties, but they are an obvious form of leverage. Although *Grant* (*1993*) has shown that Confederation of British Industry policy influence declined under Margaret Thatcher, the continued importance of individual financial donations from industry has continued under John Major. Tony Blair is attempting to reduce Labour Party financial dependence on trade unions, but it is difficult to conceive of organised labour losing all influence with that party.

A final important access point for pressure groups is local government. Since the expansion of new types of group activity (new social movements), local level protests, particularly over environmental issues, have increased.

At the local government level, policy making is in the hands of locally elected councillors working through numerous committees assisted by council officials. These provide opportunities for group activity, through either existing national pressure groups or locally formed new direct action groups designed to counter policies seen as damaging to their interests. The Wing Airport Resistance Association (1970) showed how a determined locally based group could challenge both local and central governments with good effects.

STUDENT'S ANSWER TO QUESTION 3 WITH EXAMINER'S COMMENTS

66 Interesting opening 99

It is often said that Britain has a 'representative and responsible' government. It may be responsible in a political sense but it is clearly insufficiently representative. Pressure groups contribute to our pluralistic process by representing the various regional, ethnic and economic minority groups and in this way help democracy.

Pressure groups provide essential freedoms to citizens helping them organise with like minded individuals. Without groups, the democratic process would be weaker as

66 Could use systems model here 99

many voices would go unheard. Groups help to provide better communication (alongside political parties) between those in authority and those subject to it, for example employers and employees, councils and council tenants, and producers and consumers.

Feedback from the people is essential in a democracy, the process must be 'two way'. Pressure groups allow this to take place. Essentially this is achieved by insider groups, for example during the Labour governments of the seventies trade unions played a major role in industrial policy making. Other groups may not have this type of insider influence but compensate by setting up campaigns and protests.

66 Little too general 99

As much as they may contribute to the democratic process, it can be argued that groups threaten or undermine it. The leaders of pressure groups are unelected and yet they interact with government. As they are not wholly accountable, should they have this potential influence in a democracy? Groups themselves lack a certain amount of legitimacy. Trade union meetings are often poorly attended and sometimes dominated by radical and extreme elements. Unions do not fight general elections, they do not present a manifesto to the people at regular intervals, nor do they have to take on the responsibility of government.

66 Why only trade unions 99

The freedom to organise and influence as they like makes the system undemocratic. This freedom is exploited by rich and powerful groups who are able to assert influence from the inside. The promotional type of pressure group often lacks the resources and prestige to organise coherent and influential campaigns. For example, although groups like the Hunt Saboteurs Association are well supported publicly, as an outsider group they lack the pulling power to go further.

66 Describe promotional 99

Insider groups also operate largely in secret behind 'closed doors'. This 'corporate' process between groups, ministers and civil servants is not accountable to the electorate and means decisions are made by a small elite. The public are kept in ignorance of this process until informed by the media, after the group has achieved its objectives. Sometimes groups will use the media to promote their interests further. Insider groups have an advantage over outsider groups here also.

66 Rather short explanation 99

Pressure groups both help and hinder the democratic process equally. The fact remains that they are essential in their work and without them democracy would surely fail to exist. The question that needs answering is why democracy can only be influenced by such groups? People no longer have an individual say in the conduct of their country and only through organised groups do they have a chance of influence.

66 A reasonable essay that approaches the subject in a generalised way. It shows a good grasp of pressure group theory even if it could be better expressed. More examples could be given of current groups together with academic sources to substantiate the argument. But not totally descriptive, therefore this answer is characteristic of a grade C. 99

REFERENCES IN THE TEXT

Baggot, R 1992 The measurement of change in pressure group politics, *Talking Politics*, **5** Autumn

Dahl, R 1961 *Who governs?* Yale University Press

Duverger, M 1966 *The idea of politics*, London: Methuen

Easton, D 1953 *The political system*, USA: Knopf

Finer, S E 1968 *Anonymous empire*, London: Pall Mall

Grant, W 1993 *The politics of economic policy*, Hemel Hempstead: Harvester Wheatsheaf

Hallsworth, S 1994 Understanding new social movements, *Sociology Review* September

Inglehart, R 1977 *The silent revolution*, Princeton University Press

McCulloch, A 1988 Politics and the environment, *Talking Politic*s, **1** Autumn

McKenzie, R T 1963 *British political parties*, Oxford: Heinemann

Self, P and H J Storing 1962 *The state and the farmer*, London: Allen & Unwin

PUBLIC OPINION AND ELECTIONS

POLITICAL OPINION POLLS

REFERENDUMS

THE ELECTORAL SYSTEM

GETTING STARTED

Although British political opinion polls did not have a good record in the 1992 general election, various changes have been made to polling methodologies to improve their accuracy and they are now an essential ingredient in a representative democratic system fulfilling useful functions. Referendums are a form of opinion poll on specific issues that have implications for parliamentary sovereignty. And the strengths and weaknesses of the British electoral system are well documented. The question of electoral reform is always at the forefront of British politics and academic debates usually focus on the efficacy of the system.

Questions on this part of the syllabus focus on:

- The part played by political opinion polls in the democratic process.
- The use of referendums and their relationship to the electoral system.
- Arguments for and against retaining the present British electoral system.
- Discussion of the merits of alternative electoral systems.

POLITICAL OPINION POLLS

66 Definition of polls 99

ESSENTIAL PRINCIPLES

Political opinion polls are designed to test public opinion on any number of issues and are an obvious measure of a government's popularity. Although they may not influence the Prime Minister in choice of general election date (Margaret Thatcher was said to have paid more attention to local government election results), they are considered important enough for the political parties to commission their own polls from the major polling organisations Gallup, National Opinion Polls (NOP), Harris, Market and Opinion Research International (MORI), and International Communications and Marketing (ICM).

TYPES OF POLITICAL OPINION POLL

There are six types of political opinion poll, which place questions before a representative sample of the electorate, covering the following areas:

1 **Suitability to govern**   Here the attempt is made to ascertain people's opinions on who would make the **best Prime Minister, leader, or party** for government. In the 1992 general election John Major was consistently more popular than both Neil Kinnock and Paddy Ashdown, even though the polls placed Labour ahead of the Conservatives (*Crewe 1992*). Under Neil Kinnock both the Labour Party and its leader were unpopular (1983–92). Under John Smith (1992–94), the Labour leader and the party recovered popularity. The selection of Tony Blair as Labour leader in 1994 after the sudden death of John Smith reversed the Labour Party's electoral fortunes; at the close of 1995 they were some 30 points ahead of the Conservatives. Now the popularity of a party leader, as distinct from the party, can be ascertained by polling. However, electoral opinions towards political parties are complex and can be divided on the suitability of a party to govern.

2 **Issue questions**   Issue questions concentrate on voters' opinions on which party has the **best policies**. Typical questions would focus on inflation and prices, defence, the National Health Service, education, and law and order. Since **issue** or **instrumental voting** is now considered a more important factor in voter preference, it is to be expected that parties are anxious to discover which issues are advantageous and which electorally damaging. In the 1992 general election campaign, the Labour Party generally lead on social issues like education and the NHS, whereas the Conservatives increased their dominance on prices, taxation and defence. According to *Denver* (*1992*) the fact that Labour lost the election either meant that people did not vote on the issues, or that the Conservatives picked up considerable support (last minute swing) on all the issues that mattered.

66 1992 general election 99

3 **Voting intention**   Polls on voting intention are taken throughout a general election campaign and are probably the most important political polls. First used in the general election of 1945, they are not strictly speaking opinion polls but surveys on **intended voting behaviour** and they do not predict the outcome of the general election. As snapshots of public opinion, they must be used with care for there is the tendency to freeze frame events at a particular time which may or may not be a good guide to the actual election result (*Game 1994*). The polling organisations have a mixed record on the degree of accuracy and predictability of the winning party in these sorts of poll. In the 1983 general election they correctly predicted a Conservative win. In 1987 again they were accurate in selecting the Conservative Party. In 1992 most polls made a classic error by predicting a Labour win. The five major polling organisations all had Labour to win at 40 per cent against Conservative support of 38 per cent and Liberal Democrats at 18 per cent. The actual result was 42.8 per cent Conservative, 35.2 per cent Labour and 18.3 per cent Liberal Democratic. The reasons why the polling organisations made such an error are complex. Even allowing for a statistical margin of error of 3 per cent either way, most polls failed to pick up a late swing to the Conservatives.

4 **Actual vote**   Polls on votes cast or actual voting behaviour, usually called **exit polls**, are carried out shortly after people leave the polling centre. As people have secretly recorded their vote they are less inhibited in replying to pollsters'

questions of how they voted. For this reason alone, exit polls usually have a better record of predictability of the potential election winner. In the 1992 general election, exit polls were closest to the actual result; they picked up the late swing to the Conservatives, even if presentational problems through television broadcasts failed to accurately interpret their figures, underplaying the Conservative lead (*Game 1994*).

5 **Longitudinal studies** Longitudinal studies are a common sociological method of obtaining detailed information over a period of time using the same group of respondents and returning to interview them at fixed periods. They can provide valuable insights into changing attitudes and opinions and are particularly useful for studying fluctuations in political views. As **panel polls** they are used throughout a general election campaign and thicken up the information detailing last minute vote switching, late decisions, party and leader preferences and general voter volatility. The big five polling organisations have the resources to carry out these polls, which are time consuming, expensive and difficult to run. Despite that their record is more accurate than one-off forecast polls and has a lasting relevance (*Kavanagh 1992*).

6 **Constituency opinions** **Individual constituency** polls endeavour to break down the national electorate into more quantifiable measures of public opinion. Often carried out by or on behalf of the political parties, they sometimes concentrate on opinions in marginal seats where results are not a foregone conclusion. The publication of an opinion poll (in a local newspaper) can have an effect on those intending to vote tactically. In this sense these polls are performing a useful service to local democracy for tactical voters – without this information they would not be able to evaluate the impact of their vote. The accuracy record of these polls is their greatest failing – often carried out by 'volunteers', they lack the sophistication of the big five national polling organisations with a corresponding increase in polling error.

METHODOLOGIES

❝ Sampling ❞

For validity reasons opinion polls must survey statistically significant numbers to reach quantifiable results. Sample sizes vary from 1,000 adults (the most typical) to 5,000, although polling organisations have reached 10,000 in extraordinary circumstances. Large samples of the population are not necessarily more accurate, but they do allow the achievement of a representative cross section of the electorate based on quotas of age, gender, ethnicity or class. **Sampling errors** of between plus and minus 3 per cent generally reduce the larger the sample, although these figures are regarded as acceptable in the polling industry. Apart from the margin of error argument, other explanations are offered for the poor showing of opinion polls in the 1992 general election. The most important are:

- Under-registration of Labour voters due to the effects of poll tax avoidance may have increased the Conservative vote.

- Pro-Conservative voting among Britons eligible to vote living abroad.

- Late swing towards the Conservatives too late to be picked up and registered in pre-election polls.

❝ Politically correct answers ❞

- Undecided voters had to be discounted from poll calculations adding further complexities to the final result. Many in this category were unwilling to co-operate with interviewers' questions and it is now felt that 'closet' Conservatives were prevalent in this group. *Kavanagh* (*1992*) has raised the possibility that embarrassed publics give politically correct answers for fear of offence; in the 1992 general election a public positive Labour response might have obscured private Conservative support.

Comment

Opinion poll organisations have tried to correct some of the fieldwork problems highlighted by their 1992 forecasts, for example by paying more attention to the undecided or uncooperative voter. Clearly they cannot discount for all eventualities; deliberate malicious intent to mislead pollsters is fortunately not yet of major significance and longitudinal panel surveys are helping to correct any errors in pre-election forecasting.

INFLUENCE OF THE POLLS

The publication of opinion poll results may have unintended consequences on the electorate. Psephologists (those who study elections) have long been aware of this problem although there is very little empirical evidence supporting generally held circumstantial views (*Denver 1989*). In 1967 the **Speaker's Conference on Electoral Reform** recommended that the results of political opinion polls should not be published in the three days before an election. The Harold Wilson Labour government rejected this suggestion because it was not convinced that voters were particularly influenced by the polls. Academic opinion is now divided on poll influence. Some claim a **negative impact** as polls influence the level of abstention or apathy. If polls predict a substantial win for one party, does this reduce voter turnout from those who feel powerless to influence the outcome? **Positively**, supporters of polls say they promote a higher turnout by stimulating interest in the general election. They may also act as an aid to those contemplating tactical voting by providing information on the state of the parties. Two particular political opinion poll effects have been noticed.

> Positive – negative

The boomerang effect

Opinion polls may have a **repulsion effect** by causing different types of voting behaviour to that intended. Voters might decide to remain at home instead of casting their vote for a party that is clearly going to win (according to the polls), conscious that they have little or no effect on the outcome. Alternatively, voters may decide to switch support throughout the campaign to a party that appears to be doing less well in the polls. Both these 'boomerang' effects probably have most influence on sympathy voters, the uncommitted or the alienated. According to *Crewe* (*1992*), last minute switching of votes to the Conservatives in the 1992 general election might be explained by fear that Labour were going to win induced by polls which placed that party consistently in the lead throughout the campaign.

The bandwagon effect

A widely believed idea is that opinion polls have a bandwagon or **attraction effect**. People like to be associated with winning parties; they may feel they do not want to waste their vote on a loser. Climbing on the bandwagon of a party which the polls predict as the most likely winner is a more satisfying form of political activity as it increases the eventuality of that fact occurring. Again, as with the boomerang effect, certain types of voter influenced by a bandwagon might be at the periphery of politics as uncommitted voters, floaters, detached or semi-detached. Alternatively, they could be strongly committed to a party that just happens to be in the lead according to opinion poll survey evidence. Since there are only a handful of serious contentious parties with a chance in a general election, this is bound to occur with millions of voters.

Comment

There are many theories of voting behaviour pointing to increased voter volatility since the 1960s. If the effects of opinion polls on the vote are computed in addition, it is not difficult to see why predictions of party success in general elections cannot be made with any scientific certainty. The rational voter may exist, but if any one of the effects associated with opinion polls occurred, poll results would be consistently wrong. Up to 1987 opinion poll results were consistent in their accuracy – an impressive record considering the difficulties in sampling public opinion (*Eatwell 1993*). Polling organisations' 1992 predictions (the worst on record) have damaged this reputation, however, and only a longer term view will confirm that this was a blip or something worse.

TACTICAL VOTING

The growth in support for the Liberal Democratic, Scottish and Welsh Nationalist Parties in England, Wales and Scotland, alongside traditional attachments to the Conservative and Labour Parties, introduces a bewildering choice for the voter in general and local elections. For many, to exercise that choice is to vote tactically, voting for a candidate who is most likely to defeat their least favoured party. If tactical voting is on the increase – and the evidence from both the 1987 and 1992 general elections is supportive of this (*Butler and Kavanagh 1992* and *Game 1994*) – the question of the **power of opinion polls** as an influence on voter preference is more complex.

66 Increasing importance 99

Voters in safe seats (where a one party majority is secure) have little choice but to accept the political arithmetic – they either support or oppose the dominant party in their constituency and can do little to change the system. Those in marginal seats (where the vote is more evenly balanced) have more influence if they wish to remove a sitting MP by voting tactically for a candidate who could achieve this desired effect.

Local political information on the strength of respective party support is provided by constituency opinion polls, but these are unreliable and few in number. According to *Game* (*1994*), there were approximately 80 constituency polls in the 1987 general election and less than 20 in 1992. The majority of tactical voters in marginal seats are relying on national opinion poll results to gain a snapshot of their local situation which, however, may be very different. This raises the problem that national opinion polls may be distorting the democratic process rather than adding to democracy.

OPINION POLLS AND DEMOCRACY

Publication of political opinion poll results is defended on the grounds that they aid democracy. Despite their shortcomings, they keep the electorate informed on the opinions of others and they provide some opportunity for the expression of public views between elections. Polls designed to test opinion on particular policies may also be useful to government in establishing people's attitudes or responses to them.

The main drawback of opinion polls from a democratic viewpoint is that they work to the advantage of the government and the disadvantage of the opposition. Although not a decisive influence on Margaret Thatcher's choice of election dates, Prime Ministers obviously seek to avoid (if they can) going to the country when unpopular. Governments could also be assisted by opinion polls ascertaining majority opinion on particular issues which can feed back into policy changes or adjustments, although the weight of evidence is to the contrary. Margaret Thatcher persisted with the introduction of the Community Charge or Poll Tax as a reformed system of local government finance in 1990 despite warnings from Michael Heseltine and other ministers that it would be unpopular. Had this been tested in an opinion poll beforehand, the government would have been better informed of the level of public disquiet surrounding this particular policy change.

REFERENDUMS

The government can ascertain public opinion more directly by the use of referendums – questions to the electorate on a specific issue demanding a positive or negative response. Since electorate opinions cannot be separated by issue – voting in general elections is not item by item, but taking or leaving a whole programme – it could be argued that referendums have a place in a representative democracy. Unfortunately for supporters of this idea, there is no constitutional provision for the holding of referendums in Britain even though three have been held to date.

66 Rarity value 99

Referendums are therefore sufficiently rare to be regarded as foreign to the British constitution, primarily on the grounds that an indirect parliamentary democracy cannot function by constant appeals to the electorate over the heads of its representatives. It is instructive to examine referendums from the three perspectives of representativeness, executive dominance and constitutional implications.

REPRESENTATIVENESS

It is difficult enough to ascertain public opinion on single issues; clearly there are items in a governing party's manifesto that supporters find objectionable. Despite that, British parliamentary democracy relies on a thin concept of the **mandate**. There is a tie between the electorate and the majority party elected to govern and this is generally accepted by all the mainstream political parties. However, the mandate is not binding – governments do not have to implement programmes laid before the electorate in manifestos. It is implied they will have flexibility or room for manoeuvre pragmatically responding to events as they unfold.

On this weak form of the mandate it would be possible to allow occasional referendums even if they breach the idea of parliamentary sovereignty. Some form of constitutional safeguard is offered to the people by a referendum exercise in popular sovereignty taking power back to the people (*Bogdanor 1991*).

❝ Mandate ❞

If the strong form of the mandate idea – that once elected a government is obligated to carry out policies laid before the electorate and voted on in general elections – is more acceptable to the political left, it is no surprise that two of the three referendums held in Britain to date have been under Labour governments. Either the tradition of direct democracy is stronger in the Labour Party or the referendums held were a response to difficult constitutional questions requiring bottom up agreements to changes in the status quo. The 1973 referendum held in Northern Ireland (Edward Heath's Conservative government) was an attempt to settle the problem of the constitutional position of the province – whether it should stay in the United Kingdom or join the Irish Republic. The 1975 referendum on continued membership of the EEC helped a divided Labour Cabinet (under Harold Wilson) avoid a damaging split by allowing executive dissent a public voice (*Batchelor 1992*). In a similar vein, the 1979 referendums in Wales and Scotland on the question of devolution for those countries helped James Callaghan's minority Labour government stay in power with the support of Welsh and Scottish Nationalists at Westminster. Ultimately the fact that the referendums were lost contributed to the withdrawal of this support (Labour also relied on Liberals in a Lib–Lab Pact) and the eventual collapse of the government after losing a vote of confidence in the House of Commons.

EXECUTIVE DOMINANCE

Although the executive supports the weak idea of the mandate for reasons of expediency, it is not keen to consult the electorate again between general elections. John Major made this clear in his rejection of a referendum for Britain in 1992 over the question of ratification of the terms of the Maastricht Treaty after the first Danish referendum on the issue. The Maastricht Treaty was subsequently ratified by the British government after passing the House of Commons (indirect representation), but not after a referendum consulting the people (direct representation). It is interesting that both the Conservative and Labour Parties opposed referendums on Maastricht even though the leaders did not rule out using them in the future. John Major left open the question of a future referendum in 1997 on closer ties with Europe following the 1996 Intergovernmental Conference on European Integration. John Smith, the Labour leader to 1994, promised a referendum on electoral change after rejecting the 1993 Plant Commission Report on Electoral Reform. This promise was reiterated by his

❝ Europe ❞

successor, Tony Blair, although he is on record as being unpersuaded of the need for reform.

Executive dominance of referendums is also evident in the design and mechanism of securing the vote. Since a common criticism of British parliamentary democracy is the lack of public debate on many policy issues, it could be said the public are unprepared for complex constitutional debates and cannot therefore formalise opinions on any issue. Governments must therefore overcome this lack of information by fire brigade exercises in political education. In the 1975 EEC referendum all households were supplied with pro- and anti-EEC statements before the poll, but was this enough? In the run up to the poll, additional publicity through the media was given to the respective arguments but the pro-lobby outspent the anti-lobby.

There remains the problem of the design of the survey and questionnaire. Many complex political issues cannot be reduced to a simple Yes/No response; leading questions suggesting the merits of one answer over another must be avoided. Regarding survey design in the 1979 referendum on Welsh and Scottish devolution, Nationalists felt let down by the insistence on a **qualified majority** of 40 per cent to be in favour of the proposals before the Wales Act 1978 and Scotland Act 1978 could be implemented. These Acts were subsequently repealed by Parliament because of the failure to reach these majorities.

CONSTITUTIONAL IMPLICATIONS

The British referendums held to date have all had a national or constitutional significance for the United Kingdom. It is obviously possible to design referendums having a social or moral focus, but these have been avoided as matters best dealt with by traditional representation. If more contentious referendums were held taking matters out of Parliament, parliamentary sovereignty and the role of MPs would be further undermined. In the one exception to this rule, West Wales is allowed a local referendum on Sunday opening of pubs every ten years.

66 Devolution 99

The separate referendums on Ireland, the EEC and devolution raised the question of implementation of the result. How would a government react if the people's verdict went against their recommendations? Of the three referendums, only the 1975 EEC result was regarded as **binding or mandatory** by the executive; those on Ireland (1973) and devolution (1979) were **advisory**, leaving the government the option of implementation. *Batchelor* (*1992*) makes the point that a strong positive result even in an advisory referendum would be difficult for a government to ignore. Questions on the complexity of implementation of devolution proposals were also raised by the Labour MP, Tam Dalyell. The so-called **West Lothian question** raised the spectre of Scottish MPs losing their right to vote on English matters in the Westminster Parliament if a separate Scottish assembly were established. The repeal of the Scotland Act 1978 removed this problem but it will return if a future Labour government implements proposals for devolution.

THE ELECTORAL SYSTEM

66 First past the post 99

THE BRITISH SIMPLE PLURALITY SYSTEM

The British electoral system is a **simple plurality** or first past the post system. It has many virtues and few drawbacks in the sense that no electoral system is perfect – some are simply more proportional than others.

The system is called 'simple plurality' because the winner needs more votes than any other single candidate but not more votes than all the other candidates – in fact it is rare for this to happen. Voting is a simple matter; voters place a cross against their preferred candidate and the one with the most votes wins (see Figure 10.1).

Tony Blair Labour Party	
John Major Conservative Party	X
Paddy Ashdown Liberal Democrats	
David Sutch Monster Raving Loony Party	
Dafid Wigley Welsh National Party	

Fig. 10.1 The British simple plurality system ballot slip (a hypothetical example – the leaders of the parties do not all stand in a single constituency)

Comment

The **advantages** claimed for the present British electoral system include:

- **Simplicity** It is easy to understand and simple to operate. The voter knows which party will form the government, and there is no behind the scenes manoeuvring as with coalitions.

- **Strong government** The system enables a single party to dominate Parliament and then form a government. This government in turn can claim a mandate for its policies and avoid damaging pacts or coalitions which can weaken an executive.

- **Representativeness** Electors have an MP to lobby who comes from a reasonably small, single member constituency. This ensures that MPs represent the views of all their constituents even if they did not support the MP (*Watts 1994*).

The **weaknesses** in the present system have attracted most attention, particularly from the Liberal Democrats and smaller parties who suffer disproportionately from it. At the outset it is worth remembering that until the 1920s, when the Liberals were eclipsed by the Labour Party under the existing electoral system, that party did not champion electoral reform. The main drawbacks in the simple plurality system are:

66 **Popularity and vote** 99

- **Proportionality**   One test of electoral systems is that they should produce MPs in a legislature roughly proportionate to the vote they receive. This matching does not occur in the British system. In a British constituency the candidate with the most votes is not necessarily the most popular. If there are only two candidates the winner must get a majority (over 50 per cent) but with the more usual situation of three or more, the winner may need just over one third of the vote to get elected. This can mean that more voted against the winner than for – and it certainly means that up to 70 per cent of votes cast in a single constituency are wasted. Those votes that supported other candidates are lost (not counted) and those surplus votes for the winner are also unnecessary (superfluous).

  Because votes are wasted in this way, there is no proportional link between the total votes cast for each party nationally and the final number of seats (MPs) achieved in the House of Commons. Smaller parties therefore suffer a **disproportional representation** in the allocation of seats, in what is called the electoral system effect. The figures for the 1992 general election illustrate well the problem for the Liberal Democrats who won 3.1 per cent of total seats with 17.9 per cent of the popular vote.

	Seats in Commons (MPs)	Percentage of national vote	Percentage of Commons seats
Conservative	336	42	51.6
Labour	271	35.4	41.6
Liberal Democrats	20	17.9	3.1
Scottish Nationalists	3	2.1	0.5
Welsh Nationalists	4	0.4	0.6
Ulster Parties (N. Ireland)	17	2.2	2.6

Fig. 10.2 Disproportional representation for the Liberal Democrats and minor parties – 1992 general election result

- **Minority government**   Although strictly speaking British government is majoritarian with usually a workable majority in the House of Commons from a national electorate viewpoint, many governments are elected on a minority of the popular vote. Since 1945 no government has in fact won more than 50 per cent of the popular vote and the long run of Conservative governments from 1979 were supported by less than 44 per cent of direct electorate votes.

- **Over-representation of the Conservative Party**   Although the independent Boundary Commission reviews electoral districts every ten to fifteen years to ensure constituencies do not become disproportionate in terms of electors, there is evidence that the electoral map of Britain has produced two nations – a predominantly Conservative South and a Labour North. This has partly resulted from the concentration of Labour votes in the North where votes are wasted in safe seats. Conservative strength in the South is more evenly spread thus producing more southern MPs disproportionately (*Rooker 1992*). From a party perspective, therefore, Labour is in danger of being associated as the party of the North that cannot win enough southern seats to dislodge a southern based Conservative government.

66 **Problems for Labour** 99

- **Maintenance of adversarial politics**   The present electoral system helps to maintain the artificiality of two party politics resting on an adversarial system. Each major party is encouraged by its electoral prize and stranglehold on power, to present politics in an oppositional form (*Finer 1975*). This in turn is encouraged by the existence of safe seats (approximately 70 per cent) which permanently return Labour or Conservative MPs to the House of Commons. Even marginal seats, which have the potential to produce a change of government by small swings, play into the hands of the two party system because the electoral system gives everything to the winner. The argument for a reformed voting system is even stronger on marginality grounds, for a small group of the electorate have a significance out of proportion to their number.

ELECTORAL REFORM

Mainly because of the problems of disproportionality and unfairness in the British simple plurality system, since the 1970s discussion of reform has become almost a permanent feature of the political system increasing as either Labour or Liberal Democratic parties feel more disadvantaged. For example, in 1996 with the Conservative government into its seventeenth year of consecutive administration, pressure for change accelerated. Paradoxically, as the general election approached, there were those within the Labour Party who felt 'one last push' would carry them over the electoral threshold into government under the simple plurality system. Equally, there were those who felt that Labour would again become dependent on Liberal Democratic support (as in 1976–79) in any future hung Parliament, suggesting that the price of this support could be a promise to reform the system. The fear was that should the Conservative government win a fifth consecutive term they would not change the simple plurality system and so arguments would continue.

Alternative voting systems

We have seen some of the values considered necessary in democratic electoral systems: **proportionality**, **strong government**, **representativeness** and **electoral choice**. Most electoral systems, including the British present system, embody these values, but no one system has a monopoly of all. In suggesting replacements two types of system are examined: **majority systems** that give good majorities in constituencies and **proportional systems** that ensure a proportional link between numbers of representatives and the popular vote. The following are the more important:

- **Alternative vote system (majority)** This would be the easiest form to introduce in place of the existing British system. The main difference to first past the post would be greater electoral choice placing candidates in preference order. The system was first suggested in 1910 and again by the Labour government of 1931.

Tony Blair Labour Party	1
John Major Conservative Party	4
Paddy Ashdown Liberal Democrats	2
David Sutch Monster Raving Loony Party	5
Dafid Wigley Welsh National Party	3

Fig.10.3 An alternative vote ballot paper

66 Preference vote 99

Votes are initially distributed according to first preferences – any candidate receiving more than 50 per cent is elected. If no MP emerges on the first round, then second preferences are used to build up other candidates to the required number. Although this system does not give proportional representation, it is easy to understand and ensures MPs have majority constituency support. It is used in Australia for federal elections to the House of Representatives and in State Parliament elections.

- **Party list system (proportional)** Party list or list systems are proportional in the sense that votes are apportioned to party lists according to the share of the vote received. The electorate vote for a party (not candidates) and seats are allocated according to lists supplied by the parties (see Figure 10.4).

Labour Party	
Conservative Party	
Liberal Democratic Party	
Monster Raving Loony Party	
Welsh National Party	X

Fig. 10.4 A party list ballot paper

This system is used in Israel, Belgium, Finland, Sweden and in European Union parliamentary elections outside Britain. Its main drawback is that electorates have little choice in the selection of party candidates – but its MPs are proportionately related to the actual vote.

- **Single transferable vote system (proportional)** This system is more complex than the others examined so far. Larger constituencies are involved with a number of MPs selected by respective parties. Voters express preferences (as in the alternative vote) but votes are distributed according to a formula (see Figure 10.5).

Michael Heseltine Conservative Party	6
David Steel Liberal Democratic Party	2
Gordon Brown Labour Party	8
Kenneth Clarke Conservative Party	7
David Alton Liberal Democratic Party	3
Jack Straw Labour Party	4
William Hague Conservative Party	1
Dafid Wigley Welsh National Party	5
David Sutch Monster Raving Loony Party	9

Fig. 10.5 A single transferable vote ballot paper

The formula for working out which candidates are elected is:

$$\frac{\text{number of votes cast} + 1}{\text{number of seats} + 1}$$

❝ Redistribution of votes ❞ To be elected, candidates must pass the quota. Surplus votes are then redistributed according to voter preferences 1, 2, 3, etc. A process of redistribution of votes from those who passed the quota to the less successful continues until all seats are filled. Apart from complexity, the main disadvantage with this system relates to the larger constituencies needed which could mean that MPs become more remote. This is partially offset by a greater number of MPs in each constituency and the proportionality of the system. It is used in Australia, the Republic of Ireland and Malta.

- **Additional member system (hybrid)** Some alternative voting systems are hybrid – a mix of both majority and proportional systems. The most cited example is that used in Germany (formerly West Germany), which was introduced after 1945. Here two systems are used, with voters having two votes. The first is expressed for a candidate under simple plurality, the second for a party list. Those elected by simple plurality get seats, the remaining seat allocation for each party being filled on a proportional basis according to their share of the vote. This system balances the disadvantages of simple plurality with the advantages of a proportional system.

The future

The prospects for reform of the British electoral system relate very much to the outcome of general elections. In 1996 the Labour Party seemed divided on the issue. Although they set up the Plant Commission to examine the question, they did not feel confident enough to accept the 1993 recommendations for a supplementary vote system for Parliament. A Labour Party succeeding in becoming the next government, may find their enthusiasm for electoral reform is not liable to be a priority. If unsuccessful, they will probably move closer to the Liberal Democrats who advocate a single transferable vote proportional system for Britain. In 1996 the Conservative Party remain uncommitted to reform, yet ironically their poor showing in the 1995 local elections, where they were penalised by the present electoral system (they achieved nineteen per cent of the seats on a 25 per cent share of the vote), may have an impact (*Crewe 1995*).

EXAMINATION QUESTIONS

1 Examine the argument that the regular use of referendums or initiatives in the UK would give too much power to pressure groups while at the same time reducing the role of political parties. *(40)*
(AEB)

2 Discuss the role and impact of opinion polls in British politics. *(25)*
(ULEAC)

3 How far does the present British electoral system provide a balance between representing public opinion and securing strong government? *(25)*
(NEAB)

ANSWERS TO EXAMINATION QUESTIONS

OUTLINE ANSWER TO QUESTION 1

This question demands an understanding of the constitutional position of referendums or initiatives. As initiatives (voting on specific policy issues in ordinary elections) are not generally used in the United Kingdom, concentrate on referendums. Carefully show how referendums relate to the sovereignty of the people argument and in effect bypass Parliament. You should be able to describe parliamentary sovereignty and its relationship to referendums. Develop the point about the power of pressure groups who would openly campaign on referendum issues. As there have only been three referendums in the United Kingdom, there are few examples of pressure group referenda campaigns. You could focus on the 1975 EEC referendum campaigns of both pro- and anti-EEC groups. Make some evaluation of the increased power pressure groups might gain from campaigning in possible future referendums and compare with the role of political parties. Since political parties focus on election campaigns where issues are less specific, it is possible they would lose influence in these areas. This is a debatable point and you should be prepared to argue a case for or against.

TUTOR'S ANSWER TO QUESTION 3

The current British electoral system of simple plurality or first past the post, like other systems of elections, has its strengths and weaknesses. If we define public opinion as majority opinion on specific issues, then the British system is not particularly good at transmitting particular opinions to the government. Voters elect and mandate governments on a broad platform of issues, not specifics. From another perspective the simple plurality system is not proportional – total seats gained by the parties bear some resemblance to the popular vote but they are not arithmetically proportional. In this sense the onus in the British system appears to be on parliamentary strength – strong governments are produced, but Parliaments are weak and majority electoral opinions may not be represented in the executive.

The democratic tests of any electoral system are electoral choice, representativeness and proportionality. The British electoral system scores highly on the first, but is less effective on the second and third. Electoral choice implies the electorate can vote for a spread of political parties representing all shades of opinion. In a multi-party electoral system (which the British have), there is accommodation for moderate and extremist views. Mainstream political parties (Conservative, Labour, Liberal Democratic, Scottish and Welsh Nationalists) co-exist alongside smaller serious parties like the Greens and others at the fun side or extremes of politics. Although all these parties co-exist, parliamentary representation is dominated by the big three mainstream parties. The British electoral system in effect squeezes out the smaller parties so in effect their supporters are disenfranchised and not represented.

Representativeness implies constituencies small enough for the views of the elector to be known so the Member of Parliament can be lobbied. Clearly an advantage of the present British system is that constituencies are reasonably small and theoretically MPs represent all the electorate in their area even if they did not vote for them. In alternative majority or proportional systems with larger constituencies, there is little evidence that the consultative tie between electors and representatives would be stronger.

It is sometimes claimed that the present British electoral system encourages the phenomenon of safe seats based upon large majorities which waste votes. Those voters in safe seats who did not support the sitting MP might feel inhibited from bringing their complaints to the representative. In this sense some proportional systems with larger constituencies (for example the single transferable vote system) would have more than one MP to lobby and electors could probably find at least one who was sympathetic to their views. If we take representativeness to include one vote one value, then clearly the British system is inadequate. Many votes for minority candidates are wasted (not counted) as the simple majority system merely gives the seat to the winner. From this perspective Liberal Democratic and smaller party supporters can feel aggrieved as their views (and votes) cannot be aggregated to bring effect. In a proportional system the country would either be divided into larger constituencies or one large constituency giving more weight to minor parties. A majority system would also ensure that at least the winning candidate had a 50 per cent plus majority of votes cast in a single constituency. A major drawback with the current British system is that an individual candidate can secure the nomination on a minority of the total vote.

Proportionality is the problematic feature in the British simple plurality system and has caused most controversy. There is no proportional link between the total vote cast for the winning party in a general election and numbers of seats gained. In the 1992 general election the Conservatives secured 51.6 per cent of House of Commons seats on a 42 per cent share of the national vote. Labour also did well securing a 41.6 per cent share of seats on a 35.4 per cent vote, whilst the Liberal Democrats with a 17.9 per cent national vote only secured 3.1 per cent of seats. Clearly, from the Liberal Democratic point of view, the system is disproportionate and can only be defended on the grounds of securing strong government. The over-representation of the Conservative and Labour Parties in the House of Commons ensures two things. First, the government is certain of a good majority to govern and will be able to get its programme through the House of Commons. This is an electoral advantage in one respect because the electorate know when they vote for this party (and give them a mandate) that they will be able to implement the programme without behind the scenes deals. Second, the system ensures that the second largest party has enough strength to form an official opposition party ready to take over government should that prove necessary.

Liberal Democrats and other opponents refute the points made above claiming that the British Labour and Conservative Parties are already coalitions where deals are made in secret anyway. The introduction of a proportional system might produce coalition governments in the House of Commons – and they may not be weak, and at least any deals made would be in the open.

Finally, reform of the British electoral system hinges very much on where one places priorities in a democratic representative system. If the onus is placed on Parliament and the need to secure strong (stable) government, then the present simple plurality system functions well as it has always done. The relationship between seats and popular vote is not disproportional, except for Liberal Democratic and minor party supporters. Conservative and Labour voters have the added advantage that their votes count and their parties can form strong governments if chosen. The difficulty with this argument is that as the Conservatives have remained in office consecutively for 17 years by 1996, questions about the role of the electoral system in this arrangement are bound to be asked. If the electoral system is keeping in power a government with less than 50 per cent of the popular vote, then representative democracy is not working as it should. Majority public opinion is therefore disenfranchised.

Labour attitudes to this problem are ambivalent. By promising a referendum on the electoral system, the late Labour Party leader, John Smith, went some way to acknowledge the problems in the system. But the fact that he rejected the reform proposals of the Plant Committee, and that Tony Blair is reported to be less than enthusiastic on the subject, means that we shall have to wait for the outcome of the next general election before decisions are taken on changing, adapting or reforming the system.

STUDENT'S ANSWER TO QUESTION 2 WITH EXAMINER'S COMMENTS

66 Develop introduction 99

Opinion polls were founded by Dr Gallup and were defended on the grounds that they would improve political leaders' knowledge of public opinion. So, by providing continuous feedback they could improve democracy.

However, in recent times they have come to take the role merely of racing tipsters rather than providing a wealth of information about the political mood of the electorate. Political forecasting, though, is the only objective test of how accurate polls are.

The polls in the '92 election, whilst renowned for failing to correctly predict the winning party, had a good election in other senses. Over 50 nationwide polls were commissioned in the four weeks of the campaign and stories about the polls made a tremendous amount of front page news in the time of the campaign. One polling organisation, Harris, made £200,000 from ITN alone for surveys, before collecting more from *The Observer*, *Daily Express* and the Conservative Party.

The Market Research Society commissioned a report into the reasons why the polls were so wrong in '92. Several reasons were advanced. The first is the question of sampling methods. Some critics complain that there is too much initiative left to the interviewer under the quota system. They agree more representative samples might be obtained if interviewees were picked at random. Pollsters may have picked unrepresentative sampling points, or last minute adjustments and weightings of the findings may have been insufficiently refined. Pollsters argue that their methods have produced acceptable findings on many other occasions so other factors must have come into play.

66 Any sources here 99

Another possible source of error was the effect of the Poll Tax on the electoral register. It has been argued that significant numbers of people refused to register on the electoral roll because they could be traced for non-payment of Poll Tax, and the argument runs that they were most likely Labour supporters. The Market Research Society suggested that the electorate in 1992 may have been significantly different from the population. So if two or three people in a hundred did not have a vote, yet expressed an intention to support Labour, the polls could have been thrown.

The time and day when the polls were conducted could also have been a source of error. The only survey, by Harris, to show a substantial Conservative lead was conducted over the weekend. It is claimed that this is when more Conservative supporters are available for polling, although this claim is unsubstantiated.

Last minute changes and abstentions are also pointed to as explanations for polls' errors. The late swing is the most obvious example here (as in 1970). However, cynics object that this is the pollsters' faithful standby excuse, and predictions should allow for such factors. The ITN Harris exit poll of 1992 provided the best evidence of a late surge when it found that nine per cent of Conservative voters claimed not to have decided how they would vote until election day compared to five per cent, four per cent and five per cent in the previous three elections.

An associated explanation is that a proportion of people who had told the pollsters that they would support the Labour Party did not in the event vote, whereas Conservative supporters did turn out. The impact of differential turnout has been found significant in the past, notably in 1970.

66 What about 1992? 99

The report on the polls by the Market Research Society suggested that up to half the polls' errors could be explained by last minute changes or abstentions. There are two other credible explanations why the polls got it wrong. One is that they defeated themselves, by persuading some people to vote against the outcome they were predicting and the other is that Conservative supporters consistently refused to tell pollsters their voting intentions.

In five of the last six elections, polls have overstated the support for the party in the lead. It is possible that polls have acquired a self falsifying quality, by influencing a small proportion of voters. In the last few days of the campaign the Conservatives pushed the argument that a vote for Liberals would 'let Labour in' and the opinion polls seemed to support this.

A final and more speculative factor might be that Conservative support was understated throughout the election because Conservatives disproportionately refused to declare their voting intentions. ICM, after the election, found that 'undecideds' and 'don't knows' disproportionately voted Conservative. Pollsters are reluctant to accept that some of these were deliberately lying, because if a crucial number of people lie then it raises credibility problems for their whole operation. Some Conservatives argue that this may indeed be the case; they suggest that there is a spiral of silence, in which a crucial two to three per cent of Conservatives are reluctant to reveal their allegiance because they feel that it is unfashionable. Some believe that the prevalent 'politically correct' atmosphere prevents people from admitting to uncaring, selfish preferences for lower taxes etc.

Calls have been made to ban polls during election time. However, these ought to be opposed on the grounds of freedom of expression and on the grounds of practicality as rumours of suspect 'secret' polls would abound.

Print and broadcast editors need to think carefully about their reasons for commissioning polls. Increasingly, they are becoming a form of lazy journalism, concentrating too much on the 'horse race' aspect which can go badly wrong. Polls could take more care to establish that respondents are on the electoral register, perhaps give the number of undecideds and don't knows, emphasise even more the qualifications on their findings and ask more subtle questions on crucial issues like taxation.

Calls for fewer polls, less emphasis on the standing of political parties, a greater emphasis on health warnings, more modest coverage by the media and greater attention to polls in assessing public opinion are all desirable. Editors have promised to be more cautious about polls in the upcoming election. However, we remain fascinated with the horse-race aspect of elections and, just as we turn a blind eye to the margin of error in poll findings, so we are likely to ignore the warnings of 1992.

❝ Give more detail here ❞

❝ An interesting essay strong on detail even if there is no specific reference to the Bandwagon and Boomerang effects. The balance of argument is good and it adequately answers the question. There could have been a little more discussion on the role of opinion polls in a democracy. Worthy of a low B grade. ❞

REFERENCES IN THE TEXT

Batchelor, A 1992 Referendums and initiatives, *Politics Review* **1** February

Bogdanor, V 1991 Quoted in *The Guardian* 22 November

Butler, D and D Kavanagh 1992 *The British General Election of 1992*, London: Macmillan

Crewe, I 1992 Opinion polls and the election, *Parliamentary Affairs*, **45** (4) October

Crewe, I 1995 Hanley's excuses, excuses, *The Observer* 7 May

Denver, D 1989 *Elections and voting behaviour in Britain*, Hemel Hempstead: Phillip Allen

Denver, D 1992 The 1992 general election: in defence of psephology, *Talking Politics* **5** Autumn

Eatwell, R 1993 Opinion poll accuracy: the case of the 1992 general election, *Talking Politics* **5** Winter

Finer, S E 1975 *Adversary Politics and Electoral Reform*, London: Anthony Wigram

Game, C 1994 Snapshots of public opinion, *Politics Review* February

Kavanagh, D 1992 Polls, predictions and politics, *Politics Review* **2** November

Rooker, J 1992 Face to face, *Politics Review* **4** April

Watts, D 1994 *Electoral reform: achieving a sense of proportion*, PAVIC Publications, Sheffield Hallam University

VOTING BEHAVIOUR

TRADITIONAL THEORIES OF ELECTORAL BEHAVIOUR

INTERPRETING THE VOTE

THE 1992 GENERAL ELECTION

GETTING STARTED

Traditional studies of voting behaviour tended to focus on fairly simple social determinants of electoral choice, for example social class and political socialisation (family background and life experience). Modern studies include the impact of secondary influences on the vote – political issues, instrumental or judgmental attitudes and changes in the social structure.

Although the long term trends in British voting behaviour since the sixties have been towards greater **volatility** or changeability in the electorate, this has not produced significant alternation in governments. Both major parties have had long spells in government, Labour with a broken run 1964/79 and the Conservatives since 1979. This highlights a problem in psephology, that of extrapolating from the short to the long term. Studies of general elections are snapshots of political behaviour at any point in time. They are not predictions of future behaviour. The idea that politically people do not behave in rational predictable ways is still valid.

Common themes for questions in this area are:

- The 1992 general election result and its relationship to accepted theories of electoral choice.
- Long and short term factors which have a bearing on how people vote.
- The impact of party election campaigns on the electorate.
- The electoral implications for the future of the Labour Party after a long period in opposition.

ESSENTIAL PRINCIPLES

TRADITIONAL THEORIES OF ELECTORAL BEHAVIOUR

SOCIAL CLASS

Early approaches to the study of electoral choice (**psephology**) concentrated mainly on the idea that voters aligned themselves to political parties largely on social class lines (class alignment) (*Butler and Stokes 1974*). As the Labour and Conservative Parties had dominated British politics in the post war period 1945–70, so the majority of the electorate perceived of themselves as either working or middle class. The Labour Party attracted the working class vote and the Conservative Party the middle class vote. A basic problem was to explain the success of the Conservative Party in winning general elections if a majority of the electorate (approximately 60 per cent) were working class; if the vote followed class patterns there should be more Labour governments.

66 A problem in psephology 99

Two factors were considered important:

1 **Party attachment** Class membership is related to party attachment and identity. During the fifties and sixties the majority of the electorate **strongly identified** with one of the two main parties (*Kavanagh 1990*). This strong **partisan self-image** aligned the electorate behind the Labour or Conservative Party (partisan alignment) and produced fairly consistent general election results (*Butler and Stokes 1974*). Each party could count on a 'hard vote' (as there were few floating voters) and the certainty of their own reliable class constituencies.

66 Firm votes 99

2 **Deviant voters** Class voting never followed neat patterns; there were always **deviant** voters prepared to support parties outside their class for a variety of reasons (cross-class voting) (see Figure 11.1).

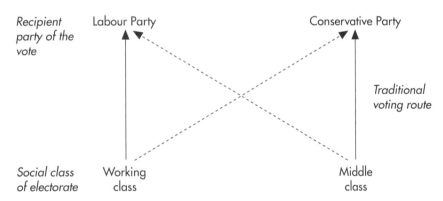

Fig. 11.1 A model of deviant or cross-class voting

Deviant voters fell into two categories:

- **working class Tories** who voted Conservative and
- **middle class radicals** who voted Labour.

66 Sociological reasons 99

Complex sociological reasons were given as explanations for this behaviour which took voters from their traditional parties.

Working class Tories

Two explanations for working class Conservative voting behaviour came from *McKenzie and Silver* (*1968*).

1 Working class Tories voted on **deferential** grounds – they deferred to the Conservative Party because in their opinion it was superior to and better able to govern than the Labour Party.

2 Those who did not fit this category were **secular** voters. They chose the Conservative Party for practical reasons.

Parkin (*1968*) and *Jessop* (*1974*) advanced a more controversial theory. For them, working class Conservative voting was explained by socialisation into Conservative and middle class values. As the **dominant value system** of British society was held to be predominantly conservative, so a large section of the working class would be influenced to vote for the party that embodied those ideas.

" Living standards and the vote "

A final traditional explanation for working class Conservative support came from *Butler and Rose* (*1960*). They suggested that as living standards rose, a greater number of working class voters experienced a middle class lifestyle which propelled them towards the Conservative Party. This causal link between living standards and party preference (**embourgeoisement theory**) has never been totally discredited and was one of the reasons why the governments of Margaret Thatcher were so successful in attracting working class support.

Middle class radicals

Two factors have always supported middle class Labour voting:

1 **Occupation** Those in public sector service employment (teaching, social work, nursing) are drawn to the Labour Party because it is perceived as more concerned with social welfare spending than the Conservative Party (*Parkin 1968*).

2 **Intellect** Intellectually certain middle class voters see no class contradiction in supporting the Labour Party; the ideas of Conservatism are not attractive. The middle class image of the Parliamentary Labour Party would also prove attractive as many first generation professionals remember the socialising influences of a working class background.

THE TWO PARTY SYSTEM

" Two party dominance "

A feature linked to the traditional pattern of voting behaviour was the existence of a fairly **stable** two party system. The Conservative and Labour Parties dominated politics throughout the fifties and sixties attracting the major share of the vote. During these years both parties secured an average vote of 87.5 per cent, leaving little room for the Liberal Party as a third force (*Crewe 1993*). Dominance by two major parties of the electoral system fitted well with the theories of class and partisan alignment and political socialisation. The majority of the electorate were said to be socialised by family background into supporting either the Conservative or Labour Parties.

POLITICAL SOCIALISATION

" Family influence "

Family background plays a major part in the formation of political attitudes. According to *Butler and Stokes* (*1974*) there is a strong correlation between the political ideas of parents and those their children will eventually adopt. Tracking this **causal link** showed how family origin conditioned educational and occupational choice. Those who had economically secure family backgrounds and a good education tended to support the Conservative Party. Labour Party supporters were drawn predominantly from those with less secure family and educational achievements.

These ideas connected **short** and **long** term social factors in a framework of voting behaviour and showed how a person's life experience – beginning with childhood – impacted on electoral choice. *Butler and Stokes* (*1974*) concentrated on the influences of housing, schooling and occupation. In their framework, *Rose and McAllister* (*1990*) included the influence of political values and party images.

INTERPRETING THE VOTE

Explanations of voting behaviour have become more complex since the 1970s for the following reasons;

1 The tie between the electorate and the two main political parties has declined (**partisan dealignment**).

2 The specific class attachment to the Conservative and Labour Parties has weakened (**class dealignment**).

" Three party system "

3 Voter **volatility** has increased to the point at which it is no longer accurate to talk about a competitive two party system. Three main parties, Conservative, Labour and Liberal Democrat compete for the vote, even if the simple majority system of election produces strong single party government.

Social, political and other factors have a bearing on electoral choice and these must be examined to complement the above features.

SOCIAL VARIABLES

The main social variables influencing political attitudes and the vote are: **age, gender, religion, ethnicity and class**. In the 1992 general election the Conservatives led the Labour Party in most of these categories, confirming long term conformity rather than volatility in the electorate (see Figure 11.2).

	Traditional Conservative lead	Traditional Labour lead	Parties supported equally
Age	✓		
Gender	✓		
Religion			✓
Ethnicity		✓	
Class			✓

Fig. 11.2 Social variables and the vote (based on 1992 general election)

Age

The connection between age and voting is subject to conflicting interpretations. It was generally accepted that the tendency to vote Conservative increased with age. Ageing is usually linked to the acquisition of more material prosperity and a general satisfaction with status quo. This conditions political outlooks which reflect in greater Conservative support. In the 1992 general election, Conservative support was greater than Labour in every category except the 25 to 34 age group.

Butler and Stokes (1974) rejected this theory of **senescence** (literally, growing old) – of voters moving to the political right as they aged – as too simplistic. They noticed a tendency for the vote to be **immunised** or **conserved** against change in political attitudes. Literally, this would imply voters remaining with the party of their first choice with loyalty increasing as they grew older. The problem with this explanation is that if the young 'conserved' their vote (and they are more radical than the old), the electorate would be gradually radicalised, over the generations.

Strong Conservative Party support from the older generations could have more basic explanations:

- middle class Conservative voters tend to live longer than working class Labour voters and
- traditionally more women voters support the Conservative Party, and women live longer than men.

66 Political outlooks 99

66 Radical youth 99

Gender

Women are more Conservative than men, but it is not greatly significant in electoral terms. *Crewe (1985a)* claimed that sex differences in the vote were of slight importance to the outcome of elections. This was supported by *Dunleavy and Husbands (1985)* who placed an estimate of five per cent difference between the sexes in terms of the vote.

In the 1960s and 1970s the gender gap between men and women voters favoured the Conservative Party. During the next decade its beneficial effects for Conservatism disappeared, only to resurface in the first general election of the nineties. In the 1992 general election the Conservative Party had the lead over the Labour Party in every age category of female vote except the young: 44 per cent of women voted Conservative against 38 per cent of men.

Research into these statistics is limited. Apart from the age factor mentioned above, most explanations for the gender gap in the vote centre around the **domestic role** of women. It is suggested that many women employed in the family home do not experience the radicalising effects of employer/employee relationships found in the workplace. Their resultant political affinities lead many women into supporting the Conservative Party.

66 Housewives and the vote 99

Religion

The connection between held religious attitudes and beliefs and party preference has received little attention from psephologists. There is sociological evidence of a decline in religious practice (**secularisation**), but it is difficult to tie this to political behaviour. Compared to Europe (France, Germany, and Italy, for example) the traditional link between religious and political attitudes in Britain is weak. The notable exception to this is **Northern Ireland** where Catholics support republican or socialist parties (Sinn Fein or SDLP) and Protestants support parties seeking to keep the United Kingdom link (Ulster Unionists).

 **European comparison**

Historically Labour received support from Non-conformists (Wesleyans and Presbyterians) in Wales and Scotland and it is still the dominant party in those regions. Catholics in England have supported the more radical Labour and Liberal Democratic Parties, whilst church-going Anglicans were said to lean towards the Conservative Party. The expression 'the Church of England is the Tory Party at prayer' links the established Church with the oldest political party, but there was never any institutional connection.

Ethnicity

The ethnic minority vote goes predominantly to the Labour Party for a variety of reasons. Labour are regarded as being more **sympathetic** to the interests of African/Caribbean, Asian and other ethnic groups partly because of their **attitude** to race relations. Of the race relations legislation passed to date, the laws controlling immigration (the Immigration Acts) have been enacted by Conservative governments. Those promoting race relations in the host society (the Race Relations Acts) have been passed by Labour governments.

Labour support is strong across the whole social spectrum of the black vote and connects with social class and party identification (*Layton-Henry 1992*). Voting Labour is often seen as a way of conforming to the predominantly working class position experienced by ethnic minority groups in general (**expressive voting**).

Ethnic representation in Parliament

Up to the 1992 general election, the Labour Party appeared to promote the **parliamentary** interests of ethnic minorities by electing a number of black MPs, admittedly to areas of high immigrant concentration. The Conservative Party's first black candidate for a safe rural seat (John Taylor in Cheltenham) was defeated in the 1992 general election. According to some observers, this was not on the grounds of race but because John Taylor was not a local candidate. Apparently the constituency had a record of rejecting candidates imposed from outside their locality. The Conservative Party did elect two black MPs at this same election and, with the other parties, has come to realise the importance of attracting the ethnic minority vote.

Class

Social class based changes in electoral behaviour were first picked up in studies of the 1979 general election and tracked in all subsequent elections. Two writers, *Sarlvik and Crewe (1983)*, were instrumental in developing the related theories of partisan and class dealignment mentioned earlier (see p. 146).

- **Partisan dealignment** describes the general declining commitment to the main political parties as the electorate becomes more instrumental in the use of its vote. The two main parties' share of the vote declined from a 90 per cent average to a 75 per cent average from the 1970s to the 1990s.

- **Class dealignment** referred to the specific reductions in class based voting for the Conservative and Labour parties, among the middle class and working class respectively. From the 1970s to the 1990s middle class support for the Conservative Party has declined from a four-fifths to a three-fifths share of the vote. Labour's share of the working class vote over the same period has fallen from two-thirds to less than a half.

The **main consequence** of dealignment is the increase in electoral volatility as voter loyalty to the main political parties declines. Voters are more willing to switch from major to minor parties with the Liberal Democrats being the main beneficiaries. According to *Denver (1993)*, switching between Conservative and Labour is less common. This has repercussions for the appeal of the parties during election campaigns, as some **floating voters** are willing to be influenced. Such behaviour over the long term relates to how elections are fought and the political appeal of the parties during the campaign itself.

The **causes** of dealignment are linked to the effects of the changing **social structure** and **class** society. Middle class political detachment from the Conservative Party is partially explained by the emergence of a new middle class or 'salariat' (*Wright 1976*). These middle class radicals work in public sector professions (teaching, social work and the civil service) and felt the insecurity of occupations dependent on public expenditure. The socialist perspective of this group complements their location in a contradictory class position, they are neither part of the traditional middle class nor are they working class.

66 New middle class 99

Apart from the traditional explanations of working class Tory voting behaviour, the fall in support for the Labour Party is also explained by the **fragmentation** of that class. According to *Crewe* (*1985b*), a new working class had emerged by the end of the seventies willing to support the radical programmes of Margaret Thatcher. This new class was predominantly more prosperous than the traditional working class and there were important differences in housing tenure, employment patterns, locality and disposable incomes, that affected the vote (see Figure 11.3).

66 New working class 99

	NEW WORKING CLASS	OLD WORKING CLASS
Voter preference	Conservative Party	Labour Party
Housing tenure	Purchasing private or state housing	Renting state housing
Employment pattern	Mainly employed in private sector	Mainly employed in state sector
Trade union activity	Weak unionisation, low membership	Strong unionisation, high membership
Locality	Live in South of England or suburban areas of Britain	Live in North of England, inner cities or declining areas of Britain
Income and standard of living	High disposable income, higher living standards, own shares in privatised industries	Low disposable income, lower living standards, no share ownership

Fig. 11.3 Differences between the new and old working classes

The significance of these divisions of working class support was also heightened by occupational changes resulting in the decline of manual employment traditionally important for the Labour vote. *Ivor Crewe's* conclusions that dealignment had damaged the Labour Party were based on the **British Election Studies** of the 1979, 1983 and 1987 general elections. Labour faced the prospect of becoming a sectional party representing a shrinking fragment of the working class. The traditional working class were still Labour, but the new working class had no interest in socialist policies or a Labour government.

Ivor Crewe's pessimistic views of the effects of dealignment on the Labour Party were not shared by *Heath, Jowell and Curtice* (*1985 and 1987*). They argued that the effects of dealignment had been exaggerated – the decline in Labour support since the 1960s was part of a **trendless fluctuation** of events rather than the result of any dramatic change in voting behaviour. The Labour Party could regain some of its lost working class support because class was still an important factor in the makeup of electoral choice. The results of the 1992 general election showed that Labour could regain lost ground among the skilled working class voters (the C2s). These had supported the Conservative Party in the long run of election victories from 1979, and were regarded as an important target for any party.

66 Skilled working class or C2s 99

POLITICAL VARIABLES

Political variables influencing the vote are generally regarded as those not totally affected by social long term factors. The main ones are: issue or judgemental voting, political perceptions and the impact of electoral campaigns. All presuppose a rational model of voting behaviour which was rejected by traditional writers as too complex.

Issue or judgemental voting

66 Voters as consumers 99

The first identification of issue or judgemental voting was made by the sociologists *Himmelweit, Humphreys and Jaeger* (*1985*). They suggested that electoral choice should be understood as the **deliberate** selection of parties, not as the product of long term political socialisation. In this **consumer model** of voting, the electorate decide on the relative merits of the parties largely on the issues. Traditionally in voter preference surveys the Labour Party does well on the issues of the welfare state, health and education; the Conservative Party on taxation, defence, and law and order. The problems with this approach in analysing electoral behaviour are **twofold**:

1 It is difficult to separate political attitudes and values from the immediate response or judgements about those issues (*Denver 1993*).

2 A party can do well on the issues in the minds of the electorate but still lose elections. In the 1987 general election the Labour Party was ahead of the Conservative Party on the main issues (jobs, health and education) but lost the election (*Crewe 1987*). Again in the 1992 general election, Labour did well in raising its issue profile – but the Conservatives still won.

Political perceptions

66 Long and short term factors 99

Electoral perceptions of the political parties are an important influence on the vote (*Heath, Jowell and Curtice 1985*). Within these perceptions long term factors (political memory) and short term factors (reacting to government policies) will play a part. In the 1960s it was argued that the electorate were largely ignorant of the different ideologies of the respective parties – one reason why *Butler and Stokes* (*1974*) felt the complexity of issue voting could not replace class voting.

66 Left–right continuum 99

Although the electorate are ill informed about politics, they are aware of what the parties stand for. Awareness of the **Labour Party** as **left** or **soft** and the **Conservative** Party as **right** or **hard** colours opinions. There is evidence that the electorate prefer Labour policies on welfarism and Conservative policies on the economy. In the last two decades they have assigned a higher priority to economic issues to the advantage of the Conservatives.

66 Competence to govern 99

As the electorate become more **volatile** and **dealigned**, general elections have become tests of competence to govern rather than arguments between competing ideologies (socialism versus capitalism). Public confidence in a party's ability to govern or 'deliver the goods' is a crucially important winning factor. During the seventies the Labour opposition image (under Michael Foot and Neil Kinnock) was of a divided party, incompetent to govern or manage the economy. Conservative general election wins under **Margaret Thatcher** were based largely on economic **feel good** factors which have been absent in the early nineties. Using an econometric model, *Sanders* (*1993*) found a strong correlation between interest and inflation rates and continuous support for the Conservative Party. It is interesting that in both these items the Labour Party trails the Conservative Party in voters' perception of sound economic management.

The impact of election campaigns

There are two different interpretations of the impact of election campaigns on voter attitudes:

1 The **traditional** sixties view of election campaigns was that they had little effect on the voter. This **neutral** view fitted well with the idea of a stable electorate bound by long term class loyalties to two main political parties. Relatively short term election campaigns would not affect the outcome.

2 The **modern** view of the impact of electioneering on electoral choice coincides with the rise of dealignment and a more volatile electorate. If more voters are detached from the political parties (**floating voters**) or are undecided, short term

66 Vote switching 99

factors like party performance in election campaigns will be **influential**. Since a considerable amount of vote switching, or 'churning', goes on during the campaign, more importance is attached to media presentation and 'packaging' of the respective parties. During the 1992 general election campaign, vote switching favoured the Conservative Party. It was estimated that 11.1 million voters changed their minds with an extra 3.2 million votes for the Conservatives against a loss of 1.81 million – a net gain of 1.39 million, enough to win the election.

OTHER VARIABLES

Electoral geography

66 Regions 99

Geographical variations in the vote have long been a feature of British electoral politics. Support for the political parties varies from region to region even within social classes. A manual worker in the South-West of England is twice as likely to vote Conservative as one in Wales. From the late seventies a regional variation in the vote between the North and South of England (**the North–South divide**) became a regular feature of general elections.

The North of England, Scotland and Wales became predominantly Labour whilst the South moved towards the Conservatives. **Social class** differences between the regions partially explain this effect with Labour working class votes concentrated in the North, Wales and Scotland. Another explanation offered by *Johnson and Pattie (1992)*, concentrates on **economic factors**. They claim that regional vote variations follow the general patterns of economic development – areas of decline have moved towards Labour, those of prosperity towards the Conservatives.

A second geographical factor influencing the vote is the **locality** or **neighbourhood effect**. According to *Denver (1993)*, the type of community conditions electoral choice. Working class neighbourhoods are predominantly Labour and condition their inhabitants to support that party. Middle class districts have a characteristic that encourages support for the Conservative Party. Critics of this theory claim a person's address is not a significant factor in the makeup of electoral choice.

The media

Election campaigns are largely fought in the media, with television playing a primary role closely followed by the press. If voting behaviour is the result of a complex mix of attitudes and values, then relatively short term media election campaigns are not going to be influential with 'hard' **loyal** voters. The greatest impact of television and press reporting of politics is on 'soft' or **floating** voters unattached to parties, but it is difficult to unpick the influences.

66 Tabloid newspapers 99

Newspaper bias for or against political parties is discounted or diffused by purchasing choice. Party choice by newspaper readership is well established. The fact that *The Sun* newspaper villified Neil Kinnock in the 1992 general election did not affect the outcome. Support for the Conservatives among readers of pro-Tory tabloids fell by three points during the campaign (*Heath, Jowell and Curtice 1994*). There is a strong relationship between the papers people buy and their political opinions but separating **cause** and **effect** is difficult. We do not know if people buy **The Guardian** because they are Labour or if the newspaper conditions them into supporting that party (*Denver 1993*).

66 Information function 99

Television reporting of politics is more balanced because of statutory controls and the public appear to accept this. The classic statement on the influence of television and political attitudes was made by *Trenaman and McQuail (1961)*. They reached the conclusion that television exposure during election campaigns had an educational effect. It did not appear to condition political attitudes or the vote, even though people were better informed of the issues in the campaign. Such a position was confirmed by later sociological studies of media consumption which demonstrated that people tended to filter or screen political messages they were not receptive to (*Seymour-Ure 1974*).

Sectoral voting

In a radical model of voting behaviour, *Dunleavy (1979)* explained voter preference by sectoral analysis. The Conservative electorate inhabited the **private** sector and the Labour electorate the **public**. Access to and consumption of education, transport,

66 Public–private split 99

housing and employment varied from one sector to the other. The public utilised state provision of services; the private supplied their own. These were the conditioning factors in electoral choice. They conveniently fit the Conservative ideology of **individualism** and the Labour ideology of **collectivism**. This view is similar to the consumer model of voting and brings together the other variables of class and locality but that does not detract from its importance.

THE 1992 GENERAL ELECTION

The 1992 general election results are important to psephologists for a number of reasons. Although the Conservatives won the election with a slightly smaller vote than in 1987, Labour appeared to regain support in the skilled 'new working class' category making predictions for the next general election more difficult (see Figure 11.4).

	Total number of votes	MPs elected	Share of UK vote (%)
Conservative	14,049,508	336	41.8
Labour	11,557,134	271	34.4
Liberal Democrat	5,998,446	20	17.8
Welsh/Scottish Nationalist	786,348	7	2.3
Others	433,870	0	1.3
Northern Ireland parties	785,093	17	2.3

Fig.11.4 The 1992 general election result

Initial reactions to the **fourth consecutive** Conservative win were mixed. *Rose (1992)* claimed that the Labour Party had suffered a shattering defeat when all the ingredients for a Labour win were present. The government were unpopular, the economy was in recession and the Labour Party were united. *Crewe (1992)*, though less pessimistic for Labour electoral prospects, also claimed the result as a devastating setback for the Labour Party. Although they **regained** a percentage of the working class vote, the evidence of class dealignment was still present and public perceptions of Labour were still unfavourable. In terms of **economic** credibility the Conservatives received most support from those who felt the Labour Party would make them worse off.

66 Labour gains 99

A different view of the 1992 general election result was taken by *Heath, Jowell and Curtice (1994)*. They extrapolated the factors working against a Labour victory and concluded their effects had been exaggerated. The following were the main features re-examined:

- Conservative bias in the press;
- Labour taxation proposals;
- popular capitalism;
- social class changes;
- Labour leadership.

66 Problems for the Conservatives 99

Their general findings were that in each of these categories Labour could improve its performance and seriously threaten the Conservative Party in the future. Only a **one per cent swing** from 1992 towards the Labour Party could deny the Conservatives an overall majority at the next election.

Changes in the electorate's perception of the Labour Party were also evident. The electorate had moved **ideologically towards** Labour on some issues (increased spending on the welfare state was one example) and a substantial proportion considered the party more moderate than before. If Labour could broaden its appeal, it stood a chance of being re-elected. The events of 1995 and 1996 and Tony Blair's attempts to repackage 'New Labour' for the middle classes can be seen against this background.

EXAMINATION QUESTIONS

1 Have issues become the dominant factor in determining voting behaviour? *(25)*
(UODLE)

2 a) What are floating voters? *(5)*
   b) Why are floating voters important, and how do the political parties
      attempt to attract their support? *(20)*
(NEAB)

3 What implications are there for the Labour Party in recent trends in voting
behaviour? *(25)*
(UODLE)

4 Was the outcome of the 1992 general election conditioned by long
term structural change in society, or was it the result of short
term factors? *(25)*
(ULEAC)

ANSWERS TO EXAMINATION QUESTIONS

OUTLINE ANSWERS

Question 2

The following points could be included in an answer.

a) 1 Define floating – uncommitted voters.
   2 Look at their characteristics, explain why they float. Give reasons – volatility, apathy, disenchantment with government, policy appeal of other parties.
   3 Most do not float between Conservative and Labour parties. Give reasons.
b) 1 Explain why they are important, provide the key to winning elections.
   2 Link with the idea of growing volatility in electorate, so becoming more numerous.
   3 Examine issues that cause voters to switch allegiance.
   4 Distinguish between long and short term factors affecting the vote.
   5 Describe Labour Party attempts to broaden appeal away from working class traditional support towards middle class.
   6 Look at Conservative government's 'feel good' factors and policies designed to attract and keep working class votes.

Question 3

This question is asking for an evaluation of the prospects for the Labour Party in future elections, based on its poor performance in the eighties and nineties. The answer could balance the work of *Crewe* on dealignment against the critical opinions of *Heath, Jowell and Curtice*, in the following form:

1 Examine the long term trends of dealignment and its consequences for Labour.
2 Discuss *Crewe's* earlier work and his conclusions on class fragmentation. Relate these ideas of the New Working Class to Labour support.
3 Comment on changes in the middle class vote (the salariat) and its implications for Labour (*Wright*).
4 Discuss *Rose's* and *Crewe's* conclusions on the outcome of the 1992 general election.
5 Balance the ideas above with the work of *Heath, Jowell and Curtice*.
6 Make some evaluation of the consequences for Labour.

TUTOR'S ANSWER TO QUESTION 4

The 1992 general election resulted in a fourth consecutive win for the Conservative Party. Although John Major's majority was smaller than those achieved by Margaret Thatcher, it did represent a significant result when all the ingredients for a Labour victory were in place (*Rose*). Long term social class and other changes are partially held responsible for this result, but they cannot be separated from short term factors like issue voting. It is possible that electoral shifts of opinion favoured the ideas of Conservatism throughout the eighties and that the nineties will see a return of a Labour government. In their study of voting trends in the 1992 general election, *Heath, Jowell and Curtice* found an ideological movement back to the left.

The Conservative Party won the 1992 general election on a 41.8 per cent share of the UK vote compared to a 34.4 per cent share of the vote for the Labour Party. This was a better result for the Labour Party than in the 1987 general election, with 271 MPs elected against the Conservative Party's 336. Analysis of the vote showed that Labour was successful in attracting back the new working class vote previously lost to Margaret Thatcher's radical brand of Conservatism. In the C2 skilled working class voter category the Conservatives polled 40 per cent in 1987 against Labour's 36 per cent. In 1992 these figures were reversed with 41 per cent going to Labour and 36 per cent to the Conservative Party.

The return of a proportion of the New Working Class vote to Labour in 1992 raises an immediate problem of analysis. If, as *Crewe* claimed, the emergence of this class represented a long term structural change which would damage Labour Party electoral prospects, the implication is of a class change or permanent dealignment. The Labour Party was still working class but the working class were no longer Labour. Clearly the 1992 result showed how short term factors overlaid the long term. The new working class also voted Conservative in 1983 and 1987 for short term policy or judgemental reasons. Popular capitalism (the sale of council housing and shares in privatised state industries) is generally thought to have been instrumental in attracting the working class vote. Conversely, the recession in the economy in the early nineties heavily affected this group in terms of unemployment and housing difficulties and this had a beneficial effect on the Labour vote in 1992.

Long term economic decline in the North of England, Wales and Scotland had helped the Labour vote (*Johnson and Pattie*) just as the expansion in home ownership appeared to help the Conservative vote. Population shifts had also produced a North/South electoral effect closely supported by neighbourhood voting, both of which fall into the structural change category. According to *Denver*, the community in which a person lives has a conditioning effect on outlooks and an impact on the vote. Working class areas tend to support the Labour Party; middle class neighbourhoods are predominantly Conservative.

The traditional patterns of voting behaviour to the 1970s were of class alignment linked to a two party system, with the Conservative and Labour Parties attracting up to 90 per cent of the popular vote. Long term social factors were said to condition voting with the emphasis on class attachment to the major parties. The working class were solidly Labour and the middle class Conservative. There had always been cross class voting with middle class socialists and working class Tories preventing a true class electoral split. *Crewe's* research into these social class changes and the vote identified dealignment as a major feature of the eighties; the question was whether these were new developments. *Heath, Jowell and Curtice* did not see dealignment as a dramatic break with class traditional voting; to them it represented a trendless fluctuation that was continuing.

Many short term political factors impact on the vote and could be said to have been influential in the 1992 general election. Political perceptions of competence to govern are an important measure of the trust of the electorate and a crucial influence on the vote (*Heath, Jowell and Curtice*). Although the Labour Party lead the Conservatives on welfare issues, it lagged behind on the crucial aspect of economic management. Attitudes and values can be deeply held and contribute to perceptions of the political parties. A substantial proportion of the electorate in 1992 remembered the economic failures of the Labour governments of Harold Wilson and James Callaghan (the Winter of Discontent). Although they did not feel well off in 1992 and the Thatcher 'feel good' factor was absent, the electorate were not prepared to trust the Labour Party with taxation and interest rates (*Sanders 1993*).

Actual election campaigns do not have much of an impact on electoral choice except on floating or undecided voters. Obviously increased voter volatility has meant more votes are 'up for grabs' by the respective parties. In the 1992 campaign a considerable amount of vote switching or 'churning' of the vote took place. But according to *David Denver* the main beneficiaries were the Liberal Democrats, for it is unusual for voters to move directly between the Conservative and Labour Parties. It has been estimated that during the 1992 campaign the Conservatives successfully attracted an extra 3.2 million voters against a loss of 1.81 million.

The Conservative handling of issues during the campaign was more successful than Labour. Although the Labour Party managed to move their winning issues up the political agenda (health, education, social services), they offered contradictory messages to the electorate. For example, the 'War of Jennifer's Ear' – a Labour political broadcast television programme attacking Conservative health policy – failed to achieve its objective, reflecting badly on the party. Neil Kinnock's public image was unattractive to many voters according to opinion polls, although *Heath, Jowell and Curtice* demonstrated that tabloid newspaper bias against the Labour leader was not a major influence with working class voters.

Finally, it is difficult to unpick long term social factors (class, socialisation, age, gender, ethnicity) from short term factors (issues, opinions, party image) in the complex mix of attitudes and values behind electoral choice. Pessimists claim to detect a long term decline in Labour Party support based on irreversible trends (*Richard Rose*). Optimists feel that long term social and structural factors are more evenly balanced between three parties – Conservative, Labour and Liberal Democrat – and that we may be witnessing a realignment in electoral behaviour.

STUDENT'S ANSWER TO QUESTION 1 WITH EXAMINER'S COMMENTS

❝❞ Could be a more precise opening

❝❞ Correctly stated

❝❞ Good reference to Crewe

❝❞ This is accurate but needs elaboration

There are many factors which influence voting behaviour, such as class, age, sex, tactical voting and issues. Often the most dominant factor of these influences changes depending on the general election.

Up until the mid 1960s the most important factor influencing voting behaviour was class. Where the increasing majority in each class voted for the party best suited and aligned to their class, so the majority of the working class voted Labour and the middle and upper class voted Conservative.

After the 1960s and especially in the 1980s, *Ivor Crewe* noticed that class alignment was losing its importance in voting behaviour as class dealignment was taking place. This was most evident in two areas. The first area was in the working class, where an increasing number were voting Conservative along the lines of non manual workers. The other group, who are not as significant as the working class Conservatives, are the middle classes who vote Labour.

There are many reasons why these two groups are dealigned. The working class Conservatives, or C2s, vote this way for a number of reasons. The majority own property (from the sale of council houses), have a car and work in non manual jobs. This has given them a new set of values and status which fit in with Conservative ideology.

On the other hand, the middle class Labour supporters, who are not such a dominant force, vote Labour often on principle. They are mainly employees in the public sector, such as teachers, civil servants and public officials. The reason for this group voting Labour is self interest – they are usually better off under a Labour government (higher wages and more resources).

Factors other than class voting are age, sex and geo-

66 Why not develop these factors 99

66 More evidence needed here 99

66 Give the 1992 election more treatment 99

graphical location. Age and sex are not a dominant force in voting behaviour as they are influenced by family background.

Geographical location may be considered a major influence as elections keep showing the North predominantly votes Labour and the South Conservative. The explanation for this connection is found in employment, the North is linked to the declining industrial working class and the South to commercial and non manual occupations.

Other factors such as issues have now become important in voting behaviour. Television is more informative on the issues of the parties so the electorate are better informed and able to make judgements. With class dealignment, the C2s and the socialist middle class are voting with the parties they value.

Issues have become a dominant force in influencing the vote but people are not rational and sometimes support parties not suited to their interests. For example, in the 1992 general election the Labour Party won on a majority of the issues, but failed to gain power. This demonstrates that although issues are important, they have not completely replaced the class influence in voting behaviour.

66 This essay is a good attempt at describing the important features in voting behaviour. Unfortunately the analytical skills are weak, there is no real discussion of the complex nature of dealignment and how it relates to issues. Within the D grade band. 99

REFERENCES IN THE TEXT

Butler, D and R Rose 1960 *The British general election of 1959*, Ilford: Frank Cass

Butler, D and D Stokes 1974 *Political change in Britain*, London: Macmillan

Crewe, I 1985a Great Britain. In I Crewe and D Denver (eds) *Electoral change in Western democracies*, London: Croom Helm

Crewe, I 1985b Can Labour rise again, *Social Studies Review* **1**

Crewe, I 1987 Why Mrs Thatcher was returned with a landslide, *Social Studies Review* September

Crewe, I 1992 Why did Labour lose (yet again)? *Politics Review* September

Crewe, I 1993 Voting and the electorate. In P Dunleavy, A Gamble, I Holliday and G Peele (eds) *Developments in British politics*, London: Macmillan

Denver, D 1993 Elections and voting behaviour. In W Wale (ed.) *Developments in Politics*, **4**, Ormskirk: Causeway Press

Dunleavy, P 1979 The urban basis of political alignment, *British Journal of Political Science* **9**

Dunleavy, P and C Husbands 1985 *British Democracy at the Crossroads*, London: Allen & Unwin

Heath, A, R Jowell and J Curtice 1985 *How Britain votes*, Oxford: Pergamon Press

Heath, A, R Jowell and J Curtice 1987 Trendless fluctuation: a reply to Crewe, *Political Studies* **35**

Heath, A, R Jowell and J Curtice (eds) 1994 *Labour's last chance?* Aldershot: Dartmouth Press

Himmelweit, H, P Humphreys and M Jaeger 1985 *How voters decide*. Buckingham: Open University Press

Jessop, B 1974 *Traditionalism, Conservatism and British Political Culture*, London: Allen & Unwin

Johnson, R and C Pattie 1992 The changing electoral geography of Great Britain. In D Denver and G Hands (eds) *Issues and Controversies in British Electoral Behaviour*, Hemel Hempstead: Harvester Wheatsheaf

Kavanagh, D 1990 *British politics*, Oxford University Press

Layton-Henry, Z 1992 Immigration and race politics in post war Britain, Oxford: Blackwell

McKenzie, R and A Silver 1968 *Angels in marble*, Oxford: Heinemann

Parkin, F 1968 *Middle-class radicalism*, Manchester University Press

Rose, R and I McAllister 1990 *The loyalties of voters*, London: Sage

Rose, R 1992 Long term structural change or cyclical fluctuations? The 1992 election in dynamic perspective, *Parliamentary Affairs* October

Sanders, D 1993. In A King, I Crewe, D Denver, K Newton, P Norton, D Sanders and P Seyd *Britain at the polls 1992*, Roundhouse Pubs Ltd

Sarlvik, B and I Crewe 1983 *Decade of dealignment*, Cambridge University Press

Seymour-Ure, C 1974 *The political impact of the mass media*, London: Constable

Trenaman, J and D McQuail 1961 *Television and the political image*, London: Methuen

Wright, E O 1976 Class boundaries in advanced capitalist societies, *New Left Review* **98**

LOCAL GOVERNMENT

STRUCTURES

MANAGING LOCAL AUTHORITIES

DEMOCRACY IN LOCAL GOVERNMENT

CENTRAL–LOCAL RELATIONS

THE FUTURE

GETTING STARTED

The study of local government (traditionally from a public administration perspective) is now over-complex because of the numerous structural reforms that have been implemented in the last decade. The effect of these reforms arising out of the Conservative government's review of local government which ended in 1995 will continue to be felt throughout the late 1990s. Substantial changes have also been introduced into the traditional central–local relationship (now moving back to an agency model) and in the ethos of local government as a provider of the sub-national services to local populations. In keeping with Conservative market thinking, the attempt (as with the civil service) has been to move local authorities towards enabling arrangements whereby they control services bought in from private contractors.

Questions on local government fall into the following areas:

- Local government structures against the background of Conservative reforms.
- The importance of local democracy and participation for the survival of local government.
- Changes in the constitutional position of local government due to adjustments in the central–local relationship.
- Reinterpretation of the role of local government.
- Internal management including relations between councillors and officers.

ESSENTIAL PRINCIPLES

STRUCTURES

⁶⁶ Different tiers ⁹⁹

The structure of local government in England and Wales at the beginning of 1996 was still essentially a **two tier** system based on counties (the top tier) and districts (the lower tier). This broad division between two levels of local authority was an historical survival pre-dating the **1972 Local Government Act**, the first serious attempt to reform the structure. This Act was in turn partially based on the proposals contained in the Redcliffe–Maud Report of 1968.

THE REDCLIFFE–MAUD REPORT 1968

Set up by the Labour government of Harold Wilson in 1966, the Redcliffe–Maud Commission was charged with examining the structure of local government with a view to making recommendations for its improvement. It was highly critical of the structures prevailing at that time, particularly:

1 **Boundaries**   Local government areas did not fit the pattern of life and work in modern Britain.

2 **Division of responsibilities**   The existing split in the delivery of services between local authorities led to fragmentation and division of responsibility which in turn made proper strategic planning impossible and uneconomic.

3 **Population and resources**   There was great disparity between population and resources. Some authorities served populations of 50,000, others up to 1 million. Functions were allocated along lines that made little administrative sense.

4 **Size**   Many local authorities were too small to function efficiently lacking qualified staffs and resources.

5 **Local democracy and relations with central government**   Possibly the most important findings of the Maud Commission (which would have far reaching effects with the Conservative governments of the eighties) were the criticisms relating to local democracy and central–local relationships. The effects of the **structural defects** existing in local government were:

■ The public perceived local government as irrelevant, with a consequent increase in apathy.

■ Central government ministers were reluctant to expand the powers of existing local authorities because of the inefficiencies in the system.

THE TWO-TIER SYSTEM OF LOCAL GOVERNMENT

⁶⁶ Types of authority ⁹⁹

Maud wanted to see a reduction in the 1,200 local authorities in England and Wales, which would be replaced by 61 large **unitary authorities** responsible for all services. In addition to this single tier system, recommendations were made for the establishment of eight **provincial councils** based on provinces of equal size. These were generally seen as a step towards regional government and possibly the beginning of a devolved system of power. These last proposals (the most radical) were not acted upon, implementation being left to the Conservative government of Edward Heath 1970–74. This government decided to implement a two tier system based on counties and districts, further subdivided between metropolitan and non-metropolitan areas. The **1972 Local Government Act** introduced 47 shire counties and six metropolitan counties providing major services, together with 333 rural (shire) districts and 34 metropolitan districts in England and Wales. London was separately organised from 1963 (London Government Act) into 33 borough councils and a Greater London Council.) This system was further modified with the passing of the **1985 Local Government Act** which removed the Greater London Council and the metropolitan counties on the grounds of inefficiency (see Figure 12.1). The removal of the Labour dominated Greater London Council and metropolitan counties paved the way for the introduction of a single tier system providing all local authority services, which would become more influential into the nineties.

Source: The Association of County Councils

	FIRST TIER MAIN AUTHORITY Major services	SECOND TIER LOWER AUTHORITY Local services
47 Shire councils	✓	
333 Rural shire districts		✓
36 Metropolitan districts	✓	
33 London boroughs	✓	

Fig. 12.1 The structure of local government 1985–95 (England and Wales)

Problems in the two-tier system

The changes introduced into the local government structure by the 1985 Local Government Act did not remove the problems which were inherent in the system. Although the functions of the Greater London Council and metropolitan counties were transferred to what in effect was a unitary (single) tier in those areas – and to separate agencies or boards (*Stewart 1995*) – the rest of the country was still administered locally through a complex mix of county, district and parish councils. For a variety of reasons (political and administrative) the central Conservative government were by 1992 anxious to move to a single tier system (paradoxically rejected in 1972 by the same party) which would prove easier to control. Critics pointed to a number of remaining problems in the structure:

❝ Complexity ❞

- From the perspective of local democracy (understanding local politics) the system was confusing.

- The provision of major services (education, housing, social services) from two levels of local authority made unnecessary fragmentations in what ought to be a 'seamless robe' or blanket covering the populace.

- Resources in terms of personnel and administration were partially duplicated by separate county and district councils serving the same area.

Politically, the Conservative government were anxious to see greater financial controls placed over local councils, and the removal of Labour dominance in much of local government. The abolition of the Greater London Council and the six metropolitan councils was seen by some critics as an attempt to remove Labour Party influence (Labour was the dominant party in those authorities) in what became oppositional authorities promoting **municipal socialism**. A further final change was the more radical attempt made to alter the culture of local government by the introduction of private business methods and outside contracting – in effect moving local authorities to **enabling** rather than **providing** authorities (*Isaac-Henry 1993*).

UNITARY STRUCTURES 1996

To move local authorities in the direction of a single unitary tier system, the Conservative central government passed the Local Government Act 1992 and introduced a complex two and a half year review of existing structures. A **Local Government Commission for England** was established (absorbing the old Local Government Boundary Commission for England) under the chairmanship of Sir John Banham, later replaced by Sir David Cooksey from 1995. The original recommendations of the commission were for the establishment of 50 new unitary authorities (providing all services) with the dismantling of only seven out of 39 shire counties (see Figure 12.2). By leaving the existing two tier county and district structures intact for the majority of the population the commission was creating a new **three tier** system across England and Wales but 'never in one area' (*Duvall 1995*).

REVIEW OF UNITARY STRUCTURES

66 Reasons for change 99

Bowing to pressure from shire county representatives and other groups, central government agreed in March 1995 to reopen the whole question of the future of county councils threatened with abolition. In the review consultation process to December 1995 the Secretary of State for the Environment, John Gummer, examined unitary plans for all the 39 English counties and agreed that with the exception of **Avon, Cleveland and Humberside** all other county councils would remain, even if in an altered format. In some counties large towns or districts were naturally hived off to form their own unitary authority, as with Milton Keynes' removal from Buckinghamshire. Both Buckinghamshire and Bedfordshire demonstrated that resourceful counties had influence with the Secretary of State by successfully removing the threat of abolition. Buckinghamshire (the last Conservative controlled county council in England and Wales at the 1993 council elections) had the support of former Cabinet Ministers Lord Carrington and Sir Ian Gilmour, and Bedfordshire was supported by Lord Pym with private backbench lobbying in both counties (*Arnold-Forster 1995*).

Evaluation of the new system

Although it is early to comment on the new unitary authorities, the introduction of what in effect is a 'hybrid' system of local government (a mix of two tier and single tier) has had a mixed reception. The intention of central government was to produce smaller authorities with average populations of 150,000 to 250,000 with regard to **local interests** and **efficient local government**. Early indications were that smaller unitary authorities would be less likely to provide full services, although in the words of *Sir John Banham* (*1995*) larger authorities could 'take in each other's washing'. The Association of County Councils were critical of the costs of reorganisation and claimed that the hybrid system would be more expensive to run. In **Cleveland**, which was replaced in April 1996 by four successor unitaries (Hartlepool, Redcar and

Sources: Map of England Crown copyright – reproduced with the permission of the controller of HMSO. Map of Wales Crown copyright – reproduced with the permission of the Welsh Office

Fig. 12.2 The structure of local government from 1996 (England and Wales) and proposed structures from 1997

| | | FIRST TIER MAIN AUTHORITY | | SECOND TIER LOWER AUTHORITY |
		England	Wales	England
36	County (shire) councils	✓		
274	Rural (shire) districts			✓
14	Unitary authorities	✓		
22	Unitary authorities		✓	
36	Metropolitan districts	✓		
33	London boroughs	✓		

Cleveland, Middlesborough, and Stockton-on-Tees), four new Directors of Education and Directors of Social Services, to take one example, added 25 per cent to salary costs (*Association of County Councils Briefing 1995*).

❝ Critics of system ❞

In the strongest academic criticism of the new structure *John Stewart*, Professor of Local Government and Director of the Institute of Local Government Studies (Inlogov), University of Birmingham, and *George Jones*, Professor of Government at the London School of Economics (*1995*) claimed the new system was an unnecessary mess. In their eyes the Banham Commission decisions were hard to justify on the grounds of consistency.

THE COMMITTEE SYSTEM

The internal structures of local authorities bring together councillors (elected representatives) and officials (appointed professionals) in a policy making and management system. Policy decisions of councils are based on a committee system with full council meetings as the ultimate authority. Management matters do not usually occupy a great deal of councillors' time (*Young and Rao 1993*). In practice (and this pattern has hardly changed) meetings of a full council handle reports or minutes from the various committees and sub-committees. Some are accepted with little debate; others arouse party political controversy and are returned to committees or sub-committees for amendment. Eventually policy making votes are taken in full council which is dominated by the ruling political party – the one with most councillors.

66 Policy making 99

Policy making and committees

Although councils have a free hand in the structures of their committee systems, they generally reflect the departmental nature in the organisation of council work (*Hutt 1990*). Chief officers (responsible for the management and implementation of policy in their departments) report upwards to their respective committees and sub-committees, which make recommendations to a Policy and Resources Committee (since 1972) before final policy recommendations to the full council. As with central government bureaucracy, departmental rivalry (**departmentalism**) pervades this structure as officers seek to advance the interests of their departments over others. Coordination of these disparate committees is also a problem as councils seek to establish a **corporate identity**. Two reports drew attention to these problems:

- **The Maud Management Report 1967** The Maud Committee on Management in Local Government Report (1967) made radical suggestions to overcome problems of coordination and policy making. Its main recommendations were:

  1 reductions in the number of committees to improve efficiency;

  2 establishment of a Management Board to assist coordination;

  3 clear separation of the respective duties of elected councillors and appointed officers.

  Although these proposals were not generally acted upon, they paved the way for the adoption of better management practices in local authorities after the publication of the Bains Report.

- **The Bains Report (1972)** The Bains Committee were expressly tasked with finding better management structures for the reformed two tier system of local government introduced by the 1972 Local Government Act. The report's main recommendations (1972) were for the creation of a **Policy and Resources Committee** interposed between the various council committees and full council meetings. In addition a **chief executive** position would be created, responsible for a senior management team following a corporate management policy. Today this procedure is the general pattern of management followed in most local authorities (see Figure 12.3).

COUNCILLOR–OFFICER RELATIONSHIPS

66 Orthodox position 99

Apart from a central government input policy making in local government reflects a compromise between councillors and their officials. The **orthodox view** of the relationship between elected councillors and paid officials is that policy making (or the political role) rests with councillors and the administrative role with officials. Yet policy and administration (as with central government) is very closely connected. Council staffs are **professionals**; councillors are **amateur**. Departmental senior staff advise council and are bound to influence decisions.

Policy identification

If policy making in local government jointly involves both councillors and officers (the Bains Committee felt it should), then officials can be publicly identified with council politics. Alternatively, it could be argued that officials and councillors formed an **elite**

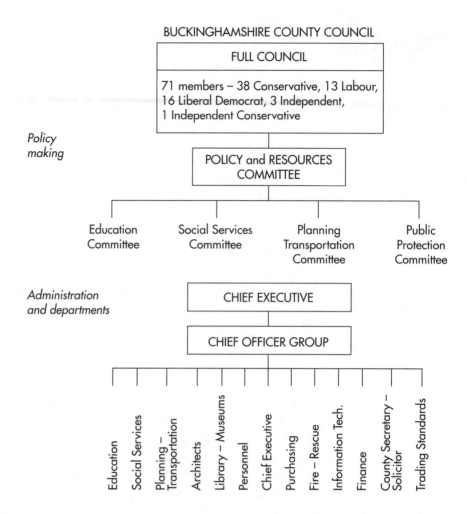

Fig. 12.3 The committee and departmental structures of Buckinghamshire county council at January 1996

governing in their own interests (*Stoker 1991*). This view is in turn countered by the idea of competing centres of power (**pluralism**) within the administrative and policy structures of local authorities. On this level there are too many other interests to be dominated by a single elite.

Policy disputes

The emphasis on management and policy implementation in local councils has produced a breakdown in some councils of the traditional trust between officers and councillors (**mutuality**). This was first noticed during the governments of Margaret Thatcher 1979–1990 as 'conviction' Conservatives entered local councils determined to implement central philosophies. Urban socialists, for their part, were determined to oppose central government policies also (*Gyford 1985*). *Laffin and Young* (*1990*) first pointed to the difficulties faced by councillors required to implement policies of which they personally disapproved.

❝ Urban socialists ❞

Increasingly, radical politicians of both Conservative and Labour persuasion have taken a greater interest in the implementation of policy in addition to its initiation. **Partisan conduct** is said to reach considerable numbers of councillors as they place party interests above representational work. This manifests itself in the attendance of officials at party group meetings and the acceptance of councillor participation in the management practices of local councils (*Young and Davies 1990*). This is a continuing problem in local government organisation to which both councillors and officers have had to adapt.

DEMOCRACY IN LOCAL GOVERNMENT

The local democracy argument has always featured in defences of the system of local government in England and Wales. Local councils and councillors as elected representatives are seen as an essential part of the democratic process, even if interest in their work is low by international standards. The Banham Committee Report (1994) emphasised the importance of local democracy in the drive to smaller unitary authorities, but did not tackle the question of the British electoral system which is held by some as partially responsible for local apathy (*Rallings and Thrasher 1994*). Equally, there is said to be no absolute correlation between the size of a local authority and increased interest in local affairs (*Newton 1982*).

PARTICIPATION

The generally held belief is that local government should be accessible and close to the people it serves. If people are to be encouraged to **participate**, local government boundaries should reflect local community feelings. Part of the reason why counties like Humberside have disappeared in the Banham Review (the Local Government Commission for England was directed by government to consult all the people in the affected counties) is presumably because local opinion sought the removal of a remote (and unnecessary) authority created in 1972. The people of Kingston upon Hull, the East Riding of Yorkshire, North Lincolnshire and North East Lincolnshire – from 1996 recreated as four unitary councils – never lost their attachment and feelings of identity with the smaller units.

Developing the ideas of attachment to localities, *Gyford (1991)* draws attention to three dimensions of local involvement:

1 **Participative** – the involvement of the local electorate in council decisions.

2 **Consultative** – where local authorities make an effort to establish what local people want.

3 **Informative** – a relationship where local councils endeavour to keep their citizens informed of local services in the most convenient ways possible.

POLITICAL IMPACTS

Local government is now totally dominated by national politics. There clearly is a Conservative, Labour or Liberal Democratic way of running councils (**politicisation**) and local electorates' perceptions of councillor value have been taken over by national political concepts (**nationalisation**). It is difficult to put a precise date on these developments; *Gyford, Leach and Game (1989)* have tracked national party political involvement in local councils and demonstrated how the national Conservative and Labour Parties came to dominate local politics after 1945. Some consequences of this are:

66 Politics in local councils 99

- **Many councillors** are returned unopposed in local elections. (All councillors serve four year terms. County councils have whole elections; districts elect by thirds).

- **Local apathy** is strong – the Widdicombe Report (1986) found turnout in British local elections at between 20 per cent and 60 per cent at the bottom end of international league tables.

- **Local voting** behaviour focuses more on national issues than local, although there is contradictory evidence for this.

The arguments

The arguments against party politics in local government now seem dated if only because of the activities of radical right and left councils since the eighties. The dependence on party labels for electoral success discourages those not standing on a party ticket. The quality of candidates for local office may be lessened by this reduction of recruitment area. The relational problem concerns the conduct of council business. The argument that party political considerations should not be allowed to affect administrative detail is clearly over. With the changing cultures of councils, the impact of the current unitary reforms and development of the 'enabling' concept, the debate has moved on. Now the **positive attributes** of party involvement in council business (defining local issues clearly for the electorate, greater participation through encouragement to get involved, the advantage of party discipline giving coherence to the programme) are joined in structural debate over a **revival or decay** of local government and what 'business' it is in (*Isaac-Henry 1993*).

CENTRAL–LOCAL RELATIONS

❝ Balance ❞

THE CONSTITUTIONAL POSITION

Local government is a form of **self-government** in the sense that local authorities are given considerable independence from the centre. Relationships between these two levels of government (both impacting on the citizen) traditionally involved a delicate balance between control and independence; partnership and separation. Controls fall into three areas – **parliamentary, executive** and **judicial** – although local authorities do not have three sets of controllers.

Parliamentary control

The powers of local authorities are conferred by parliamentary statutes emanating from central government. Councils therefore work within the broad general framework of central government policy. They do not legislate except in the sense of local by-laws which are also subject to executive controls.

Executive control

Executive or administrative control over local government is substantial and covers all the activities of council work. The following are the more important:

1 **Controls over service provision** to maintain standards in, for example, education, child protection and social services. This embraces reserve or **default power** to supply services if local councils refuse and includes an **inspection power** over education and children's services.

2 **Control over local government officials**   Under the Local Government Act 1972 central government laid a broad duty over local councils to employ certain officials including Chief Education Officers and Directors of Social Services. Some of these appointments have detailed ministerial control over the types of people that can be employed. The Department of Social Security approves the qualifications of Directors of Social Services and the Home Secretary approved the appointment of Chief Constables when police authorities were under the control of local government. (They are now run as separate autonomous combined authorities.)

3 **Ministerial approval**   Local authorities require ministerial approval for a long list of functions including development planning, compulsory purchase orders and settlement of disputes between individuals and councils.

4 **Financial control**   The financial controls over local government are now quite significant and include expenditure capping, council tax regulations and standard spending assessments, all designed to bring council tax spending within central government plans for public expenditure. In addition, control over spending and value for money is examined by the Audit Commission established by the Local Government Finance Act 1984 to replace the traditional district auditor system.

Judicial control

Judicial control over local government is not as significant as in the early nineteenth century because of the development of central control. The courts can rule local authority power as being beyond its statutory remit or *'ultra vires'*. In 1981 the courts rejected the GLC's arguments for subsidising public transport in the 'Fares Fair' case. They can also decide whether matters are within the competence of a local authority.

THE THEORETICAL POSITION

❝ Local versus central ❞

As the functions of local government have changed, so the traditional relationship between the centre and localities has had to adapt. Under a unitary form of central government, local authorities cannot be completely independent units administering services irrespective of the policy dictates of the majority party in government. On the other hand, local government enshrines important principles of local democracy and does not simply act as an agent of central government. These various positions find expression in theoretical models that place a differing emphasis on local power (**localism**) in its relationship to central authority (**centralism**). We can identify four models in the theory of the central–local relationship.

1 **Oppositional view** Many councils (mainly, but not entirely, Labour led) saw the growth of central government powers over local government as reducing local autonomy, particularly in the fields of education and social service provision. This attitude produced a deterioration in the relationship between the Department of the Environment and many councils. In April 1995 some councils were prepared to set illegal budgets because central government refused to finance in full the teachers' pay settlement that year. Councils were told to make administrative cost savings to find the money.

2 **Partnership View** The traditional picture of central–local relations is as a partnership with each side bringing different skills to the table. The Redcliffe–Maud Report of 1968 clearly defined central government responsibilities as focusing on provision of a standardised service, or where decisions could only be taken at the national level. Local government was best suited to provide services (like education) where the level of local opinion was important even if this should be done within a framework of national policy making.

3 **Power–dependence view** This position tends to focus on the central–local relationship as one of consultation. Each level of government has its own power base which it can use in negotiation with the other side. Central government is not all powerful and local government is not powerless; they are mutually dependent on each other. A good example of this relationship is provided by the annual meetings of the Consultative Council on Local Government Finance (first established by the Labour government of 1975) which brings together the Secretary of State for the Environment and leaders of the counties, districts and metropolitan authorities in discussions of future council spending settlements.

4 **Agency view** Despite the above comments some writers feel that central–local relations today are characterised by an agency relationship where local authorities carry out functions entirely controlled and financed by central government (*Isaac-Henry 1993*). Since the election of a Conservative government in 1979 the trend for local government to act as an agent of central government has become more marked, particularly in the areas of finance, functions and roles.

   ■ **Finance** Central government controls over finance have increased with the replacement of the community charge by the **council tax** in 1993. **Standard spending assessments** (SSAs) have been introduced as the basis for the calculation of local authority grants. Finally, **capping** (since 1991) has been used to restrict the amount local councils can raise by the council tax. These three features – plus the activity of the Audit Commission – are devices now restraining local government finance and overspending.

   ■ **Functions** Possibly the biggest single change affecting the function of local councils was the introduction of market forces techniques into the supply of services. The free market was seen as the most efficient way of serving the customer. The 1988 Local Government Act introduced the practice of **compulsory competitive tendering** (CCT) which places a duty on local councils to allow outside contractors (in some cases council direct labour organisations can be considered) to bid for the provision of services in a competitive manner. Here the intention was to achieve two things: a) drive down council costs by purchasing the cheapest service and b) treat the elector as a consumer buying services that provided the best value for money.

   ■ **Role** The overall role of local government has been reduced under the Conservative governments of Margaret Thatcher and John Major. Where services could not be contracted out, as with education, social services and housing, attempts have been made to break up the bureaucratic nature of local authority provision. Local government monopoly in educational provision has been broken into by the introduction of local management of schools allowing direct control over budgets and by opt-outs (grant maintained schools) allowing independence from local government control. The effects of this one change have forced some councils to drastically reduce their headquarters educational staffs as services have been amalgamated. The 1988 Housing Act further reduced local government freedom in council housing adding to the right to buy scheme allowing tenants to purchase local authority housing. This Act specifically introduced the idea for the first time that local authorities should be enablers of housing rather than providers by allowing private sector landlord competition into the municipal housing market (*Gray and Jenkins 1994*).

THE FUTURE

❝ Enabling concept ❞

It is difficult to predict the end result of the changes now taking place in local government. The Labour Party appear committed to a form of unitary local government plus a system of directly elected regional assemblies. The Conservative government reforms have their critics and supporters. Those who support the enabling concept and private sector methods of delivering services generally point to a revival in the fortunes of local government. Better management practices and improved procedures are said to be leading to lower costs and less bureaucratic waste with attendant prospects for customer care. Pessimists opposed to recent structural and organisational reforms feel there is little to be gained and much to be lost by moving to unitaries. There is said to be less accountability than before as appointed quangos (boards, trusts and authorities) take over many of the traditional functions of local authorities, thus reducing their significance in public life.

EXAMINATION QUESTIONS

1 Evaluate the arguments for and against a unitary system of local government throughout England and Wales. *(25)*
(NEAB)

2 Why is local government so continuously being reformed? *(25)*
(UODLE)

3 'Local authorities are undergoing a fundamental transformation from being the main providers of services to having responsibility for enabling their provision.' Explain and discuss this view of contemporary local government. *(25)*
(NEAB)

ANSWERS TO EXAMINATION QUESTIONS

OUTLINE ANSWER TO QUESTION 3

This question requires an understanding of the broad philosophical reasons why the Conservative governments of Margaret Thatcher and John Major changed the 'service' ethos in local government. Points that could be included in an answer are:

1 Show how Margaret Thatcher and Nicholas Ridley developed the enabling concept.

2 Examine the response made by the Conservative governments to Labour controlled oppositional councils. Link this to the drive to efficiency and removal of functions of local government.

3 Explain how the process of enabling authority works. Discuss the removal of service functions (housing, education) reducing the traditional provider role of local government.

4 Focus on compulsory competitive tendering and the marketisation of local government designed to open councils to market forces.

5 Make some evaluation for and against the enabling concept showing an understanding of Conservative thinking.

TUTOR'S ANSWER TO QUESTION 2

There has never been a time when local government has not been subject to some degree of change in the powers delegated to it, the structures within which it operates or the overall pattern of financing. From the nineteenth century to the present, local government has been subject to a bewildering series of changes which developed a subordinate system of government acting on the citizen at the local level. Central government concentrated on national administration and was content for most of the first half of this century to leave local decisions affecting people to locally elected councils to administer. Education, housing, environmental protection, social care and other immediate services were delivered by local governments to citizens within recognisable boundaries of counties or districts.

As population pressures on resources grew, so local councils became more dependent on central government grants to assist locally raised revenues (rates). Inevitably governments of both Labour and Conservative persuasions would have to tackle problems of resources, needs and structures against changes in consumption patterns, living and working arrangements. The first governments in the modern period to tackle these problems were the Labour governments of Harold Wilson in the 1960s.

The Wilson government of 1964–66 faced the problem of irrationality in the various structures of local government (counties, county boroughs, rural districts, urban districts) which had not been reformed structurally since its inception in the 1880s. By setting up the Redcliffe–Maud Commission (1966–69) Harold Wilson hoped to find a rational solution to the problem of duplication, confusion and inefficiency in the administration of local government services, caused by population changes, transportation developments and increasing demand. Although the government accepted Maud's recommendations for a single tier unitary system as the most efficient form possible (including the proposal for regional reorganisation), it was left to the incoming Edward Heath Conservative government of 1974 to implement any accepted changes.

The basic structure of a two tier system that is still in existence (in modified form) has its origins in the adaptations made by the Heath government to the Maud proposals of 1969. This government introduced the first major structural change to local government with the Local Government Act 1972 bringing in a two tier system based on counties and districts. London government had previously been reformed with the London Government Act 1963 setting up a Greater London Council and 32 London borough councils sharing services with education in the centre run by an Inner London Education Authority. These London councils (mainly Labour dominated) would be abolished in 1986 by another Conservative government following more right wing principles than those adopted by the Heath government.

Throughout the second Labour administration of Harold Wilson 1974–76 and that of James Callaghan 1976–79 relations between central and local government continued in the traditional partnership pattern with regular consultation between the two sides. For example, the Consultative Council on Local Government Finance was established in 1975 bringing together for the first time central government ministers in direct talks with local government representatives. However, by the end of this period the Labour government had begun to restrict local spending by reducing the levels of rate support grants from 1974. This in turn paved the way for the considerable changes that would be introduced by Margaret Thatcher and her radical reforming Conservative government.

The government of Margaret Thatcher (1979–90) adopted a radically different perspective to local government from their Labour predecessors. They had a mandate to overhaul the rates system of local finance and were also determined to continue the restrictions placed over local government spending in line with their general drive to restrict public expenditure. The rates as a form of local taxation badly in need of reform had been examined by the Layfield Committee in 1977 who suggested their replacement by a local income tax. This proposal was not acted upon – instead a community charge (or poll tax) was introduced in 1986. The object of this new charge was to spread the cost equally on all users of local government services in line with New Right Conservative thinking irrespective of incomes or situation.

Other changes introduced into the local government dimension by the Conservative government (it has been estimated that approximately 124 Acts of Parliament passed during the 1980s had some effect on local government) included the abolition of the Greater London Council and the metropolitan counties in 1986, in effect establishing single tier authorities in those areas. Although these councils did duplicate some of the work taken on by the lower tiers and were removed because they were seen as an unnecessary burden on local government finance, critics have linked this action to the philosophical position taken by Margaret Thatcher that these councils were oppositional to her overall policies because they were invariably controlled by the Labour Party. There is evidence to show that the GLC and metropolitan counties were led by new 'urban socialists' determined to use local government as a challenge to the dominance of a radical Conservative government at the centre. Some of the policies of these councils were therefore seen as extravagant and responsible for the high costs of running councils in those areas.

Following a radical programme of 'conviction' politics, Margaret Thatcher began the process of altering the role of local government away from provider to enabler of services within the passage of various Acts. The Local Government Planning and Land Act 1980 began the process of compulsory competitive tendering (CCT) and market testing, whereby local authorities were obliged to contract out certain services including highway repair, grounds maintenance, catering provision and cleaning services. From the early eighties council tenants were given the right to buy council houses and the Housing Act of 1988 reduced further the role of local government housing by encouraging the activities of Housing Action Trusts. The last major service of local government, education, was also radically altered by the Education Act 1989. Now schools were encouraged to operate in a market for services by being allowed to opt out of local authority control through local management, the ultimate intention being to secure the opting out of all schools from local authority control.

The Major government from 1990 further adapted and redefined many of the above changes impacting on local government. Possibly the most significant reform was the removal of the unpopular community charge in April 1993 and its replacement by a more acceptable council tax based on ability to pay. In addition, John Major continued with the capping arrangements introduced to control council spending together with standard spending assessments which restricted the level of grants paid by central government to the councils.

The final most recent reform introduced by the John Major government with implications through 1996 and 1997 was the passing of the Local Government Act 1992. This Act established the Local Government Commission for England under the chairmanship of Sir John Banham (Sir David Cooksey from 1995) charged with examining the existing shire county system of local government. Its main recommendation was the creation of 50 new unitary authorities but keeping the majority of existing counties. This 'hybrid' system has attracted its own critics who basically do not see how it solves the structural problems still remaining in local government. As the Banham Commission responded to local opinion by surveying all those affected, it cannot be charged with being unresponsive to the local democracy argument.

Local government has given the appearance of being continuously reformed throughout the eighties and nineties because Conservative governments have tackled long overdue problems in finance, structure and central–local relations. If a date had to be found when local government ceased to be purely 'administrative' and became 'political', one would choose 1979 with the election victory of Margaret Thatcher and her new brand of Conservatism. This government (for ideological reasons) was determined to change the face of local government from the traditional decentralised partnership arrangement towards centralised agency status. We do not know what will happen to this system under any future Labour government, but what local government needs is a period of consolidation to absorb the many changes of the last decades.

STUDENT'S ANSWER TO QUESTION 1 WITH EXAMINER'S COMMENTS

❝ Strong introduction ❞

```
The problem with any local authority reorganisation is
that it is a simple matter to work out in theory a pre-
ferred system, but in practice the implementation of such
a change on a working system of government is very diffi-
cult and, as it has been shown, throws the best intentions
into turmoil. The very involvement of a local authority in
a reorganisation distracts the authority from its core
business, costs time and money, and creates resentments.
```

It appears that one of the main debates of both the Maud Report and the 1995 Local Government Review is for or against a unitary system of local government.

This debate was in a lot of ways flawed from the outset because a system of local government that was truly unitary would be unworkable either because it was too small, or if it was larger too remote. There are always going to be differing levels, from parish and town councils to joint arrangements or regional authorities, involved in local government. If we take the unitary solution as being a system of local government when one authority has responsibility over a geographical area with layers below (smaller) having their budgets and responsibilities delegated, and layers above (larger) taking representatives from the unitary authority, then we have a more clear cut argument.

Good argument

The argument for or against unitary authority is often actually one of size. People argue that to be effective, a unitary authority must be large enough to make and implement strategic decisions and to raise a large enough budget to be *able* to implement them. This is usually thought to be at least 250,000 people and this would make them too remote to be truly local. It is usually then the logical step to say a lower tier is required and this becomes a two tier system, i.e. the unitary is not viable.

If the unitary authority is planned to be small enough for local accountability, it will still probably require parish councils beneath and more importantly, strategic joint working arrangements above. This size of unitary authority has less power and although perceived to be closer to the people, is less remote. In reality the councillors (elected members) would still represent their own local ward, as in the larger size unitaries, but the resulting council would have to have many joint arrangements to effectively deliver services such as special education, a comprehensive library service, waste management, highways transport and planning, *and* present an effective voice to the central government.

If you take on board the fact that a unitary system provides less duplication and at the correct size more effective delivery of service, then why has this system not been implemented? What are the arguments against?

Evidence of evaluation

Having two authorities working in the same area provides a system of checks and balances. The very conflict that occurs between such authorities, even if good natured, curbs the 'enthusiasm' of a headstrong or reckless authority. If a district council makes a planning decision that the county believes is unsound, it can comment in the first place and challenge the decision legally if required. The workload of the elected members is split, often with county members having meetings during the day and district having them in the evening, thus encompassing differing types of representatives. In a unitary authority the workload of the councillor, taking on all aspects of district and county work, combined with representing their division on parish councils, town councils and on joint or strategic committees, would increase dramatically and change the nature of the position fundamentally. The electorate, whilst feeling that an effectively sized unitary authority may be the ideal solution, probably would not be ready for full time, properly remunerated councillors.

> If all authorities were of a consistent make-up, it
> would enable local authorities as a whole to have a coor-
> dinated voice to central government and it is this fact
> that probably is the main reason why such a system will
> not be implemented in the near future.

  ❝❝ An enjoyable essay to read displaying a very detailed knowledge of the practical problems of reorganisation. There is little academic support for points made but the overall treatment is analytical. Characteristic of a grade B. ❞❞

REFERENCES IN THE TEXT

Arnold-Forster, J 1995 Two counties to be let off unitary hook, *Local Government Chronicle* 24 February

Association of County Councils (ACC) 1995 Briefing, September

Bains, M A 1972 *The new local authorities*, Norwich: HMSO

Banham, Sir J 1995 quoted in *The Times Educational Supplement*, 12 January

Duvall, J 1995 Author's interview with Jim Duvall, Public Affairs Manager, The Association of County Councils 29 November

Gray, A and B Jenkins 1994 Local government. In B Jones (ed.) *Politics UK* 2nd edn. Hemel Hempstead: Harvester Wheatsheaf

Gyford, J 1985 *The politics of local socialism*, London: Allen and Unwin

Gyford J 1991 *Citizens, consumers and councils: local government and the public*, London: Macmillan

Gyford, J, S Leach and C Game 1989 *The changing politics of local government*, London: Unwin and Hyman

Hutt, J 1990 *Opening the town hall door*, London: Bedford Square Press

Isaac-Henry, K 1993 Local government – revival or decay, *Politics Review* April

Jones, G and J Stewart 1995 Academics slam 'futile' review, *Local Government Review* **17** 16 January

Laffin, M and K Young 1990 *Professionalism in local government*, Harlow: Longman

Maud, J 1967 *Management of local government*, Norwich: HMSO.

Newton, K 1982 Is small really so beautiful? *Political Studies*

Rallings, C and M Thrasher 1994 Electoral accountability and local government, *Politics Review* February

Stewart, J 1995 Change in local government, *Politics Review* November

Stoker, G 1991 *The politics of local government*, London: Macmillan

Young, K and M Davies (1990 *Local government since Widdicombe*, York: Joseph Rowntree Foundation

Young, K and N Rao 1993 *Coming to terms with change? The local government councillor in 1993*, York: Local Government Chronicle in a joint series with the Joseph Rowntree Foundation

CONFEDERATION →
THE UNITING OF STATES INTO
A LEAGUE.

FEDERATION → GROUP OF
STATES INDEPENDENT IN LOCAL
MATTERS BUT UNITED UNDER A
CENTRAL GOV. FOR PURPOSES SUCH
AS DEFENCE.

THE EUROPEAN UNION

DEVELOPMENT OF THE EUROPEAN UNION

IMPACT OF MAASTRICHT

EUROPEAN UNION INSTITUTIONS

PARTIES AND THE EUROPEAN DEBATE

GETTING STARTED

Membership of the European Union (formerly the European Economic Community) has had a profound effect on British political life in terms of external relations and foreign policy, political sovereignty and the impact on the internal cohesion of the political parties. The movement towards European integration offers a number of options for the future direction of British governments: remain in the EU under present developing intergovernmental relationships (confederation), resist the drive towards a supranational Europe (federation), or move to a twin track variable geometry situation combining both approaches allowing a longer term period of adjustment. Whichever position is ultimately taken, future governments will have to settle problems of monetary union in the shorter term (by 1999) and decide whether Britain remains at the centre or periphery of other European developments.

Examination questions on this topic fall into the following general areas:

- The impact and influence of membership of the European Union on British political life.

- The effects of European Union membership on parliamentary and political sovereignty.

- How the European debate has divided the Conservative and Labour Parties.

- The constitutional implications of Britain's continued membership of the European Union.

Useful definitions

- **Supranational** – the process whereby European institutions are created over and above the institutions of the nation states with powers that are superior to those of each constituent country.

- **Intergovernmental** – a Europe based on a system of confederal institutions whereby each constituent member state is able to veto policy that is contrary to their national interests.

- **Deepening** – the passing of European Acts which take the European Union closer down the road of integration to a federal or supranational structure.

- **Widening** – expanding membership of the European Union to include the poorer industrial countries of Europe which increases problems of economic, political and social integration.

DEVELOPMENT OF THE EUROPEAN UNION

ESSENTIAL PRINCIPLES

66 Post war developments 99

The origins of the European Economic Community (EEC) – the term European Union (EU) was not adopted until after the passing of the Treaty on European Union, or Maastricht Treaty, in 1992 – lie in the post war economic arrangements primarily agreed between Germany and France in the Schuman Plan of 1950. Although British Prime Minister Winston Churchill was instrumental in floating the idea of a United States of Europe as early as 1946, both Labour and Conservative governments kept Britain out of European arrangements because of commitments to the Commonwealth and a special relationship with the United States. As a result, the six European powers (France, Germany, Italy, Belgium, The Netherlands and Luxembourg) established the **first supranational institution**, the European Coal and Steel Community (ECSC), in 1952. This was closely followed by the creation of the European Atomic Energy Community (EURATOM) and the European Economic Community (EEC) in 1958. The primary objective of these early organisations (established by separate treaties of Rome and merged in 1967) was economic – to bring about increases in trade by the abolition of barriers and customs duties and the free movement of goods in a common market. The secondary objective was political – a hope that these trading nations would move towards a closer union as they transferred powers of regulation to the supranational EEC (*Geddes 1993*). It was this factor that successive British governments found objectionable.

BRITISH ATTITUDES TO EUROPE

66 Why Britain opposed 99

Apart from opposition to the EEC for reasons of trade, successive British governments were opposed to membership on the grounds that **national sovereignty would be damaged**. By agreeing to join the EEC, countries were subjugating their Parliaments to the supranational organisations of the EEC. The British preferred to negotiate from the point of intergovernmentalism, maintaining state identities through the use of a veto in protection of national interests should that prove necessary. Fortunately the adoption of the 1966 Luxembourg Compromise introduced the idea of consensus or unanimity voting in place of qualified majority voting in the institutions of the EEC, which softened the effects of supranationalism taking it partly towards intergovernmentalism which was more acceptable.

After two unsuccessful attempts (1961 and 1967) Britain finally joined the EEC in 1973 under the Conservative government of Edward Heath, a committed European. By clinging to the intergovernmental idea, the British Conservative government of Edward Heath and Labour government of Harold Wilson (from 1974) were able to sell the idea of EEC membership to a sceptical public and the anti-Europeans. From this perspective the initial difficulties of British membership could be presented as worthwhile. They included:

1 High cost of subscription in the short term as a new member.

2 Loss of cheaper food sources from the Commonwealth as EEC tariffs were applied.

3 Less benefit from the Common Agricultural Policy (CAP) because British farming was efficient.

4 Acceptance of existing EEC regulations developed before Britain was a member.

66 Sovereignty 99

On the important question of national sovereignty, the Heath government were able to claim that British sovereignty was not affected because ultimate sanction still rested with the Westminster Parliament rather than the EEC.

British membership of the EEC was popularly tested in a referendum by Edward Heath's successor, Harold Wilson, in 1975. By voting to stay in the Community (67 per cent were in favour) the British electorate helped Harold Wilson overcome difficulties in his own Cabinet and party over attitudes to the EEC. These would not be solved until opposition to Margaret Thatcher's Conservative government from 1979 convinced the Labour Party that the institutions of the EEC could keep socialism alive because the left played a significant role in the making of pro-Labour Community legislation.

for finance in the member states. Its main work comprises approval of Commission proposals and the issue of regulations and directives which are binding on all EU members. The voting procedure is a majority system which means member states cannot overrule decisions reached. The Councils are assisted in their deliberations by

COREPER

a Committee of Permanent Representatives (COREPER) which acts as a secretariat preparing papers and agenda. Occasionally decisions taken in COREPER are accepted by full council meetings with very little change.

EUROPEAN COUNCIL

European Council meetings bring together the heads of government of the separate member states to settle strategic decisions for the whole European Union. They are mainly used to break policy disputes in the EU or decide important new policy directions. The European Monetary System, the Single European Act and Treaty of the European Union (Maastricht) were all decided by heads of government meeting in council session in the country of the member state holding the EU presidency.

EUROPEAN PARLIAMENT

The European Parliament (EP) is not a Parliament in the strict legislative sense – the Commission initiates policy which is approved by the Council of Ministers – but Parliament has certain basic powers. It can offer opinions on legislation, examine the work of the Commission and Council, influence the EU budget and theoretically dismiss the Commission. These original consultation powers have been supplemented since the Single European Act of 1987 and the Maastricht Treaty to include **cooperation procedure** (the ability to influence the Council of Ministers by greater involvement in procedure) and **co-decision powers** which give the EP the right to veto or reject legislation (*Nugent 1994*). The addition of these powers to the EP means a reassessment of its role from a weak institution to one of increasing influence. However, there are a number of problems associated with the institution.

EP evaluation

Although the EP is the only other elected Parliament that could challenge the sovereignty of the Westminster national Parliament, its democratic representational credentials are not strong. British turnout in the 1994 European elections at 36 per cent was among the lowest in the EU. Public apathy on the role of the EP and European institutions is high with the result that claims of a mandate for any particular vision of Europe are hard to substantiate. This argument could therefore be used to support a future Conservative or Labour referendum on the replacement of the pound by the Euro-currency.

EUROPEAN COURT OF JUSTICE

The European Court of Justice is charged with the upholding and administration of EU laws. As all directives, decisions and laws in the EU are based on the written treaties of the EU, the European Court plays the primary role in interpreting the meanings of these treaties and their applicability to member states. European law is binding over member states and in this sense does not need enactment in the separate Parliaments. Citizens of member states are thus given rights and obligations without recourse to their own legislatures and can appeal directly to the European Court. The power of the European Court over national legislation contravening

Supremacy of European law

European law was demonstrated in the **Factortame Case** of 1990 whereby the Court ruled that sections of the British Merchant Fishing Act of 1988 were incompatible with European law. In March 1996 Spanish fishermen were granted leave by the Court to sue the British Government for £30 million for being excluded from British waters.

PARTIES AND THE EUROPEAN DEBATE

LIBERAL DEMOCRATS AND LABOUR

Of the three main political parties only the Liberal Democrats are united in their commitment to a federal Europe and greater political integration. The Labour Party has gone through periods of pro- and anti-Europeanism. Some on the left of the party see the institutions of the European Union as a capitalist club offering little to the working classes of the member states. Others adopt a more pragmatic approach, particularly the moderniser supporters of Tony Benn. During the years of opposition to the Conservative government of Margaret Thatcher 1979–90, there were those in the Labour Party who looked to Europe for socialist support in opposition to what they regarded as sectional policies harmful to the working class. They can point to the adoption of the Social Chapter by the majority of European governments with the exception of Britain as an example of Conservative opposition to legislation protecting the manual working class. The Conservative government have always taken the view that industrial and labour relations are internal national matters that do not concern the supranational institutions of the European Union.

CONSERVATIVES

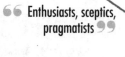
Enthusiasts, sceptics, pragmatists

The Conservatives as the governing party since 1979 have been most affected by schisms surrounding the position of Britain's relations with Europe. The struggle to ratify the Maastricht Treaty bears witness to an issue that brought John Major's government close to collapse in 1993. Margaret Thatcher herself and a number of her senior ministers eventually lost office over European integration issues and John Major has survived a number of crises including the withdrawal from the Exchange Rate Mechanism and a challenge to his leadership in 1995. Simplistically, Conservatives are divided between enthusiasts, sceptics and pragmatists. Enthusiasts wish for greater influence in Europe, either through intergovernmentalism or federalism, to secure the benefits of greater prosperity. Sceptics are opposed to greater European integration – some are anti-marketeer nationalists, others fear for loss of British sovereignty. Finally, pragmatists do not belong to either category – according to *Geddes* (*1993*), they are characterised by a common sense approach and accept membership of the EU as inevitable.

SOVEREIGNTY AND FEDERALISM

According to *Bulmer* (*1994*), debates over British sovereignty centre around two aspects. Firstly, parliamentary sovereignty is the notion that the House of Commons has always had legislative primacy. This is now removed by European Union law and legislation. Secondly, there is the idea of national sovereignty, whereby the UK has the policy freedom to operate as it wishes. By joining the European Union, Britain has lost some of this exclusivity. Decisions are now taken in Brussels which have the potential to divide political parties in the foreseeable future.

EXAMINATION QUESTIONS

1 Examine the effects of European issues on British party politics. *(25)*
(UODLE)

2. 'Membership of the European Community seriously threatens the British constitution.' Discuss. *(25)*
(NEAB)

3. How and why are both the Conservative and Labour Parties divided over the European Union? *(100)*
(ULEAC)

ANSWERS TO EXAMINATION QUESTIONS

OUTLINE ANSWER TO QUESTION 3

This question demands an appreciation of the different factions in both the Conservative and Labour Parties and their attitudes to Europe. With the Labour Party you could mention the fact that they have changed their stance from one of anti-Europeanism to pro-Europeanism since the 1970s. Discuss the impact of the long period in opposition since 1979 and the acceptance of the idea that socialism was a stronger force in the European Parliament. Greater integration was therefore to be encouraged for the reverse reason that it offered an alternative to the policies of Margaret Thatcher and John Major that could not be countered by the Labour Party in the Westminster Parliament.

An examination of the factions within the Conservative Party and attitudes to Europe could begin with the Edward Heath government of 1970–74 that finally succeeded in taking Britain into the EEC. Discuss Margaret Thatcher's early enthusiasm for Europe (for reasons of economic trade and free markets) and her later conversion to scepticism as the institutions of the EEC moved to closer integration. Mention her successes (the EC budget) and failures (EMU) culminating in her loss of ministers and her own removal from office. Explain John Major's attitude to Europe against the background of his difficulties in securing the passage of the Maastricht Treaty. Examine his success in securing opt-out clauses and subsidiarity with the possibility of moving to a variable geometry approach to monetary union. In all these discussions you should set the position of federalists and intergovernmentalists in perspective, noting that the pragmatists are the largest European group within the Conservative Party.

TUTOR'S ANSWER TO QUESTION 2

See the answer to the same question in Chapter 3, The Constitution (p. 31).

STUDENT'S ANSWER TO QUESTION 1 WITH EXAMINER'S COMMENTS

After 1945 moves towards the greater economic and political integration of West European states were encouraged by the wish to promote peace and Franco-German cooperation. There was a belief that the combination of sizeable economies would lead to a more powerful Western Europe capable of exerting greater international influence than separate medium sized states.

66 Other factors important 99

Britain, though strenuously courted by other states, stood aside from the early stages of integration for a number of reasons. One was a sense of superiority and national pride resulting from the defiance of Hitler and victory in the war – the other countries involved were either occupied or defeated during the war. Britain also had a lot of international status, close links with the USA, standing in the Commonwealth and so on, so why choose to be merely a European influence? A final reason was a sense of difference. Britain had a more secure experience of nationhood. Another difference was that most of the other six countries had frequently experimented with coalitions and proportional representation. They had multi party systems and written constitutions. One may also add the sense of difference stemming from Britain's insular separation from her neighbours.

But British political leaders in the late fifties and sixties became aware of the faster economic growth of the

EC states, as well as of the weakening of Commonwealth ties and the 'special relationship' between Britain and America. As a result, two attempts were made in the sixties to gain British entry into Europe (one by Macmillan in 1961 and the other by Wilson in 1967); both failed. In 1971 British entry was achieved and the terms were approved by Parliament, but Labour opposed until the referendum which approved membership by a two-to-one 'Yes' vote.

The impact of the EEC on Britain has been seen in a variety of areas, for example in political and constitutional matters. It has involved the introduction of the device of the referendum, the relaxation of collective Cabinet responsibility (in the 1975 referendum and in the form of electoral system for the direct elections in 1977), and the introduction of a large element of a written constitution, with a consequently greater role for the courts and a limit to parliamentary sovereignty.

> **Good collation of impacts**

Labour was bitterly divided over Europe until the mid 1980s when it abandoned its withdrawal policy. In 1989 it won a resounding victory in the elections to the European Parliament. Currently the Conservatives are deeply divided over further integration, with a pro-European group and another, commonly known as the Euro-sceptics, who follow the distinctly unenthusiastic line spelt out by Mrs Thatcher in her 1988 Bruges speech.

Already though, Europe has practically transformed British politics. Britain freely entered and is now locked into a quasi-federal system. It retains a theoretical right to withdraw but in practice it simply resists the further transfer of power to the EU, and asserts the principle of subsidiarity to protect national power against what is seen as the centralising encroachments of federalism. The idea of an increasingly powerful centralising body is one often exploited by Euro-sceptics on both sides of the House of Commons and the government has yet to calm this fear which resides in much of the population.

Dismay, reluctance and protest cannot do much to change the policy consequences of EU membership. Over significant areas policy now has to be developed collaboratively, negotiated and agreed within the framework of the EU. This is a new and uncomfortable experience for British governments accustomed to their 'winner takes all' system of

> **Some compression here**

absolute power. Also, for a Conservative government which is currently the most right wing in Europe, this means many considerable compromises in policy. This is in sharp contrast to other European national governments which are often coalitions.

Prime Ministers have seized the promotional opportunities of European summitry. It helps if the Prime Minister is a first rate negotiator and diplomat; Margaret Thatcher's warrior approach to her fellow Community heads of government proved damaging. Thus the job of the British Prime Minister has been changed significantly through membership of the Community.

As far as the influence of the EU over a range of policy areas is concerned, the EU framework includes the substance of macroeconomic policy, conditions of employment, regulations of industry and agriculture, commerce and the environment, welfare provision and immigration. The accession

66 Valid points 99

of Britain to the Exchange Rate Mechanism brought a significant restraint on economic policy making and the freedom of manoeuvre of the Chancellor of the Exchequer. But, in or out of the ERM, British governments have yielded some freedom in matters both fundamental and politically sensitive, such as border controls and taxation.

Departments of state and the civil service have had to adjust to a European dimension in their work. So what was traditionally regarded as 'low politics' has been elevated with many higher civil servants having to get involved in the complexities of policy making whilst regarding the all important European consensus.

The influence of Parliament has been diminished. Many right wing Conservatives are dissatisfied with this process as they see Parliament as sovereign representing a successful liberal democracy not to be encroached upon by any form of outside body. However, in place of this diminished national sovereignty, ministers go bargaining in Brussels and cannot be pursued there by Parliament. International negotiations always lie beyond the reach of legislatures and under the EU, substantial areas of domestic policy are moved beyond Parliament's grasp.

66 Give more detail here 99

Apart from major policy, Parliament does have the right to scrutinise European legislation. The difficulty lies in the sheer bulk of the documentation and the shortage of time and expertise.

European law has primacy over national laws, where it is applicable, and the courts in consequence have to engage in the novel function of reviewing the constitutionality (that is conformity to European law) of Acts of the British Parliament and government. This means imposing a written constitution upon a governing party which relies on pragmatism and flexibility in the case of Britain.

However, Europe has had a divisive effect on both major political parties. In 1975 Harold Wilson hoped to resolve the divisions in his Cabinet and party by device of the referendum, but divisions reopened later, and the European issue in part motivated the SDP breakaway from the Labour Party in 1981. In 1983 the Labour manifesto included a commitment to leave the EC. This was at a time when the left of the party had considerable influence and the EC was portrayed simply as a capitalists' club. However, by 1992 the party was officially committed to vigorous participation in the Community.

The Conservatives' divisions were evident most prominently at the fall of Mrs Thatcher to some of her senior colleagues with more pro-European views. John Major's policy is summed up in the deliberately ambiguous formula 'at the heart of Europe but fighting for British interests'. This is similar to the Labour position. The Liberal Democrats are the only party to be enthusiastic for Europe, without much qualification. The forward policy set out in the Maastricht Treaty poses a severe test for both Labour and the Conservatives. Despite the disruptive consequences for the political parties, membership of the EC has not had a sharp impact on popular politics. The concerns of the political elites have not been fully shared with the public, except in the referendum campaign of 1975.

66 More elaboration needed 99

It seems now that both major parties will continue to

push the argument that in an economically hostile world
Britain (as well as other members) will benefit from joining together as a trading group with the rest of Western
Europe. The question has now evolved from whether Britain
should stay in the Community to what sort of Community it
is to be.

66 The strengths in this answer relate to the detail in the broad sweep of influence over the institutions. There is little discussion of supranationalism and federalism but it is still a good essay. A B grade is probable. 99

REFERENCES IN THE TEXT

Bates, S 1995 Why a vote by MPs cannot change course of EU fishing policy, *The Guardian* 20 December

Bulmer, S 1994 Britain and European integration. In B Jones (ed.) *Politics UK* 2nd edn, Hemel Hempstead: Harvester Wheatsheaf

Delors, J 1995 Delors disowns Maastricht, *The Sunday Times* 1 October

Geddes, A 1993 *Britain in the European Community*, Manchester: Baseline Books

Jones, B and L Robins 1992 *Two decades in British Politics*, Manchester University Press

Lynch, P 1993 Europe's post-Maastricht muddle, *Politics Review* November

Nugent N 1994 *The government and politics of the European Union*, Basingstoke: Macmillan

Waigel, T 1995 EC sticks to 1999 deadline, *The Sunday Times* 1 October

REVIEW SHEET (CHAPTER 2)

1   Give a definition of political culture.

_____

_____

2   What were the main conclusions drawn by Almond and Verba on the British political culture?

_____

_____

_____

3   Briefly show how deferential political attitudes relate to the political system.

_____

_____

_____

4   What do instrumentalism and ambivalence mean when applied to working class political attitudes?

a) _____

_____

b) _____

5   Why is the past so important to an understanding of current political practice?

_____

_____

_____

_____

6   Explain the term 'culturally homogeneous society'.

_____

_____

7   Why do ethnic minority voters preponderantly support the Labour Party?

_____

_____

8   Briefly, is Celtic Nationalism any longer a threat to the United Kingdom?

_____

_____

_____

9   What was the importance of the embourgeoisement debate to an understanding of working class attitudes?

_____

_____

_____

10   How do the new working class differ from the old working class?

_____

_____

11   What divides the middle class?

_____

_____

12 Explain the term 'political consensus'.

_____

_____

13 Give two important features of the post war consensus.

1) _____

2) _____

14 What was 'Butskellism' and how did it relate to consensus?

_____

_____

_____

_____

15 Why was Margaret Thatcher so opposed to consensus politics?

_____

_____

_____

16 Is there a new consensus in the nineties?

_____

_____

_____

17 What is the important difference between criminal and anti-political acts?

_____

_____

18 Give two features that threaten the consensus of the nineties.

1) _____

2) _____

REVIEW SHEET (CHAPTER 3)

1 Why is the lack of a written document not a handicap when describing the British constitution?

_____

_____

_____

2 Briefly explain the difference between a prescriptive and descriptive constitution.

_____

_____

3 What is the significance of the separation of powers principle?

_____

_____

4 Give one advantage and one disadvantage of a flexible constitution.

a) _____

b) _____

5 Explain the term 'evolutionary nature' when applied to the British constitution.

_____

_____

6 What was the main idea behind the balanced constitution argument?

_____

_____

7 Briefly summarise the difference between the Whitehall and empirical views of the constitution.

_____

_____

_____

_____

8 Name the five sources of the constitution:

a) _____

b) _____

c) _____

d) _____

e) _____

9 Why do Acts of Parliament constitute the most important source of the constitution?

_____

_____

10 Give two examples of conventions and briefly assess their contribution to the constitution.

a) _____

b) _____

11 How does European Union law impact on the British constitution?

_____

_____

_____

12 Explain the term 'parliamentary sovereignty'. How important is it?

_____

_____

_____

13 What are *A V Dicey's* three features of the rule of law?

a) _____

b) _____

c) _____

14 Why did devolution become a constitutional issue from the 1970s?

_____

_____

15 Briefly explain *one* problem in the constitution.

_____

_____

16 Why did demands for a new constitutional arrangement become clearer after the 1970s?

_____

_____

_____

17 Distinguish between the Liberal and Traditionalist approaches to a reformed constitution.

_____

_____

_____

18 Why does *Phillip Norton* feel that demands for a new constitution are unrealisable?

_____

_____

_____

_____

19 Give one argument for and one argument against a written constitution.

a) _____

b) _____

REVIEW SHEET (CHAPTER 4)

1 Why are Prime Ministers more powerful than in the past?

_____

_____

_____

_____

2 Give a *brief* description of the Prime Ministerial government debate.

_____

_____

_____

3 What are the principle advantages in the Cabinet government debate?

_____

_____

_____

4 How did John Major 'restore' Cabinet government?

_____

_____

_____

5 Give *two* criticisms of John Major's premiership.

_____

_____

_____

_____

6 What did John Major gain by winning the 1995 Conservative leadership election and what did he lose?

_____

_____

_____

_____

7 Why are core executive theories now regarded as important additions to the analysis of Prime Ministerial power?

_____

_____

_____

8 Isolate and explain *one* important difference between Margaret Thatcher's and John Major's style of leadership.

_____

_____

_____

_____

9 *Briefly* state how a Prime Minister depends on the Cabinet.

_____

_____

_____

10 How and for what reasons did John Major survive the Conservative leadership election contest in July 1995

_____

_____

_____

_____

11 Name the *three* variables in the Prime Minister's environment.

_____

_____

_____

12 Why is it necessary for a Prime Minister to keep good relations channels open to his backbenchers.

_____

_____

_____

_____

13 Why have successive Prime Ministers refused to create a separate Prime Minister's Department?

_____

_____

_____

_____

14 What difficulties do governments face in trying to satisfy public expectations?

_____

_____

_____

15 Give *two* reasons why the dissolution threat from a Prime Minister to critical backbenchers is unrealistic.

_____

_____

_____

_____

16 Can a Prime Minister be 'sold like a product' by the media to the electorate?

_____

_____

REVIEW SHEET (CHAPTER 5)

1 Why is the Cabinet both an administrative and political body?

_____

_____

2 Briefly when and how did the Cabinet emerge in government?

_____

_____

3 What is the advantage in having a Cabinet government system based on conventions?

_____

_____

_____

_____

4 Briefly explain the difference between the narrow and the broad view of the Cabinet.

_____

_____

5 What determines the size of the Cabinet?

_____

_____

_____

6 Give three features within the convention of collective responsibility.

a) _____

b) _____

c) _____

7 What did the resignation of Michael Heseltine tell us about Margaret Thatcher's way of running the Cabinet?

_____

_____

_____

_____

_____

8 Briefly show how the following affect collective responsibility:

a)   Media leaks

b)   Publications

_____

_____

_____

_____

9 What were the 'agreements to differ'? How did they contribute to Cabinet government?

_____

_____

10 Explain the following terms:

a) Inner Cabinet

_____

_____

b) Partial Cabinet

_____

_____

11 What is 'departmentalism'? How does it affect the working of the Cabinet?

_____

_____

12 Refute the charge that Cabinet minutes are cosmeticised or changed by the Prime Minister.

_____

_____

_____

_____

13 What is the main function of the Cabinet Secretariat?

_____

_____

_____

_____

14 Give two advantages of the Cabinet committee system

a) _____

b) _____

15 Briefly describe the 'Overlords' experiment'. Why did it fail?

_____

_____

_____

_____

_____

16 Why did Leo Amery suggest the establishment of a 'Policy Cabinet'?

_____

_____

17 On what grounds was the Central Policy Review Staff (CPRS) abolished? Do you think this was a good idea?

_____

_____

_____

_____

REVIEW SHEET (CHAPTER 6)

1   Briefly summarise the following perspectives on Parliament:

a)   Legal institution

_____

b)   Westminster

_____

c)   Transformative

_____

2   Which MP 'crossed the floor' of the House of Commons in late 1995 and why?

_____

_____

3   Why is the Speaker expected to be impartial?

_____

_____

4   What is the essential point about:

1)   A one line whip?

_____

2)   A two line whip?

_____

3)   A three line whip?

_____

5   Who were the 'whipless rebels' and why did they rebel?

_____

_____

_____

_____

6   Is there a pattern to backbench dissent in the House of Commons?

_____

_____

_____

_____

7   Explain the difference between:

a)   Private member's bill

_____

b)   Government bill

_____

c)   Private bill

_____

8   Why are private members' bills not usually successful?

_____

_____

9   Which legislative stage do you consider most important and why?

_____

_____

_____

10   Give one advantage and one disadvantage of Question Time in the House of Commons.

a) _____

b) _____

11   Why was the Nolan Committee on Standards in Public Life set up?

_____

_____

_____

_____

12   Briefly explain the value of the House of Commons departmental select committees.

_____

_____

_____

_____

_____

13   What is the difference between the representative and delegate theory of the MP?

_____

_____

_____

_____

14   Explain the 'convergence' theory of class background of MPs.

_____

_____

15   Why was Lord Salisbury's Convention established in the House of Lords?

_____

_____

16   How do 'backwoodsmen' affect the political arithmetic of the House of Lords?

_____

_____

17   Give one argument for and one argument against retaining the House of Lords.

_____

_____

REVIEW SHEET (CHAPTER 7)

1 Summarise briefly the main ideas of the following approaches to the civil service:

a) Liberal Democratic

ORTHODOX VIEW THAT CIVIL SERVANTS DO WHATEVER MINISTERS TELL THEM.

b) Constitutional Bureaucracy

DUE TO NATURE OF MINISTERS ETC. SOME ELEMENT OF PERMANENCE NEEDED

c) Power Bloc

CIVIL SERVANTS CANNOT OPPOSE RADICAL OR REFORMIST GOV. OBJECTIVES

d) Bureaucratic Over-Supply

EXPANSIONISM + OVER-STAFFING

e) Whitehall Community

'COSY WORLD' OF WHITEHALL - MINISTERS + CIVIL SERVANTS WORKING TOGETHER.

2 What was the significant feature of the Northcote–Trevelyan Report 1854?

DIVIDED CIVIL SERVICE (ENTRY) INTO MECHANICAL + INTELLECTUAL CLASSES.

3 Briefly describe the thinking behind the Fulton Report 1968.

NOT EFFICIENT ENOUGH — MANAGERIALISM NOT EQUAL OPPORTUNITY WITHIN - CLASSLESSNESS

4 Give two criticisms made by Fulton of the civil service.

a) *SECRECY - NOT 'OPEN' ENOUGH*

b) *TRAINING - ONLY ON THE JOB - NOT SPECIAL SCHOOL AS IN FRANCE.*

5 Why did the Fulton reforms take so long to be implemented?

HIGHER CIVIL SERVANTS TOOK OPPOSITION

6 What is the origin of the philosophy of the amateur and what does it mean?

TOO GENERALIST — MORE RELEVANT DEGREES NEEDED.

7 How and why is 'Oxbridge' bias in recruitment to the higher civil service defended?

STATISTICALLY MORE APPLICANTS MOST ABLE GRADUATES TRADITION OF APPLYING

8 Write brief descriptions of the following features:

a) Permanence

CIVIL SERVANTS ARE PERMANENT WITHIN DEPT.

b) Expertise

GAIN VALUABLE EXPERTISE WITH TIME

c) Anonymity

DO NOT GET BLAMED FOR SUCCESSES OR FAILURES

d) Impartiality

POLITICALLY NEUTRAL - WHATEVER POLITICAL COMPLEXION

9 Why has it proved difficult to examine the relationship between a permanent secretary and a minister?

NOT SURROUNDED IN PUBLICITY - VERY SECRETIVE.

10 What do you understand by the term individual ministerial responsibility?

MINISTER IS FULLY RESPONSIBLE FOR ALL SUCCESSES + FAILURES OF THEIR DEPT.

11 Explain the difference between role responsibility and personal responsibility.

ROLE - POLICY MISTAKES ETC. (DUGDALE) PERSONAL - PRIVATE LIFE (MELIOR, MATES, YEO + PARKINSON)

12 On what grounds do ministers tend to resign today?

TO PROTECT THE GOV. AS A WHOLE E.G. LEON BRITTAIN - 86 - WESTLAND RICHARD LUCE LORD CARRINGTON FALKLANDS HUMPHREY ATKINS — TO PROTECT THATCHER.

13 What was the prime purpose of the Rayner 'Scrutinies'?

TO INCREASE/IMPROVE MANAGERIAL EFFICIENCY + REDUCE WASTE WITHIN THE CIVIL SERVICE

14 Briefly explain why the Next Steps programme was introduced?

TO SEPERATE ADMINISTRATORS FROM POLICY ADVISORS - 'IMPROVING MANAGEMENT IN GOV'

15 How does management theory relate to Next Steps?

HORIZONTAL - NOT VERTICAL

16 Why do the reforms introduced under Next Steps threaten the traditional role of civil servants?

B THREATENS TO BREAK UP NATIONAL CIVIL SERVICE + PARLIAMENTARY SOVEREIGNTY.

REVIEW SHEET (CHAPTER 8)

1 Explain Robert Michell's 'Iron Law of Oligarchy'.

_____

_____

2 Briefly summarise the following degrees of apolitical behaviour:

a) Apathy

_____

b) Cynicism

_____

c) Alienation

_____

3 What is the difference between a mass party and an elite party?

_____

_____

4 Why does Britain have a dominant party system?

_____

_____

5 Who are median voters and how do they relate to the party system?

_____

_____

_____

_____

6 Give two advantages of two party competition.

a) _____

b) _____

7 What is the pendulum theory of party competition?

_____

_____

8 Briefly explain the following models of party competition:

a) The economic model

_____

b) The adversarial model

_____

9 In what sense does Britain have a multi-party system?

_____

_____

_____

_____

_____

10 Briefly give three features explaining the electoral success of the Conservative Party.

a) _____

b) _____

c) _____

11 Give one central feature of Conservatism.

_____

_____

12 Explain one difference between One Nation Conservatism and Liberal or New Right Conservatism.

_____

_____

13 Why is the Conservative Party organisation described as unitary?

_____

_____

14 How did the ballot election of the Conservative leader affect his/her authority?

_____

_____

_____

_____

15 Briefly explain socialism as interpreted in the Labour Party.

_____

_____

16 What was the difference between Labour fundamentalists and revisionists?

_____

_____

17 What was McKenzie's thesis on power in the Labour Party?

_____

_____

_____

_____

_____

18 Why did the Labour Party change the method of electing the leader in 1981?

_____

_____

19 In what sense are the Liberal Democrats related to the old Liberal Party?

_____

_____

REVIEW SHEET (CHAPTER 9)

1   Why is pluralism the main theoretical approach to pressure groups?

_____

_____

2   *Briefly* explain countervailing power.

_____

_____

3   What was tripartism?

_____

_____

4   Give **three** differences between a political party and a pressure group.

_____

_____

_____

5   What is the difference between a sectional and a cause group?

_____

_____

_____

_____

6   Why do insider groups generally have more influence with government?

_____

_____

7   Explain the term representativeness as applied to groups.

_____

_____

8   Why are public demonstrations taken as a sign of weakness with policy makers?

_____

_____

9   Explain the term direct action politics.

_____

_____

10   Which access or influence point do you consider the most important and why?

_____

_____

_____

_____

11   How do certain pressure groups acquire sanction power over government?

_____

_____

12 What is the clientele relationship and why is it important?

_____

_____

_____

_____

_____

13 Give *one* example of a local action group in your area and say what its aims are.

_____

_____

14 Why should Tony Blair seek to change the sponsorship link between the Labour Party and the trade unions?

_____

_____

_____

_____

_____

15 *Briefly* describe the public interest. How does it differ from the sectional interest?

_____

_____

16 Distinguish between a) equilibrium theory and b) conspiracy theory of pressure group politics.

_____

_____

_____

_____

_____

17 *Briefly* explain how and why pressure group activity has changed in the nineties.

_____

_____

REVIEW SHEET (CHAPTER 10)

1   Briefly explain the object of the following types of political opinion polls:

a)   Suitability to govern

_____

_____

b)   Issue question

_____

_____

c)   Voting intention

_____

_____

d)   Actual vote

_____

_____

e)   Longitudinal studies

_____

_____

f)   Constituency opinions

_____

_____

2   Give two reasons why opinion polls failed to predict the Conservative general election victory in 1992.

1)   _____

2)   _____

3   Why did the Harold Wilson Labour government reject the recommendation of the 1967 Speaker's Conference?

_____

_____

_____

_____

4   How does the boomerang effect apply to voting behaviour?

_____

_____

5   What is the bandwagon effect?

_____

_____

6   What is the connection between tactical voting and opinion polls?

_____

_____

_____

_____

7 Give one advantage and one disadvantage of opinion polls.

1) _____

_____

2) _____

_____

8 Briefly say why referendums are foreign to the British constitution.

_____

_____

9 Explain the concept of the mandate.

_____

_____

10 Name the object of the following referendums:

a) 1973 _____

b) 1975 _____

c) 1979 _____

11 Why did the devolution referendums fail?

_____

_____

12 What was the West Lothian question?

_____

_____

_____

_____

_____

13 Why is the British electoral system described as 'simple plurality'?

_____

_____

14 Give two advantages and two disadvantages of the British electoral system.

a) _____

b) _____

c) _____

d) _____

15 What is the difference between a majority and proportional electoral system?

_____

_____

16 Briefly summarise the position of the Conservative, Labour and Liberal Democratic Parties on electoral reform.

_____

_____

REVIEW SHEET (CHAPTER 11)

1 Explain the deferential vote.

_____

_____

_____

_____

2 How is voting Conservative linked to working class living standards?

_____

_____

_____

_____

3 Give *two* reasons for middle class support for the Labour Party.

_____

_____

_____

_____

4 How does family background influence the vote?

_____

_____

5 Why did explanations of voting behaviour become more complex after the 1970s?

_____

_____

_____

6 Give three social variables affecting the vote.

a) _____

b) _____

c) _____

7 What was the theory of senescence?

_____

_____

_____

_____

8 Why proportionately do more women vote Conservative than men?

_____

_____

_____

9 Give *one* explanation for ethnic minority support of the Labour Party.

_____

_____

10 *Briefly* explain the difference between class and partisan dealignment.

_____

_____

_____

_____

11 Who are the new working class and why are they important?

_____

_____

12 What is the consumer model of voting?

_____

_____

13 Why are issues important to the vote?

_____

_____

_____

_____

14 What is the 'feel good' factor and how did it relate to the Conservative election victories of the eighties?

_____

_____

_____

_____

_____

15 Do election campaigns influence the vote?

_____

_____

_____

_____

_____

_____

16 Can the Labour Party draw any comfort from the 1992 general election result?

_____

_____

_____

_____

_____

REVIEW SHEET (CHAPTER 12)

1   Briefly explain the main findings of the Redcliffe–Maud Commission.

_____

_____

_____

_____

2   Give two problems in the two tier system of local government.

a)   _____

b)   _____

3   Why was the Conservative government of Margaret Thatcher keen to see greater financial controls placed over councils?

_____

_____

4   What was the main objective of the Banham Commission (the Local Government Commission for England 1992)?

_____

_____

5   Why did the Major government re-open the review of shire counties in March 1995?

_____

_____

_____

_____

_____

6   Explain the term 'hybrid system' as applied to local government structures in 1995/1996.

_____

_____

7   On what grounds did Professors John Stewart and George Jones criticise the unitary system?

_____

_____

_____

8   Give one problem of the committee system in local government.

_____

_____

9   What did the Maud Management Report of 1967 recommend?

_____

_____

10 What were the two main recommendations of the Bains Report 1972?

1) _____

_____

2) _____

_____

11 Is local government dominated by a single elite or a series of elites?

_____

_____

_____

_____

12 Explain the terms 'conviction' Conservative and 'Urban Socialist'.

a) _____

_____

b) _____

_____

13 Briefly what is the local democracy argument?

_____

_____

14 Give one consequence of the domination of councils by party politics.

_____

_____

15 Briefly summarise the following theories of local-central relations.

a) Oppositional _____

_____

b) Partnership _____

_____

a) Power-dependence _____

_____

b) Agency _____

_____

16 Explain the importance of compulsory competitive tendering (CCT) to current Conservative thinking on local government.

_____

_____

_____

_____

REVIEW SHEET (CHAPTER 13)

1 Briefly what are the three possible approaches facing the British government in relations with the EU?

CONFEDERATION
FEDERATION
TWIN TRACK - BOTH (LONGER PERIOD OF ADJUSTMENT)

2 Why was the EEC set up originally?

ECONOMIC - TO BRING ABOUT INCREASES IN
TRADE BY THE ABOLITION OF BARRIERS + CUSTOM
DUTIES + THE FREE MOVEMENT OF GOODS IN
A COMMON MARKET.

3 What major factor kept successive British governments out of Europe?

FEAR THAT NATIONAL SOVEREIGNTY WOULD
BE DAMAGED.

4 How did the Heath government present the question of sovereignty to the public after joining the EEC?

REFERENDUM - 1975
67% IN FAVOUR TO STAY IN THE COMMUNITY

5 Give one positive and one negative criticism of Margaret Thatcher's attitude to Europe.

1) WANTED A FAIRER BRITISH CONTRIBUTION TO
THE WHOLE EEC BUDGET.

2) OPPOSITION TO THE 'SOCIALIST CHARTER' - PURELY
BEING PHILOSOPHICAL - AGAINST IMP. SOCIAL PROTECTIONS.

6 How did John Major placate the Euro-sceptics in his party over the Maastricht Treaty?

SECURED A NO. OF CONCESSIONS FOR BRITAIN →
'CLOSER UNION' RATHER THAN FEDERAL ARRANGEMENT
SOCIAL CHAPTER PLACED IN SEPERATE PROTOCOL
'OPT-OUT' CLAUSE TO SINGLE EUROPEAN CURRENCY
PRINCIPLE OF SUBSIDIARITY WAS CONCEDED

7 Briefly explain the problem of elitism in European integration. How was it overcome?

CLAIMED THAT THE DRIVE TO FURTHER
EUROPEAN INTEGRATION WAS LED BY POLITICAL
ELITES RATHER THAN ORDINARY MEMBERS OF THE STATES.

8 What are the practical difficulties of EMU (Economic and Monetary Union)?

MEETING THE CRITERIA (+ BY 1999 DEADLINE)
• CONVERGENCE OF ECONOMIES
• ADOPT COMMON POLICIES ON INTEREST RATES, PRICE
STABILITY + INFLATION (ESP. HARD FOR BRITAIN
AFTER LEAVING E.R.M IN SEPT. 92)

9 What is the role of COREPER?

COMMITTEE OF PERMANENT REPRESENTATIVES
- ACTS AS A SECRETARIAT PREPARING PAPERS +
AGENDA FOR THE COUNCIL OF MINISTERS.

10 Explain the following European Parliament proceedings:

a) Cooperation THE ABILITY TO INFLUENCE COUNCIL OF
MINISTER BY GREATER INVOLVEMENT IN PROCEDURE.

b) Co-decision GIVES EP THE RIGHT TO VETO OR
REJECT LEGISLATION.

11 What was the significance of the Factortame Case 1990?

DEMONSTRATED THE POWER OF THE EUROPEAN
COURT OVER NATIONAL LEGISLATION CONTRAVENING
EUROPEAN LAW.

12 Summarise the position of the following Conservative groups:

a) Enthusiasts GREATER INFLUENCE IN EUROPE (INTER-
GOVERNMENTALISM OR FEDERALISM), TO SECURE
BENEFITS OF GREATER PROSPERITY

b) Sceptics OPPOSED TO GREATER EUROPEAN
INTEGRATION- SOME ANTI-MARKETEER
NATIONALISTS, OTHERS FEAR LOSS OF BRIT. SOVEREIGNTY

c) Pragmatists

13 What two aspects are involved in discussions over British sovereignty and the EU?

INDEX

Access points 121
Accountability 50
Acts of Parliament 24
Ad hoc committees 56
Administrative group (civil service) 86–7
Adversarial model 102
Ambivalence 8
Annual party conference 106
Apolitical behaviour 100
Assimilation 9
Attitudinal issues 7

Backbench dissent 65
Backwoodsmen 78
Balanced constitution 23
Bandwagon effect 132
Bicameral legislature 64
Bureaucracy 84
Bureaucratic coordination model 40
Burkean theory 74

Cabinet 37–9, 41, 49–63
Cabinet committees 56
Cabinet secretariat 56
Celtic nationalism 10
Central/local government relationship
   166–8
Centre ground 13
Charter 88 29
Civic culture 7
Civil servant 84
Civil Service 83–98
Civil service selection board 88
Class and voting intentions 148
Class culture 9
Class divisions 10
Clause IV 107
Coercion 14
Collective action 116
Collective ministerial responsibility 52
Collectivism 107
Committee system 56–7
Common law 25
Conscience issues 66
Consensus 11–15
Conservative ideology 104–5
Conservative party 103–6, 178
Constitutional safeguard 77
Constitution 21–30
Constitutional bureaucracy 84
Constitutional disputes 14
Constitutional reform 30
Consumer model of voting 150
Continuity in the state 8–9
Conventions 25
Core executive 40
Council of Ministers 176–7
Criminal Justice Act 27
Crossbenchers 77
Cultural diversity 9
Cultural norm 7

Dealignment theories 10
Deferential vote 145
Delegate theory 74
Departmental select committees 66
Descriptive constitution 22
Deviant voters 145
Devolution 27–8, 135

Direct action 120
Dissident MPs 67
Dissolution of Parliament 43
Dominant value system 145

Efficiency unit 93
Election campaigns 150
Electoral college 108
Electoral reform 137–9
Elite parties 100
Embourgeoisement debate 10, 151
Environment of Prime Minister 42–3
Ethnic pluralism 9
Ethnicity 9, 148
Ethnicity and voting intentions 148
EU see European Union
Euro 176
Euro-sceptics 41, 44, 53
European Commission 176
European Council 177
European Court of Justice 177
European law 25
European Parliament 177
European Union 121, 173–82
Executive 21

Fabian Society 107
Federalism 178
Feel good factor 150
Fields of authority 43
First past the post voting system 135
First, second and third readings 70
Foreign affairs 55
Fragmentation of policy making 39
Free votes 66
Fulton reforms 85–6
Functional school 7
Functionalism 128
Functions of MPs 75

Gender and voting intentions 147
General election 152
Golden Age of Parliament 64
Government bills 68
Government by committee 64, 73
Group politics 116
Guillotine 69

Hegemony 8
Hereditary peers 77
House of Commons 66–73
House of Lords 76–8

Ibbs Report 93
Instrumentalism 8
Issue voting 130, 150

Judiciary 21

Labour party 106–9, 177
Leaks 52, 53–4
Legal institutional model of parliament 65
Legislation 68
Legislature 21
Legitimation crisis 13
Liberal constitution 24
Liberal Democrat constitution 24
Liberal Democrats 109–10, 177
Life peers 77

Lobbying 128
Local action groups 122
Local government 122, 158–72
Lord Salisbury's convention 76

Maastricht Treaty 43, 175–6
Mandarins 84
Marxists 8, 29
Mass parties 100
Members of Parliament 73–6
Memoirs 54
Minor parties 110
Moderate government 14
Monetary Union 175–6
MPs *see* Members of Parliament
MPs' pay 75
Multi-party systems 103

Neo-corporatist view of state 117
Neo-liberal view of state 117
New Labour 109
New middle class 149
New working class 149
Next Steps Report 93–4
Nolan Committee 71
Northcote-Trevelyan Report 85

One line whip 67
One party system 101
Opinion polls 130–3
Over centralisation 37
Overlords 57–8
Oxbridge bias in civil service recruitment
    87–8

Parliament 64–82
Party attachment 145
Party systems 101–3
Party unity 44
Patronage 29
Peers 77
Personalities of Prime Ministers 40
Pluralism 116, 123
Policy cabinets 57
Political consensus 11
Political culture 6–20, 128
Political parties 99–114
Political socialisation 146
Political world 7
Polls 130–3
Prescriptive constitution 22
Pressure groups 115–28
Prime Minister 35–48
Private bills 68
Private members bills 68, 122–3
Problems in the constitution 28–30
Procedural consensus 13–15
Psephologists 132
Psephology 145
Public bills 68
Public opinion 129–43

Quangos 29, 94
Question Time 43, 71
Quiet action by pressure groups 120

Race Relations Acts 9–10
Radcliffe Committee 54
Redcliffe-Maud Report 1968 159
Referendums 26, 133–5
Reform of civil service 85–7
Reform of Parliament 73
Reform of the House of Lords 78
Register of Members' Interests 71
Religion and voting intentions 148
Report Stage 70
Representative theory 74
Resignations from cabinet 52, 92
Revision (for examination) 5
Revisionists 107
Role of civil service 84
Royal assent 70

Sampling 131
Scotland 27, 28
Scott inquiry 90
Scrutiny 70
Second chamber 76
Secrecy in cabinet 53
Sectional view of the state 117
Sectoral divisions 10
Segmented decision making model 39–40
Select committees 71
Senescence 147
Separation of powers 22
Social background of MPs 74–5
Social Charter 175
Social world 7
Socialism 106–9
Sovereignty 26, 174, 178
Speaker of the House of Commons 66
Standing committees 56, 69
Star Chamber 56
Statutory Instruments (SIs) 70
Syllabuses (examination) 2–5

Tactical voting 132–3
Three line whip 67
Toleration 14
Traditionalism in civil service 85
Transformative model of parliament 65
Two line whip 67
Two party system 101, 146
Two-tier system of local government 160

Unitary state 27
Unitary structures 161

Voting behaviour 144–57

Wales 27, 28
Westminster model of parliament 65
Whips 44, 66–7